THE WEEK-END BOOK:
A SOCIABLE ANTHOLOGY

The Week-End Book was first published in June 1924.
With various editions and alterations it was reprinted in
England thirty-four times. In "criticism" of its commercial
success, Virginia Woolf once commented:

"The Hogarth Press may not make any money
- but at least we did not publish
The Week-End Book."

The first Duckworth edition of
The Week-End Book was published
in 2005. This new edition contains all new
material from the 1920s and 1930s, and specially
commissioned pieces for the 2006 edition by
Julian Fellowes, Rory Stewart,
Ian Benfold Haywood and
David Atkinson.

The
Week-End Book:
A Sociable Anthology

A Nonesuch book
published by
Duckworth Overlook
London · New York · Woodstock

This edition published in 2006 by
Duckworth Overlook
in association with The Nonesuch Press

LONDON
90-93 Cowcross Street
London EC1M 6BF
inquiries@duckworth-publishers.co.uk
www.ducknet.co.uk

WOODSTOCK
The Overlook Press
One Overlook Drive
Woodstock, NY 12498
www.overlookpress.com
[for individual orders and bulk sales in the United States,
please contact our Woodstock office]

NEW YORK
The Overlook Press
141 Wooster Street
New York, NY 10012

A CIP catalogue record for this book is available
from the British Library

ISBN 0 7156 3595 6 (UK)
EAN 9780715635957
ISBN 1-58567-813-9 (US)
EAN 9781585678136

Typeset by Ray Davies
Printed in Great Britain by
Creative Print and Design Ltd, Ebbw Vale

WEEK-END

The train! The twelve o'clock for paradise.
Hurry, or it will try to creep away.
Out in the country everyone is wise:
We can be only wise on Saturday.
There you are waiting, little friendly house:
Those are your chimney-stacks with you between,
Surrounded by old trees and strolling cows,
Staring through all your windows at the green.
Your homely floor is creaking for our tread;
The smiling tea-pot with contented spout
Thinks of the boiling water, and the bread
Longs for the butter. All their hands are out
To greet us, and the gentle blankets seem
Purring and crooning: "Lie in us, and dream"

Harold Monro

THE CONTENTS

THE CONTENTS

"Weekends are a bit like rainbows; they look good from a distance but disappear when you get up close to them."

—John Shirley

"One should always be wary of anyone who promises that their love will last longer than a weekend."

—Quentin Crisp

THE GOOD GUEST

The Good Guest

We hear a great deal about how to entertain. How to cook, how to dress, how to decorate, there are books on these which sell in their thousands, but there is very little information on how to be a good guest and yet, heavens, what a difference it makes when you are.

Bad guests can be a nightmare. My parents were once forced into having a couple to stay at the end of the war. They came for a week and they stayed. And stayed. And stayed. And then at last it was time to say goodbye, a moment which, by some miracle, had been reached without the smiles ever cracking. The door shut with a click and my parents raced upstairs to celebrate. My mother leaped onto a table and started to dance a flamenco, swishing her skirts and petticoats to and fro, while my father circled below her, stamping his heels, clapping, whistling and laughing with glee. "They've gone!" they shouted, "They've gone! They've gone!" Then they stopped. The guests were standing in the drawing room door.

"We forgot to leave our key," they said.

Being a guest is a skill. It's also a kind of work. It is something you can be good at. So many people see the role of a guest as a reactive thing, a passive response to the work of entertaining by the host. But this is not so. My training began early because one night, when I was about eleven, somebody chucked for a dinner and my mother realised with horror that the party would number thirteen. I was told (not "asked," you understand, in those very different days) to change and come downstairs to join the gathering. "When I look down the table," said my mother, who was generally a

3

funny woman but could also be quite fierce, "I want to see you talking to your neighbours."

"But what am I to talk about?" I asked in a wavering treble.

"Nobody cares what you talk about," she said. "Just *talk!*"

Anyone who has sat through dinner with a companion who answers in monosyllables and never asks one single question will understand exactly what she meant.

The key factor which one should never lose sight of is a simple one: this is not your house and you are not paying. Therefore you do not have the control over your own comfort that you enjoy in even the dingiest hotel. And frankly, if the arrangement does not suit, then you should simply stay away. Or, if you must go, then make it for luncheon or dinner and not overnight. That way you can still visit and they will not hate you by the end. Reader, understand only this: no bill equals no rights.

It is often hard for people (especially the elderly) who live alone to grasp that they have entered the World of Compromise when they accept an invitation for the weekend. When you hear that dinner will be served at least two hours later than you like it, you must hold your tongue. Anyone who says: "That's a little late for me," will almost certainly never be asked again. In truth, I don't understand why folk cannot eat later or earlier than they might like *for one night*. What are they afraid of? Will their hunger pangs render them unable to walk unaided? Will their digestion never recover? I went into our kitchen not long ago at about half past six to find a painter-friend finishing a large bowl of cereal because "I was hungry." He was not however hungry for the four-course dinner that was laid before him at nine. The same holds true for your accommodation. "The mattress is very soft. Do you have a board that I could use?" No, we do not. And next time, don't leave home.

We run a fairly relaxed house but we do have one iron rule: once the burglar alarm has been switched on, no guest may venture down until the house has been opened up in the morning. Inevitably, one dark night, we started awake, jerked bolt upright by the jangling of bells. In terror of hearing the swooping sirens of the local police approaching, we tore down to discover an indignant American standing in her pyjamas.

"I thought we said not to come downstairs," said Emma.

"That's ridiculous!" she replied. "I only wanted a banana."

The magic rule is simply that one must try to "fit in". Even if, these days, there are degrees. Few hosts now expect vegetarians to eat meat even if an amazing number will still slop gravy over the vegetables and then wonder why the plate is left untouched. It is also just about possible to get away with a real allergy and most of us are fairly nut conscious. Having said that, claiming an allergy is a privilege that must not be abused. Americans, especially, have come to believe that it is socially acceptable to say they are "allergic" to things when what they mean is that they don't like them. "I'm allergic to fish," as a rule translates as "I do not like fish," "I'm allergic to eggs," "I'm allergic to offal," "I'm allergic to citrus," all these are generally no more than a list of dislikes. We even had a recent case of "I'm allergic to cabbage."

"*Nobody* is allergic to cabbage," said my wife firmly. "But if you do not want any, you shall not have it."

In truth, to the English, food fads are always tiresome. "No cauliflower for me!" is enough to set a British hostess's teeth on edge. Most of all, let no guest be under the illusion that they are somehow rendered interesting and even spiritual by getting out horrible little tins and bags and sacks of things that look as if they should be used to clean decanters, and then sprinkling the contents over their plates. The ideal guest simply takes as little of the offending material as he may without being conspicuous. If he can force himself, he puts his jaw into overdrive, and swallows it. If that is truly not possible and if he wants to come back another time, then he just cuts up the cauliflower, moves it around ... and leaves it. I was recently faced with a plate of glistening, spongy snails while sitting on the hostess's right. I was a child of the 1950s and I am generally equal to getting at least *some* of the food

5

down my gullet but as I lifted the cunning tool to prize out the greyish, oleaginous slime, I thought, just for a moment, I was actually going to be sick and so I decided against it. I busied myself with the bread and sopped up the garlic butter but when the maid returned to remove the platter, the gleaming gastropods were still there in all their repulsive glory. What makes this tale peculiarly English was that, at no point, did I make any reference to the fact that I was choking back vomit and nor did my delightful companion once refer to my leaving her costly and elaborately prepared dish untouched. The British do not like fussing but they respect hypocrisy and nobody will criticise you for disliking your food in silence. Just don't be a bore.

Emma is a vegetarian and so is obliged to negotiate this most un-English position through various country houses at regular intervals. Her ideal is when hostesses don't know and so make no preparations. She is then free to pick around among the vegetables until she is content. Her nightmare is that moment when the hostess gives the weary smile of the much-put-upon and says "We've made something just for you." This is usually the precursor to real anguish. As it happens, she would rather eat a live rabbit than a courgette quiche but when it's been made specially she knows there is No Way Out. She is a good guest. She understands the task before her, takes her helping and forces it down.

The rules of dining in other people's houses are pretty simple: come about ten minutes after the time you were told, check that you are wearing the clothes the hostess wants you in, admire the house, admire the food, try to eat everything, talk to your neighbours, ask them questions, laugh at their jokes and don't be the last to leave. Staying for the weekend is more or less the same: check the clothes, admire the house, admire your room, eat everything and like everybody. Although I suppose the Rules of Arrival for a weekend make it a little bit different. Above all, come when you say you are coming. An astonishing recent development is the number of people who will suddenly telephone and say "We won't be there for Friday dinner after all," or they will announce at breakfast, "We're leaving before lunch to avoid the traffic." Presumably they do not give house parties themselves or they would know that by doing such things, they are hurling sticks of dynamite into the plans of their host.

A lot of people today forget to leave a tip for the staff (including the invisible daily) when they go. This is irritating as it means these unfortunates have the burden of extra work with no compensation. Sometimes the hostess just pretends and runs round the bedrooms sticking £20 notes under the dressing table ornaments but this is really unfair on her. Another perilous area is that of presents although, by and large, the form is simple: if you are over thirty, never take anything to a dinner party and always take something to a weekend. It is a good idea to avoid giving flowers in the country but, if you must take flowers, then take them growing in a pot or already arranged in a vase. The *last* thing any sane hostess wants is to find herself struggling with scissors, stems and thorns just as her guests are arriving.

Above all, steer clear of the misconception that you, the guest, have a part to play in the shaping of the entertainment, or that your opinion on what has been planned is a valid one. Nor are the proposed outings optional.

"We're all going for a walk on the beach."

"You go. I'll stay here and read. Don't worry about me."

This will swiftly earn you the reputation of being "rather a tiresome guest." Obviously, not all houses are the same and in some there is a margin for independence. Not every suggested activity is compulsory, but beware. It is up to the guest to use their antennae to discover the truth, the difficulty being that the British, particularly the posh British, never say what they mean. When you ask: "Would you mind frightfully if I skip lunch? I'm not really hungry." You may be answered with a warm grin, "Of course not! Don't even think of it!" When in truth the hostess, who has spent the last few days running through menus and queuing in Waitrose, wants you dead.

7

Then again, conversation isn't all plain sailing. It can be tricky and a bit of homework never hurts. As a deb's delight of nineteen, I remember stating gaily at a dinner that I was "mad about Christine Keeler" to be greeted by a thunderous silence. It seemed the famous uncle of one of my companions at the table had been ruined in the scandal. My father once asked my mother about the wine they were drinking. "This is really *filthy*. Where on earth did you get it?" My mother indicated a fuming guest on her right. "Patrick brought it as a present," she answered brightly. Emma's mama is pretty good at this sort of thing. Not long ago, we had a delightful musician staying and, as a compliment, we put on one of his recordings during lunch. As the melody wafted into the dining room, my mother-in-law looked up. "What is that *ghastly* noise," she groaned.

It is common among people who are anxious to give the impression they are well bred to make a great show of keeping away from "forbidden" subjects. "I never discuss religion or politics," they say, or, worse, "I don't really care for gossip." I suppose it's possible these were once strict rules in good society but I rather doubt it since they would have disposed of every subject worth discussing. At any rate, today, the genuinely smart have few such restraints and will happily launch into any controversial view. I have in the past suspected some hosts of deliberately trying to make their guests cross, to beef up the evening a bit. As most of us know, there is nothing better than a good argument at the dinner table, best of all between a husband and wife. But, assuming one does not want to play at fisticuffs oneself, perhaps a useful guide is to remember to keep it light. Most opinions are acceptable in a discussion if they are not expressed too forcefully. Of course, if the views of the company are really disgraceful, then one always has the option of leaving rather than hear more. Should this truly be the only course open, then go quietly. Above all, avoid flouncing out. There must be no dramatic statement in your departure.

The only topic which it probably *is* best to steer clear of is money. Most people feel they have too little of it, which makes for uneasy listening, and those few who might be considered to have too much—or, at the very least, enough—should probably keep silent for fear of depressing their friends. Of course, as I have pointed out before now, the upper classes may not talk about money but they never think about anything else.

In the end, I suppose the chief maxim of the Good Guest is that he or she must not be a problem. They must not be unhappy. A friend once had to endure one of their own dinners being high-jacked by a sobbing woman, recently discarded by her husband, until the entire table had fallen silent under the weight of her misery. To make matters worse, she had only been brought along to make up numbers by someone thinking the evening "might cheer her up." Nor was she in the least beguiling as a personality. At the end, having pushed her, still wailing, into a taxi, the hostess turned to me: "Spare me the troubles of an unattractive stranger," she sighed. Just as a good host tries to make their guests feel comfortable, so a good guest must always create the impression that they are at ease, untroubled, having a lovely time. This obligation goes beyond the weekend or dinner in question. Good guests should not be discontented in their jobs or their homes or with their spouses. They may enjoy some humour at the expense of their families but only for the purpose of a merry anecdote. It must never seem that difficult relatives are actually causing sorrow. Their lives, in short, must be going well. They can complain about the state of the nation or, Lord knows, the government, to their heart's content, but not about anything that might make others feel ill at ease.

Above all, a guest must absolutely *never* invite pity. My great aunt used to say that, in society, nobody should be "more difficult than they're worth" and one of the most difficult people to entertain is surely the guest with any form of grievance. Certainly, it is odd how many men and women feel entitled to complicate social gatherings with imagined slights, as they pour out endless detail of some carefully preserved wound to their spirit. "What do you think he really meant by that?" they mutter grimly. Of all tedious inflictions by the bad guest, for me anyway, taking offence is the worst. It manages to be infuriating and incredibly boring at the same time. In the end, one dreads the sight of those of your acquaintance who are always nursing some chip or other, feeling let down, feeling ignored or under-valued or "taken for granted". Sorry. Life is too short to spend any of it with people who are looking for trouble. Some might say this indicates a lack of charity on my part but I would argue that it stems more from a modern inability to gauge the degrees of friendship correctly. While I do think one has the right to expect a weekend guest to eat food they do not like and talk to people who bore them and go for walks they do not want, I don't believe they are obliged to come running in the small hours when the tank bursts, or to listen to wracking sobs when genuine tragedy strikes. That stuff should be, must be, reserved for one's *real* friends. These, as all the world knows, form quite a different group, and anyone who cannot tell the difference has no future as a social being.

Probably, herein lies the key: being a Good Guest is a performing art. It has little to do with lifelong friendship. Real friends will take one in when all performance is beyond one. But their number is not legion. A dozen true friends testify to a life well lived and most of us must make do with less. For the friendly acquaintance, and I have nothing to say against this most cheerful of relationships, different rules apply. They have the right to demand we play our part when invited to their tables. Play it right and you will have a busy and rewarding time of it for as long as you may care to do so.

Julian Fellowes

PARLOUR GAMES & SPORTING FUN

How to Brighten Cricket

I HAVE been watching cricket. You pay sixpence and enter an enclosure which contains a large open lawn of level turf surrounded by rows of seats. Thousands of people enjoy this pastime and manifest extreme emotions of pleasure when runs are hit or wickets bowled down. There are two wickets set up about twenty or thirty yards apart in the centre of the open space. Two batsmen come out from the pavilion to defend these wickets with a bat against the attempts of nearly a dozen men of the other side who constantly endeavour to throw them down with a leather ball. The theory of the game seems to be this: either you strike the ball away and run from wicket to wicket as fast as your legs will carry you, or else you miss the ball and it scatters your stumps. In the latter event you go back to the pavilion and another member of your side takes your place. Several of the players made a worthy effort to realise these alternatives, and, while they did so, it seemed to me to be a most fascinating spectacle. You were always in suspense as to what would happen. Would it be four runs or a wicket down? There was another delightful possibility: the striker might smite the ball with a resounding crack high into the air, then one or two of the opposing side would rush to catch it before it fell. There were some moments of breathless suspense while the ball was in mid-air, with the batsmen legging it to and fro at the top of their speed. I declare that I clapped and shouted as heartily as anybody at these incidents; but, alas! the came seldom, considering that the game lasted for five or six hours and was, I was informed, to continue day after day. There were a good many of the bowlers who seemed unable to hit the

13

wickets, even when the batsman missed the ball. There were some batsmen who seemed so confident of this that they made no real attempt to strike the ball. At such times I could not imagine a more lugubrious pastime, especially as all the players displayed an almost excessive gravity of mien and solemnity of deportment. Every now and then they would all stop batting and bowling and march across the ground in a very slow and dignified manner, which tried my patience almost beyond endurance. There were two stout, elderly men on the ground who took no active part in the game. From the extreme ceremoniousness of their manner and from the fact that they wore long white robes, I concluded at first that they were priests; but this, I learn, was an error. They are there to detect and thwart any attempt at foul play, to which, one is sorry to be informed, cricketers are excessively prone. I myself saw one batsman furtively kicking the ball with his heel as it passed him, and I saw bowlers who deliberately ambushed themselves behind the umpires. And yet I conceive that at one time this game must have been conducted in a singularly upright spirit, since we still hear the phrase "It's not cricket" used as if "cricket" were synonymous with "honour".

To me it seemed remarkable that so many people, obviously by their appearance belonging to quite humble walks of life, could afford the entrance money and the time to watch this game for the whole day. There were long intervals while the players retired for meals, or rested between the innings, or tramped from place to place. Nor were the cricketers really expert at their business. The sorriest juggler in the cheapest music hall performs far more successfully and audaciously than these men. He never drops a ball, even when he has half a dozen in the air at once; but these men were constantly dropping the ball or letting it slip between their hands. I had heard cricket spoken of as a manly English sport, but I could not see anything particularly courageous in the play. There would perhaps have been some risk of injury from the fast bowlers, but the batsmen were guarded against that by padded leg-guards and gloves. When a ball did hit them elsewhere they were far from stoical in their behaviour. In the matter of hitting difficult balls most of the batsmen were very far from temerarious.

From the conversation of my neighbours it appeared that some of my criticisms are supported by facts. It seems that six or seven counties are on the verge of bankruptcy, that the attendance of spectators is rapidly dwindling, and that various newspapers have been discussing the question of how to brighten cricket. The latter seems to me a topic well worthy of the present season, and I hope to make some contribution to its proverbial silliness by the following suggestions:—

1. Realising that what spectators of sport generally desire is a quick and clear result which admits of a ready settling of bets, I should shorten the innings, and, if possible, have six innings on each side to last about two hours each. The spectators could bet on the result of each innings. I should not expect all the bowlers to bat any more than I should expect all the batsmen to bowl.

2. I should give the bookmakers a far more important position on the ground. I should divide the ground up into sixpenny rings, shilling rings, half-crown rings, and pound rings, each with their own staff of bookmakers. The merry cries of the bookmakers and the shouts and oaths of the backers would introduce a far brisker atmosphere into the cricket field. Patient plodding would not be tolerated.

3. Mr Keary's maxim, "Get on or get out", would be the guiding principle of the batsmen. The stonewallers and the crooked bowlers would be automatically eliminated by the demands of the ring. But, if necessary, it would be easy to pass a new rule that any batsman who received six consecutive balls without a *bonâ-fide* attempt to score a run should have to retire. He might perhaps be allowed to try once again later on, but I would absolutely prohibit the practice known as "playing yourself in". In some sides it

15

appears to be the accepted rule that no batsman must attempt to make a run until he has been at the wicket for about ten minutes.

4. I should firmly suppress all but the most necessary intervals. At the end of each over I should compel the fieldsmen to run to their other places by allowing the batsmen to score runs as fast as they could until every fieldsman had taken up his new position. As the bowlers and batsmen would not generally be the same people, there would be no need of an interval between the innings.

These few and simple reforms would, I fancy, be found to effect a complete alteration in the character of the game. At all events, we must settle in our minds for whose benefit the game of cricket is designed. If for the pleasure of the players, well and good. Let them play it as they like, but do not let them expect to be paid for doing so, or complain of our lack of support. If they are amusing themselves, they should not charge for admission. On the other hand, if the game is intended for the amusement of the spectators, let us frankly inquire what amuses the spectators most. If anyone is amused at old Joe Vine watching Iremonger's off-balls going by, let him say so now, or for ever hold his peace.

Indoor Games

EARTH, AIR, WATER, FIRE

The players sit in a ring. The one to start the game is provided with a handkerchief or scarf. He moves round the ring on the inside.

Suddenly he throws the handkerchief on the shoulder or in the lap of one of the players, and says, "Earth. Two—Four—Six—Eight—Ten." Before the caller has reached "Ten", the player chosen must name an animal that lives on the earth. If he gets the name out in time, the caller must try someone else. If he does not succeed in doing so, he must take the handkerchief and change places with the caller.

The caller may make any of the four calls—"Earth", "Air", "Water", or "Fire". Any flying creature will do as a response to "Air", and any creature that lives in the water as a response to "Water". A player who names the wrong kind of animal is out; he is not given the chance to correct himself.

None of the creatures may be named twice in the same game.

The call "Fire" should be given only when the caller has been unsuccessful a good many times. The response is "Salamander", and all change places. This gives the caller a chance to find a seat. The one who is left out in the general move becomes the caller.

Some players are rather slow when they begin to play this game. At the start the count may be "One—two—three——" up to ten, and not merely the even numbers; but the counting can soon be speeded up.

POST GOES

This is one of the liveliest of party games.

The company are seated in a circle, one going to the middle of the ring. Every chair must be occupied.

Each member of the company takes the name of a station. The Leader, who is to direct all the journeys, hears the names as they are being said. If the company is large, he may write the names on a slip of paper, so as not to leave anyone out of the game.

When all is ready, the Leader says, "Post goes from Leeds to Newcastle." Leeds and Newcastle must then change places. Whilst they are doing so the man in the centre tries to get into one of the vacant places. If he succeeds, the man he displaces must off to the centre and must give his station to the man who replaces him.

Skill may be shown in dodging the man in the centre when changing places. If the centre man stays near one station, the other player may steal up and be ready to slip into the place as soon as it is vacated.

The Leader must be ready with another journey as soon as the first is completed. When he gives the order "General Post", all the players must leave their chairs and find new ones. The one left out goes to the centre.

The success of the game depends largely on the ability of the Leader to keep things on the move. He should think out his next move whilst the excitement of the present one still exists. He should always be ready with a "General Post": (i) when some people have been seated too long, and need livening up; (ii) when any player has had too long a period in the centre and is ceasing to be amused; (iii) when any player, on the contrary, is trying to monopolise the centre part of the game. The last-named difficulty may be solved by two "General Posts" in quick succession.

Numbers may be used instead of place-names, but the latter give a more lively effect.

TWO'S COMPANY

One of the company goes to the centre. The others form a ring in two's, each couple linking arms. Another player is ready to link arms with one of the couples. As soon as he does this, the player on the other side of the group must run off and link arms with another couple. The outside member of this group must then run off and link arms with still another couple. And so the movement goes on.

The object of the man in the centre is to touch the unattached man before he can link arms with another couple. The object of the other is to avoid capture by touching. Anyone captured goes to the centre, and the one who captures him then becomes for the moment the man who has to link arms with one of the couples.

This game should be kept going at a good speed. Agility in getting away, and so eluding capture, adds greatly to the fun. Players should see that everyone has a part in the game, and the Leader should do his best to ensure this; though occasionally it is good fun to have a specially lively member of the company pursued relentlessly.

SERGEANT'S ORDERS

The company march round in a circle. They have to be ready to obey the Sergeant's orders exactly.

The fun of this game depends largely on the Sergeant. Some of his orders should be simple and straightforward: "About turn"; "Hands above heads"; "Hands stretched sideways."

But the Sergeant should always be ready with unexpected orders: "Hop on one foot"; "Walk on all-fours"; "Sit on the floor"; "Walk like a rabbit"; "Run on the spot (without moving forward)"; "Catch hands in a circle"; "Raise knees high"; "Face out and walk sideways"; "Bow as you walk"; "Touch toes"; "Hands on the shoulders of the one in front".

19

GRUNT, HONEY, GRUNT

Silence should be observed by all who take part in this game, except for legitimate noises. Any extraneous noises spoil the chance of the unfortunate man in the centre.

The company sit in a ring. The odd man out goes to the centre. He is blindfolded with a scarf, and is then given a cushion. The procedure of the game is explained by the Leader.

All the company change places, and then keep quiet. The man in the centre moves across and gropes about till he touches one of the company. He puts the cushion on this person's knee, sits on it, and says "Grunt, honey, grunt".

The person called upon gives a grunt or a squeak in a disguised tone.

The man in the centre guesses who it is by the sound of the voice. If he guesses wrongly, the company hiss, and he must try someone else. When at last he is successful the company clap. The one whose voice has been guessed goes to the centre to be blindfolded.

And so the game proceeds until it has gone on long enough.

The Director of the game may do a little quiet arranging, so as to bring as many as possible into it. He can, for example, turn the blindfolded man to parts of the ring that have not previously been visited.

SITTING WITHOUT CHAIRS

This is always an amusing item for an odd moment. The company stand close together in a circle, face to back all the way round. At the work of command each sits on the knees of the person behind.

With a little practice everyone can sit down and rest comfortably on the knees of the one behind.

THE BELLS OF ST. CLEMENT'S

Anyone who tries this will find the effect really beautiful.

We want about a yard (or rather more) of thin string and two spoons. The spoons are tied to the ends of the string.

The string is passed over the head and held down to the openings of the ears with a finger at each ear.

The spoons are then made to clash together. Each clash causes a tinkle which is heard as a beautiful, strong, bell-like note.

Several sets of spoons and string may be provided and handed on from one to another of the company.

THE ZOO GAME

Half the company turn their chairs so that the backs are to the front. They then get behind the chairs as thought they were in cages.

Each player chooses an animal that makes a distinctive noise: donkey, cat, lion, wolf, pig, bear, and so on. Each player should choose an animal that he can imitate fairly well. Any who are good at mimicry should certainly be included in the Zoo.

The Keeper walks up and down and names the animals: "We have here, ladies and gentlemen, the noble donkey, famed for his long ears; and here the prowling lion, and here the melodious pig. Over here you will recognize the bear by its attractive growl." And so on, naming each animal in turn.

When an animal is named, it must give its distinctive cry for ten seconds. When the Keeper mentions the Zoo, all must give their cries at once.

On the second round the Keeper mentions the animals quickly, so as to have as many as possible going at once. He may have them going in pairs and threes, and work up finally to the whole Zoo. "This is a most magnificent Zoo. There is no Zoo like it. It is the Zoo of all Zoos." The end should be a climax of sound, and then, when the Keeper raises his hand, sudden silence.

The Keeper bows and the game ends.

NECROMANCY

We need two packs of cards for this game, and they had better be old packs.

The Necromancer sits in the middle of the floor with one pack in front of him. He is draped with an Eastern shawl.

The other pack is distributed to the company. The one to start the game asks a question, probably mildly and possibly outrageously slanderous. "Who got up late this morning?" will do as an example.

The Necromancer turns up the top card in his pack—say the 8 of diamonds. "Who has the 8 of diamonds? You, William?" So William is declared by the cards to be the one who got up late.

Then William has the privilege of asking a question, and the next card turned up by the Necromancer decides the answer. And so the game proceeds until the pack has been gone through. It is great fun when a slanderous question comes back on the questioner.

When the cards have nearly run out, and there is no danger of being hoist with your own petard, there is the opportunity of being really slanderous.

The questions asked should begin with "Who is ——" "Who is the greatest thief in the company?" "Who is contemplating murder?" "Who didn't put on a clean collar?" "Who beats his grandmother?" "Who steals library books?" And so on.

If the cards are collected as the game proceeds, it is good fun to try to make the last questions appropriate to those left with cards.

DETECTING BY EYES

This game is played by two teams, A and B.

A sheet, or a screen of some kind, is hung up near the door. There is a hole in the screen just big enough for the eye to be seen through.

Team A go out. One by one they line up behind the screen in such a position that one eye just shows.

Team B discuss who each one is, and after discussion announce the team's guess. They score one point for each correct guess.

Team B then goes out, and the roles are reversed.

GUESSING BY SHADOWS

This is a game similar to the last, and again played by two teams.

The room is darkened and a screen is hung up near the door. Behind the screen is a lighted candle.

Team A go out. Each in turn stands between the candle and the screen, so that his or her shadow falls on the screen.

Team B discuss whose shadow is thrown on the screen, and announce their decision. A point is awarded for each correct guess.

Team B then go out, and the roles are reversed.

The flickering shadow thrown by a candle is better for the purpose of this game than the more definite shadow thrown by electric light.

HIDDEN ANIMALS

Cards are pinned up here and there with sentences written on them in which the names of animals are hidden. Each card has a number.

Members of the party find the cards and try to find the hidden animals. Each is supplied with a slip of paper on which to write the solutions. At the end of a specified time the one with the most correct solutions is the winner. Each animal discovered counts a point.

Here are a few suggestions:

1. Along he came, limp, and aching. (Camel, Panda.)
2. They went to war, tho' goodness knows why. (Warthog.)
3. I don't like wishy-washy enamel brooches. (Hyena.)
4. Ha! Realise all or nothing. (Hare, Seal.)
5. They were shaken with fear, mad, ill, or had lost all I (on Monday) had seen them with. (Armadillo, Stallion.)
6. I saw her pant. Her heart beat rapidly. (Panther.)
7. Ill fares the land where, look, a pious man drills plodding or hasty men. (Eland, Okapi, Mandrill, Dingo.)

23

8. Should an author select his own publisher? (Horse)
9. I saw a monk eyeing a peachlike lady. (Monkey, Ape.)
10. Yesterday a King's robe arrived, eerily enough, from Paris. (Yak, Bear, Deer.)
11. He swung to and fro, going up, up, and up to a drier land. (Frog, Pup, Toad.)
12. Harris and Co. will sell enormous emeralds and finest agates. (Cow, Mouse, Stag.)

TOWNS AND PLACES

The Director in this game has a list of twenty or more questions to which the answer is a place-name. He reads them out one by one. The first to supply the correct answer scores a point. The highest score wins. Here are some suggestions; many more can readily be found.

1. A town that might stop a bottle. Cork.
2. A town that goes first. Leeds.
3. A town for a modern Noah. Newark.
4. A town to make one weep. Leek.
5. An island for cars. Rhodes
6. A town for the blackout. Wick.
7. Mr. Pegg's sister. Winnipeg.
8. A hard county. Flint.
9. A town with an atmosphere. Ayr.
10. A town on board a ship. Crewe.
11. An incendiary capital. Berne.
12. A town where farmers get a rest. Stockholm.
13. No place for the Black Friars. Whitechapel.
14. A lazy mountain. Everest.
15. A river on the dinner-table. Plate.
16. "You goose!" to a gentleman. Uganda.
17. A cape for those who don't want to score. Spurn Point.
18. A secretive wilderness. Exmoor.
19. An islet for the legs. Calf of Man.
20. An island for air pilots. Skye.
21. A fishy country. Finland.

22. A badly fed country. Hungary.
23. A town for hikers. Rome.
24. Where the church bells don't ring. Belfast.
25. Where they ought to know twice times. Dublin.
26. A country for Christmas. Turkey.
27. Where an old coin is kept up to date. New Guinea.
28. No place for pessimists. Cape of Good Hope.
29. Where they almost read. Peru (almost Peruse).
30. Not my rope. Europe.
31. The unplaced river. Forth.
32. Town for the hungry. Eton.
33. Wooden business town. Deal.
34. Republican town in England. Barking.
35. Grain rampart in England. Cornwall.
36. Brittle country. China.
37. Not the lake I'm on. Lake Huron.
38. Where you might take legal action against a whole tribe. Sudan.
39. State that brags of its debts. Ohio.
40. A slippery country. Greece.

PROBLEM DRAWING

Every member of the company has a long slip of paper and a pencil. The company are given three minutes to make the best "problem drawings" they can at the top of the paper.

Each drawing should tell some kind of story. At the bottom of the paper the artist writes what the picture is intended to be, and then turns up the paper so that no one can see what has been written.

The papers are passed on. Half a minute is allowed to study the picture and write at the bottom what it is. Once more the papers are turned up and passed on. This continues until the available space has been used up.

The captions to each picture are read out, and finally the artist's own description of what he intended.

COMPETITION RACE

On a number of cards are written instructions for various small competitions. The cards should be pinned where they can be read without being moved, but they should not be too conspicuous.

Each card has a number. On the table is any apparatus necessary for the competition, and beside it the corresponding number.

Players are given slips of paper. Then each hunts for the instructions and does his best to solve the little problems quickly. The first to return a set of correct answers is the winner.

The competitions may be any of the following, or similar problems. (It should be understood that no marks are to be made on the apparatus, and the order of cards, etc., is not to be changed.)

1. Which letters of the alphabet are missing? (The letters are on small squares and three or four are missing.)
2. Make two five-letter words from the given letters. (The letters AELPS are written on a card. There are several anagrams: lapse, leaps, pales, peals, please, sepal.)
3. Which card is missing from the suit? (12 cards of one suit are mixed and placed in a pile.)
4. Name one flower of each of the given colours. (Several colours are written on a card.)
5. Count the number of peas in the saucer. (Some odd number of peas—79 or 87. Two saucers of peas may be provided.)
6. Make the name of an animal from the jumble of letters. (*E.g.* FABOFUL = BUFFALO.)
7. Which is the most frequently recurring word in the last paragraph of the book? (Choose a book in which the last paragraph is not too long.)
8. Choose the words from the list that are fuels. (A list of words is written on a cared. The list should include

COAL, PEAT, WOOD, GAS, OIL, TALLOW.)

9. Name the capitals of the given countries. (The names of several countries are written on a card.)
10. Find the middle letter of the given sentence. (A rather long sentence is written on a card.)

THE LABYRINTH

This is a very popular game to precede supper. A number of "favours" or souvenirs should be provided, two of each kind. Tissue paper novelties or penny toys will answer the purpose. If it is a "mixed" party, two balls of coloured string are necessary, blue for the girls and red for the boys. The string should be cut into as many lengths as there are players. Then one end of each string is tied to the parlour chandelier and the other end fastened around some piece of furniture. Sometimes the strings of the labyrinth are even turned around the banisters and carried to an upstairs room, but this is rather a complicated proceeding. To the "far end" of every blue string is attached one of the souvenirs, and its duplicate is fastened to the end of a red string. Then the players are assembled, the chandelier strings are cut and one of the proper colour is given to each player, who proceeds to wind up until he reaches his hidden souvenir. Care must be taken not to break the stings wherever they cross in the labyrinth. When all are untangled, the players holding duplicated souvenirs become partners at supper. The favours are worn as badges, and if they are funny, the meal is sure to begin in merriment.

BLINDMAN'S BUFF

Consists in one person's having a handkerchief bound over his eyes so as to completely blind him, and thus blindfolded trying to chase the other players, either by the sound of their footsteps, or their subdued merriment, as they scramble away in all directions, endeavouring to avoid being caught by him; when he can manage to catch one, the player caught must in turn be blinded, and the game be begun again. In some places it is customary for one of the players to enquire of

Buff (before the game begins), "How many horses has your father got?" to which enquiry he responds, "Three." "What colours are they?" "Black, white, and grey." The questioner then desires Buff to "turn round three times, and catch whom you may," which request he complies with, and then tries to capture one of the players. It is often played by merely turning the blindfolded hero round and round without questioning him, and then beginning. The handkerchief must be tied on fairly, so as to allow no little holes for Buffy to see through. In Europe they have a modified way of playing at blindman's-buff, which, though less jolly than our American method, may be followed with advantage on birthdays and holidays, when boys and girls are dressed in their best, and careful parents are averse to rough clothes-tearing play. The party are not scattered here and there over the ground, but take hands and form a circle. In the midst stands Mr Buff, blindfolded, and with a short thin stick in his hand. The players keep running round in a circle, generally singing, while Buff approaches gradually, guided mostly by their voices, till he manages to touch one of the twirling circle with his stick. Then the dance stops, and the dancers become motionless and silent. The player who has been touched must take the end of the stick in her hand, while Buff holds the other; and she must distinctly repeat three times after him, any word he chooses to name—"Good morning" or "Good night", for instance of course, disguising his or her voice as much as possible. The blind man tries to guess the name of his captor by the voice. If he succeeds, the person caught becomes blind man: if not, Buff must try his luck again.

ONE OLD OX OPENING OYSTERS

This is a capital round game, and will tax the memory and the gravity of the youngsters. The company being seated, the fugleman says, "*One old ox opening oysters*," which each must repeat in turn with perfect gravity. Any one who indulges in the slightest giggle is mulcted of a forfeit forthwith. When the first round is finished, the fugleman begins again: "*Two toads, totally tired, trying to trot to Troy*," and the others repeat in turn, each separately, "*One old ox opening oysters; two toads, totally tired*," etc. The third round is, "*Three tawny tigers tickling trout*," and the round recommences:—"*One old ox*, etc.; *two toads, totally*, etc.; *Three tawny tigers*, etc.*" The fourth round, and up to the twelfth and last, given out by the fugleman successively, and repeated by the other players, are as follows: "*Four fat friars fanning a fainting fly; Five fair flirts flying to France for fashions; Six Scotch salmon selling six sacks of sour-krout; Seven small soldiers successfully shooting snipes; Eight elegant elephants embarking for Europe; Nine nimble noblemen nibbling nonpareils; Ten tipsy tailors teasing a titmouse; Eleven early earwigs eagerly eating eggs;* and *Twelve twittering tomtits on the top of a tall tottering tree*." Any mistake in repeating this legend, or any departure from the gravity suitable to the occasion, is to be punished by the infliction of a forfeit; and the game has seldom been known to fail in producing a rich harvest of those little pledges. Of course, a good deal depends on the serio-comic gravity of the fugleman.

MAGIC MUSIC

One of the players is sent out of the room, and a handkerchief, a pair of gloves, a brooch, or other small article, is hidden in some cunning nook. The signal is then given for the banished one to return; and a lady or gentleman acquainted with music takes up a position at the piano. It is for the musician to indicate, by the strains of the piano, when the seeker is approaching the object hidden. As he recedes from it, the music falls to a low tone, and a mournful cadence; as he approaches it, the notes swell out loud and clear, and bursts into a triumphal strain as he lays his hand on the prize. If properly managed, the magic music may be made to have almost magnetic power in drawing the seeker toward it.

Another way of playing the game, and an improved one, is to set the seeker some task to perform, instead of finding the handkerchief. Say, for instance, he is to take a book from a bookcase, and present it to a lady. As he walks round the room, the music increases in sound as he approaches the bookcase, but falls as he passes it. This tells him in what locality his task is. He takes a book, and the music sounds loudly and joyously. He begins to read—no! the music falls at once; he is faltering in his task. He carries the book round the room. As he approaches the lady, the notes burst forth loudly again, concluding with a triumphant flourish as he presents the volume to her with a gallant bow. In case of failure, a forfeit is exacted, and each player must have a task set him, or her, in turn.

TWIRLING THE PLATE

The players sit or stand around a table covered with cloth, and one of them takes up a wooden or metal plate, which sits on its edge, and gives it a spin. As he does this he names one of the players, who is obliged to catch it before it has done spinning, or pay a forfeit. The player so called on sets the plate spinning in turn, calling upon some other player to stop it, and so on around.

INDOOR GAMES

HOW DO YOU LIKE IT? WHEN DO YOU LIKE IT? AND WHERE DO YOU LIKE IT?

This is a guessing game. One of the company retires, while the rest fix on some article or object—for instance, light, an apple, money, etc. The person who has gone out is then recalled, and proceeds round the circle, asking each player in succession, "How do you like it?" Supposing the thing thought of to be *money*, the first may answer, "In abundance," the second, "Ready", and so on. The questioner tries to gain from the answers thus given some clue to the nature of the thing thought of. The second question, "When do you like it?" will probably help him. One of the players may reply, "When I have to pay my bills;" another, "When I want a new coat," and so on. The third question is almost certain to help a judicious questioner out of his puzzlement. "Where?" "In my pocket," one of the players will reply; another, "At my banker's," and so on. Someone is almost sure to drop a hint which will set the guesser upon the right track. Three guesses are allowed him. If he succeeds, he must point out the player whose answer gave him the clue, and the latter pays a forfeit and goes out to be puzzled in his turn. Failing to guess in three trials, the first player must try another question. The art of the game consists in choosing words with more meanings than one, such as cord (chord); for then the answers may be varied in a very puzzling manner. One will like a *cord* round his box; another a c(h)ord in a piece of music; another on the piano, etc.' thus key (*quay*), bark, vessel, are good words to choose.

WHAT IS MY THOUGHT LIKE?

The party sitting round as usual, one of them thinks of some person, place, or thing: the Emperor Napoleon (the first or third will do), New York, a coal-scuttle, the Island of Tahiti—anything, in fact, that first occurs to him; and then he asks each of the company in turn, "What is my thought like?" They, in complete ignorance as to the nature of the

31

said thought, reply at random. One says, for instance, "like a steam-engine"; another, "like a cavern"; a third, "like a tea-kettle". When an opinion has thus been collected from each one, the questioner tells what his thought was, and each player, under penalty of a forfeit, has to give a reason for the answer made to the first question. We will suppose, continuing the instance just begun, that the questioner says to the first in the company, "My thought was Napoleon III. Now, why is Napoleon III like a steam-engine?" The answer is ready enough: "Because he goes at an uncommonly fast pace." "Why is he like a cavern?" "Because his depth is one of his distinguishing qualities," replies the second. "Why is he like a tea-kettle?" "Of course, because he boils over occasionally," says the third player, triumphantly; and so the game goes merrily on through the circle. There is an anecdote told of the poet Moore, which is worth repeating. Moore was once at Lord Holland's house, among a distinguished circle of guests, and "What is my thought like?" was the game of the evening. When the question came to him, the poet replied, "a pump." The thought happened to be, "Lord Castlereagh," a statesman famous for the absurd speeches he made in Parliament. Among other strange assertions, he had said of an opposition member, "The honourable gentleman came down to the house *like a crocodile, with his hands in his pockets.*" Well, every one thought Tom Moore was posed; but the poet, with a merry smile, gave not only an answer, but a poetical answer to the query; he replied:

"Because it is an empty thing of wood,
Which up and down its awkward arm doth sway,
And coolly spout, and spout, and spout away,
In one weak, washy, everlasting flood!"

CUPID'S COMING

A letter must be taken, and the termination "ing". Say, for instance, that P is chosen. The first player says to the second, "Cupid's coming." "How is he coming?" says the second.

"Playing," rejoins the first. The second then says to the third, "Cupid's coming." "How?" "Prancing," and so the question and reply go round, through all the words beginning with P and ending with ing—piping, pulling, pining, praising, preaching, etc. Those who cannot answer the question on the spur of the moment pay a forfeit.

CROSS QUESTIONS AND
CROOKED ANSWERS

The company sit round, and each one whispers a question to his neighbour on the right, and then each one whispers an answer; so that each answers the question propounded by some other player, and of the purport of which he is, of course, ignorant. Then every player has to recite the question he received from one player and the answer he got from the other, and the ridiculous incongruity of these random cross questions and crooked answers will frequently excite a good deal of sport. One, for instance, may say, "I was asked 'If I considered dancing agreeable?' and the answer was, 'Yesterday fortnight.'" Another may declare, "I was asked 'If I had seen the comet?' and the answer was, 'He was married last year!'" A third, "I was asked 'What I liked best for dinner?' and the answer was, 'The Emperor of China!'"

CONSEQUENCES

This is a round game, to play at which the company must be seated at a table. Each player has before him, or her, a long, narrow piece of writing-paper and a pencil. At the top of the paper each writes a quality of a gentleman. "The fickle", for instance, or "the insinuating", or "the handsome", "the ugly", or any epithet, in fact, that may occur to the mind at the moment. But nobody may see what the neighbours to the right and left have written. The top of each paper is then folded down, so as to hide what has been written, and each one passes his paper to his neighbour on the right, so that every player has now a new paper before him. On this he writes a gentleman's name; if that of one of the gentlemen in the company, so much the better. Again the papers are passed to the right after being folded over; the beauty of the game being that no one may write two consecutive sentences on the same paper. *The quality of a lady* is now written. Fold and pass the paper—*The lady's name*—then where *they met*—*what he said to her*—*what she said to him*—*the consequence*—and *what the world said*. The papers are now unfolded in succession, and the contents read, and the queerest cross questions and crooked answers are almost sure to result. For instance, the following will be a specimen:— "The conceited Mr Jones (one of the company) and the accomplished Miss Smith met on the top of an omnibus. He said to her, 'Will you love me then as now?' She said to him, 'How very kind you are.' The consequence was, 'they separated forever', and the world said 'Serve them right.'" Another strip, on being unfolded, may produce some such legend as this: "The amiable Artemus Ward and the objectionable Mrs Grundy met on the mall at the Central Park. He said to her, 'How do I look?' She said to him, 'Do it.' The consequence was 'a secret marriage', and the world said, 'We knew how it would be.'"

PROVERBS

One of the company who is to guess the proverb leaves the room; the remaining players fix upon some proverb, such as "All is not gold that glitters"—"A bird in the hand is worth two in the bush"—"Birds of a feather flock together"— "Train up a child in the way he should go"—"A miss is as good as a mile". A proverb being chosen, the words are distributed in rotation through the company, each player receiving a word which he must bring in in the answer he gives to any question asked by the guesser. We will suppose the proverb, "Train up a child in the way he should go", to have been chosen. The first person will receive the word "train", the second "up", the third "a", the fourth "child", the fifth "in", the sixth "the", and the seventh "way", and so on. The person who has gone out is now called in, and begins his questions with the first player, something in the following manner: *Q.* "Have you been out today?" *A.* "No, I must *train* myself to like walking better than I do." He turns to the second player. *Q.* "Are you a member of the National Guard?" *A.* "No, I gave it *up* some time ago." The third player has an easy task to bring in the word *a*, but the fourth, with the word *child*, finds his work more difficult. *Q.* "Are you fond of reading?" *A.* "Any *child* might answer that question." Now, the guesser, if he be a sharp reasoner, will see that this answer is evasive, and only given to bring in the word *child*; he will, perhaps, guess the proverb at once; but if he is a cautious personage he will go on, and finish the round of questions before committing himself by a guess, for he is only allowed three. If he succeeds in guessing the proverb, he has to point out the person whose answer first set him on the right track, who must then pay a forfeit, and go out in his turn to have his powers tested.

THE EMPEROR OF MOROCCO

This is one of those games in which the art consists in preserving an immutable gravity, under every provocation to laugh. In "the Emperor of Morocco," two of the players, generally one of each sex, advance with measured steps into the middle of the room, and ceremoniously salute each other, and the following dialogue takes place, the speakers being compelled to look one another full in the face:—

FIRST PLAYER: The Emperor of Morocco is dead. SECOND PLAYER: I'm very sorry for it. FIRST PLAYER: He died of the gout in his left great toe. SECOND PLAYER: I'm *very* sorry for it. FIRST PLAYER: And all the court are to go into mourning, and wear black rings through their noses. SECOND PLAYER: I'm *very* sorry for it. They then bow again and retire to their places, while another pair comes forward to go through the same impressive dialogue; and so on, till the game has gone all round the circle, a forfeit being the penalty for the slightest approach to a giggle.

ORANGES AND LEMONS

A good children's game. Two of the players take each other's hands and hold them up in the form of an arch (as in the "Sir Roger de Coverley" dance), and the others, taking hold of each other's coats and dresses, pass under the arch one after the other, while the archway players chant the following ditty:

"Oranges and Lemons, say the bells of St Clements.
 You owe me five farthings, say the bells of St Martin's.
 When I grow rich, say the bells at Shoreditch.
 When will that be? say the bells at Stepney.
 I do not know, says the great bell at Bow.
 Here comes a candle to light you to bed,
 And here comes a chopper to chop off the last,
    last, last man's head."

And as the last man comes to the arch, it descends like a portcullis, and cuts him off from his companions. His captors then ask him if he prefers oranges or lemons, and according to his reply he is sent into the right or the left corner of the room; the chant then recommences, and continues till all the last men's heads have been duly cut off, and the players are divided into two parties on opposite sides. They then take hold of each other round the waist, and the foremost players grasp each other by the hands. The party that can drag the other across the room wins.

PIGEONS FLY

The players are seated at a table, and each puts his two forefingers on the board before him. The leader cries out, "Pigeons fly!" and suddenly lifts his hands in the air to imitate the action of flying; all the players have to do likewise. The leader raises his hands each time he calls out a name; but the others must only remove their hands from the table at the names of such creatures as really fly. The leader's object is to entrap them into incurring forfeits by lifting their hands at the wrong time, which, under judicious management, some of them are sure to do. Thus, the leader cries in rapid succession: "Crows fly!—Eagles fly!—Gnats fly!—Sparrows fly—*Horses* fly!" In the excitement of the game, some are sure to lift their hands from the table, oblivious of the fact that horses do *not* fly, and they pay forfeits accordingly.

RED-CAP AND BLUE-CAP

Is a good game, and used to be very popular at sea, in the olden times, among the little middies. The penalty of a mistake was cobbing with knotted handkerchiefs; but, of course, in polite society, this part of the ceremony is dispensed with—a forfeit, or something similar, being substituted. The players sit round in a circle, and represent tailors. Each has a name, and one is the master. One man takes the name Blue-cap, another is Red-cap, a third Yellow-cap, a fourth Black-cap, and so on, through as many colours as there are players. The leader then pretends to examine the work, and says: "Here's a false stitch; who made it, Blue-cap?" Blue-cap immediately answers: "Who, sir?—I, sir?" "Yes, you, sir!" "Not I, sir." "Who then, sir?" "Yellow-cap, sir." Yellow-cap must at once take up the word, and the same dialogue is repeated. "Who, sir?—I sir?" etc., another workman being named as the delinquent. Any one who fails to answer to his name pays a forfeit. If briskly kept up, the game is a thoroughly good one.

CONCERT

The players represent an orchestra, each one taking charge of an imaginary instrument, and going through the motions of playing upon it. Thus, "Fife" too-toos on an imaginary instrument about nine inches long; "Drum" bangs away at an invisible parchment; "Trombone" puts one hand to his mouth, and shifts the other to and fro as he grumbles out an accompaniment; "Cymbals" clashes his two hands together,

37

and each and all are kept in order by a conductor, who stands in the midst, beating time energetically. At a signal from the leader, they all go off simultaneously; but when he holds up his hand, they must stop instantaneously. He then pretends to find fault with one or more of the players, who must instantly answer with some excuse adapted to their instruments; violin pleading that he has no rosin; harp, that a string is broken; and so on. Any hesitation at once entails a forfeit, as does, also, an answer not immediately connected with the instrument of the person challenged.

PRUSSIAN EXERCISE

This game furnishes a good joke, but must be played circumspectly, that no offence may be given, and no unpleasant consequences arise. The company are drawn up in line, with a sergeant and captain—the former standing at the head of the line, the latter in front of the regiment, to give the word of command. The two officers must be in the secret, and act in concert. The captain gives the order, and puts his men through their drill, they taking the time from the sergeant. After a few ordinary commands, such "Heads up", "Eyes right", etc., the word is given to "Ground right knees", whereupon all the men kneel down on the right knee. Then comes, "Right hands forward", whereupon the sergeant stretches out his right arm and hand horizontally in front of him, at full length. "Left hands backward", and the left arms are thrust back as nearly horizontal as possible with the shoulders. Now comes the word "Fire!" at which the sergeant gives his neighbour a push; he, taken unawares, tumbles against the next man, and down goes the whole row like a house of cards.

"MY LADY'S TOILET"

Is very like the "family coach". Each person represents some necessary of the toilet—brush, comb, soap, scent, brooch, jewel-case, etc., and the lady's maid stands in the middle of the circle, and calls for any article her lady is supposed to want. The personator of that article must then jump up, or be fined a forfeit for negligence. Every now and then the Abigail announces that her lady wants her whole toilet, when the whole circle of players must rise and change places. The lady's maid herself makes a bolt for a chair, and the player who is left chairless in the scuffle becomes lady's maid.

YES AND NO

One of the players thing of any person or thing, and the rest sit round and ask him questions about it, which he answers with "yes" or "no", taking care to give no other explanations. From the information thus gained, each gives a guess as to what the thought was. If the questions are ingeniously framed, the solution is generally discovered, unless the "thought" be peculiarly abstruse. The game is a very good one, and we herewith emphatically recommend it, particularly as affording an opportunity of "cooling down" after a romp.

COPENHAGEN

First procure a long piece of tape or twine, sufficient to go round the whole company, who must stand in a circle, holding in each of their hands a part of the string; the last takes hold of the two ends of the tape. One remains standing in the centre of the circle, who is called "the Dane" and who must endeavour to slap the hands of one of those who are holding the string, before they can be withdrawn. Whoever is not sufficiently alert, and allows the hands to be slapped, must take the place of the Dane, and, in his turn, try to slap the hands of someone else.

HUNT THE HARE

The company all form a circle, holding each other's hands. One, called the hare, is left out, who runs several times round the ring, and at last stops, tapping one of the players on the shoulder. The one tapped quits the ring and runs after the hare, the circle again joining hands. The hare runs in and out in every direction, passing under the arms of those in the circle, until caught by the pursuer, when he becomes hare himself. Those in the circle must always be friends to the hare, and assist its escape in every way possible.

THUS SAYS THE GRAND MUFTI

In this game one of the company sits in a chair, and is called the Mufti, or the Grand Mufti. He makes whatever grimace or motion he pleases, such as putting his hand on his heart, winking, sneezing, coughing, stretching out his arm, smiting his forehead, etc. At each movement he says, "Thus says the Grand Mufti," or "So says the Grand Mufti." When he says, "Thus says the Grand Mufti," every one must make just such a motion as he does; but when he says, "So says the Grand Mufti," everyone must keep still. A forfeit for a mistake is exacted.

HUNT THE RING

Is a good substitute for the old game of "hunt the slipper", which has become almost impracticable in these days of crinoline. A long tape, with a ring strung on it, is held by all the players, as they stand in a circle, with one in the middle. They pass the ring rapidly from hand to hand, and it is the business of the player in the midst to hunt the ring, and try to seize the hands that hold it; while the other players, on their part, make his task more difficult by pretending to pass the ring to each other, when it may really be in quite another part of the circle. The person in whose hands the ring is found has to take his turn in the middle.

TRANSPOSITIONS

A capital game to sharpen the wits, and one from which amusement for many hours may be extracted. The company sit round a table, and each person is provided with a pencil and a scrap of paper. Each one writes on his or her scrap a name of a city, country, river, mountain, or, if preferred, of some historical personage, transposing the letters so as to make the recognition of the word as difficult as possible, and accompanying it with a few written words of explanation; for instance, if a town is selected, the explanation must give some particulars of situation or circumstance, to set the guesser upon the right track; if a personage, the date at which he flourished and the country which gave him birth ought to be given. Then the papers are folded together and deposited in the middle of the table; and when they have been well mixed, a folded paper is drawn by each player, and those who cannot decipher the transposition which has fallen to their share are condemned to pay a forfeit. When all have been read, the game begins anew. The following transpositions of words may serve as hints to those who wish to introduce this very amusing pastime among their friends:

Ann Filkr—The name shared by two great discoverers, one of whom visited an unexplored region, and the other explored a region he had never visited.

Simon Ficar ran—A celebrated general of the Revolution, who rarely commanded over fifty men, and yet was more dreaded than those whose followers numbered thousands.

Voosarinlimb—A soldier who gave his country a government, and died while in arms against the government he created.

Jack Wanders? No—A man who rose from obscurity to the highest position in the country; who became a soldier, without a military education; and received the highest degree a university could confer, without learning.

Lollcomew River—A potent sovereign, who ruled a nation with despotic sway and profound wisdom, advancing her glory and consolidating her power, but whose name is not recorded among her kings.

TISHY-TOSHY

An early version of the game is said to have taught Bosanquet the googly. You need a table (rectangular, the largest possible) and a tennis-ball. Two players stand at opposite ends, and throw the ball to each other in turn; the Server may roll, bounce or full pitch the ball, but it must not drop off the sides of the table (only off the ends) and must only leave the table between imaginary parallel lines continuing the sides of the table. The Receiver may not put his hands over the table, or touch it with his hands or any part of his person. If he does so, or if he fails to catch the ball, the Server scores one point. If the Receiver catches the ball lawfully, neither scores. But the Receiver scores a point if the Server sends the ball off the sides of the table. Game is for any number of points agreed upon—say five. The very expert can make a rule to use one hand only, or to bar catches made against the body. Remember always that this is a game of skill, not of strength; and the ball must never be thrown at all fast.

FLOUNCE-FLORIN

Put a Florin in the middle of a shiny table. Four people stand one on each side of the table with a tennis-ball for each opposite pair and bounce the tennis-balls on the table, trying to knock off the coin by a direct hit. Each catches the ball of his partner opposite and tries to knock the coin off in his turn. The table *must* be very shiny.

The man who wins pockets the coin and the others have to put up the new stake. Originating with war-profiteers (but which war?) the game is *now* usually played with pence or halfpence, but keeps its extravagant name.

UP-JENKYNS!

Orders can only be legally obeyed when given by one of the Captains; and if the team which is hiding the Sixpence obeys any other order, it loses. The "In" team, which is hiding the coin, must put up its hands the instant the opposing Captain calls "Up-Jenkyns!" but he ought to allow them at least five seconds before he calls. He can keep their hands in the air as long as he likes, for examination purposes; the "Down" calls are "Down-Jenkyns" (hands can be put down as players please); "Smashums!" (hands must be crashed down on the table); "Crawlers!" (hands placed quietly on the table, and fingers quietly undone till the hands lie flat); "Open Windows" (hands must lie on the table with all the fingers, but not the thumbs, apart); and "Lobster-Pots" (fingertips only to rest on the table, and fingers to be held at an angle to the palm). In lifting the hands, only the Captain's order must be obeyed; but he should allow free and fair consultation to his own side first. Scores can be played for, by the number of separate "wins", or the show of hands on the table when the Sixpence is discovered. *Before* the game starts, all rings and spurs to be removed. *After* the game, let the provider of the sixpence see that he gets it back!

HANGING

One member of the company is picked out and told that he is deemed guilty of murder and will be hanged at the end of five (or ten) minutes unless he can prove himself innocent. All the rest of the company are *omniscient* witnesses and have to answer any question he puts to them. He questions them in turn, and is acquitted if he can find any contradiction or flat inconsistency in their story. The wildest improbabilities are allowable, and are to be encouraged, in their answers, but witnesses cannot abrogate the laws of nature, though they may play tricks with artificial human ones. E.g. You may make the criminal travel by a non-existent train, but if you make him arrive at his destination before he started, he is acquitted.

TASKS FOR REDEEMING FORFEITS

Now that we have shown our friends so many ways of getting rid of their property, under the guise of forfeits, it is but fair that we should give them a few directions concerning the methods by which they may win them back, and therefore we give, for the benefit of all players of games of forfeits, the following selections, from a large variety of tasks to be executed by those players whose gloves, handkerchiefs, and other properties have been laid under embargo for their owners' shortcomings during the game. The usual method of proceeding in redeeming forfeits is this: A lady, who undertakes to cry the forfeits, sits on a chair or sofa, and another player, who is to pronounce the various sentences, sits or kneels on a low stool before her. One of the forfeited articles is held up by the lady on the sofa, over the head of the doomster, who must not see what it is. The following formula is then gone through:

"Here's a pretty thing, and a very pretty thing;
What shall the owner do, now, of this very pretty thing?"

"Is it fine (belonging to a gentleman), or superfine (belonging to a lady)?" asks the pronouncer of sentences, and, according to the reply, he selects a task appropriate for a boy or a girl. The task having been selected, the article is held up to be owned.

Among the penalties most frequently inflicted are the following:

To Perform a Grecian Statue—This is a boy's forfeit, and he achieves his task by mounting on a chair or table, when each one of the company advances, in turn, and puts him in a different attitude, in which he must remain until it is altered by the next person. The fun consists in the ridiculous postures the unfortunate victim is compelled to assume by his tormentors.

To Pay each Person in Company a Compliment, and then Spoil it—This will exercise the quickness and wit of the performer, and enable him, besides to take a little harmless revenge on those of his friends who have been harassing him during the evening. To one, for instance, he says, "You have a finer voice than anyone in this present company; but," he adds, as the person addressed bows to the compliment, "it's a pity that you never give it any rest." To another, "You have certainly a great amount of wit, *only* you always exercise it at the expense of your friends," and to a third, "Your eyes are certainly very bright, and is that the reason why they're always searching for their own reflection in the looking-glass?" and so on, until you have finished your round.

To Brush off the Dime—This is a trick which may be played off on a novice, and will excite much merriment if well managed. The owner of the forfeit is told that he will have to shake off a dime from his forehead, and a coin is shown him. The dime is then enclosed in a damp handkerchief, and pressed hard against the forehead of the victim, who is not allowed to put his hands up to his head. Feeling the impression of the dime on his brow, he will have no doubt that it has been really fastened on, and not suspecting its removal in the handkerchief, he will begin shaking his head from side to side, and even rubbing it against projecting pieces of furniture, to the delight of the spectators, in persevering efforts to get rid of what is not there.

Bow to the Wittiest in the room, kneel to the prettiest, and kiss the one whom you love best.

To Play the Judge—This consists in sitting on a chair in a conspicuous part of the room, and listening with the most perfect gravity to the complaints brought by the rest of the company, who try, by all kinds of ridiculous reports and artifices, to upset the stolidity of the learned gentleman on the bench.

Compliments under Difficulties—Pay six compliments to six different persons, avoiding the use of the letter *l* in every one.

Prison Diet—A glass of water and a teaspoon are brought into the room, and the person who has to undergo "prison diet" is blindfolded, and a teaspoonful of cold water administered to him by any of the others, until he guesses who is feeding him, which seldom happens, unless he be born under a fortunate star, till the glass of water is half empty.

Repeating a Piece of Poetry, or telling an anecdote, is a very favourite way of redeeming a forfeit. Singing a song, either humorous or sentimental, is also admissible.

The Knight of the Rueful Countenance—The knight whose forfeit is to be redeemed is marched slowly round the circle of company by his squire, who kisses the hand of every young lady (and the cheeks of all under a certain age), wiping the mouth of the knight after each salute. If the

knight's countenance relaxes from a rueful expression into a
smile, his forfeit is not returned until he has gone through
some other task.

Other penalties for forfeits there are in abundance, such as
to laugh, cry, cough, and sneeze in the four different corners
of the room; to count forty backwards; to kiss your own
shadow, without laughing, four separate times; to compose a
rhymed verse; to hop on one foot three times round the
room; to ask a riddle of each person in company; to repeat,
without hesitation or mistake, some such brain-puzzle as the
following:—

> "Robert Rowley rolled a round roll round;
> A round roll Robert Rowley rolled round;
> Where rolled the round roll Robert Rowley
>   rolled round?"

Or the still more heart-breaking epic:—

> " There was a man and his name was Cob;
> He had a wife, and her name was Mob;
> He had a dog, and his name was Bob;
> She had a cat, and her name was Chittrybob.
> 'Bob!' says Cob.
> 'Chittrybob!' says Mob.
> Bob was Cob's dog;
> Mob's cat was Chittrybob;
> Cob, Mob, Bob, and Chittrybob!' "

And when all these pains and penalties have been gone
through, if there should still be some pledges remaining, we
recommend that a general amnesty be published, and such
pledges returned to their respective owners, the penalties
being remitted. Above all things, let these round games, like
all others, be pursued in a hearty and generous spirit; and let
us, in concluding this chapter, remind our young readers that
the real way to enjoy them is to preserve a hearty good
humour in the heat of playing.

Outdoor Games

I SPY

is a good game for the playground or the field. The players separate into two parties; one party must hide their eyes in a chosen base or *home* (and no peeping allowed), while the rest seek out the best hiding-places they can find. One of the hiding party waits until his companions are hidden, and then ensconces himself in some nook, crying "Whoop" as he does so, as a signal to the opposing party that they may sally forth. The object of the hidden ones is to rush out suddenly, and touch one of the opposing party, before they can retreat to the shelter of the "home". On the other hand, if one of the seekers can detect the lurking-place of any foe, he gives the alarm by crying—"I spy Jones!" or "I spy Robinson!" whereupon the said Jones or Robinson must come out and try to touch one of the retreating crew, who scour away home at his appearance. Every one thus touched counts *one* toward the side of the player who touched him. When all that are of one side have come out of their concealment, the opposite party take their turn at hiding; and the side which manages to touch most of the enemy's men, wins the game.

BASTE THE BEAR

The boys who are to play at this game begin by twisting their handkerchiefs into the form of whips, with a knot at the end—a thing which most boys can do uncommonly well. A boy is then fixed upon to act "Bear". He crouches down, holding a cord in his hands, while another boy, who represents his master, seizes the opposite end. The boys try to hit the bear with their pocket handkerchiefs, while the master's aim is to touch one of them, without letting go the

rope, or overbalancing the bear, who, from his squatting position, is easily overturned by a jerk of the rope. The first boy touched takes the bear's place, while the late bear becomes bear-leader, and the leader joins the assailants. This is a capital game, requiring the three qualities we like to see developed by all boys—temper, ability, and endurance. Care must be taken, however, that the handkerchiefs are not knotted too tightly, and that the assailants are forbearing with the bear, whose position would otherwise become unbearable.

PITCH-STONE

This game is played by two boys, each of whom takes a smooth, round pebble. One player then throws his pebble about twenty feet before him, and the next tries to strike it with his stone, each time of striking counting as one. If the two pebbles are near enough for the player to place one upon the other with his hand, he is at perfect liberty to do so, and it will count one for him. It is easy enough to play at this game when the pebbles are at some distance apart; but when they lie near each other, it is very difficult to take a good aim, and yet send one's own pebble beyond the reach of the adversary's aim. Two four-pound cannon-balls are the best objects to pitch, as they roll evenly, and do not split, as pebbles always do when they get a hard knock. The game is ten, and whoever gets ten first, wins the game.

AMERICANS AND ENGLISH

This is a very merry old game, and one of the simplest kind. Two captains are named, who choose their men alternately, until all the players are divided into two equal parties. A line is chalked or scratched on the ground, and all the players take hold of each other as represented in the engraving. The object of each party is, by dint of judicious pulling, to draw their adversaries over the line. This is not a mere matter of strength. It depends in a great measure upon the skill of the leaders, who show their skill by letting their respective followers know, by a secret sign, when they are suddenly to slacken their hold, and when to give a long pull, and a strong pull, and a pull altogether. We have seen, assisted, and led this game, hundreds of times, and never failed to find it productive of very great amusement. The game is not to be considered as won, unless the entire side has been dragged over the line.

COCK-FIGHTING

This game, which is productive of fun, is a trial of skill between two players. It is also called "trussing". The players are made to sit down on the ground, and draw their legs up, clasping the hands together below the knees. A stick is then passed under the knees, and over the elbows of each player, as shown in the cut; and then the two players, being placed face to face, try to overbalance each other, by pushing with the points of their toes. Of course, the hands may not be unclasped; and when a combatant rolls over, he lies quite helpless, until set up again by the spectators, or by his backers. The cock who overturns his adversary twice out of three times is considered to have won the fight.

PRISONER'S BASE

This is a capital game. It is a war in miniature, with attack, retreat, stratagems, bold sallies, with defeat and imprisonment for the vanquished, and honour and credit for the victors. The various incidents of this game, its exciting character, and the scope it affords for the display of activity, readiness, and ingenuity, give "Prisoner's Base" an undoubted right to the first place among playground games, not requiring toys. It is played in the following manner:

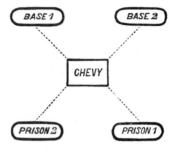

The players should be about sixteen to twenty in number. They are divided into two parties, the men being chosen alternately by two leaders or captains, so as to make the forces as equal as possible. Two bases are then marked out side by side, one for each party, and two prisons or smaller bases opposite the first, at about twenty yards distance—the prison belonging to base No. 1 being opposite to base No. 2 (see diagram), and *vice versa*. A player now runs out from base No. 1, to the space between the bases and the prisons, and standing still, cries out, "Chevy, chevy chase, once, twice, thrice," which is considered as a challenge to the opposite party in base No. 2; one of whom, accordingly, runs out to try and touch the challenger before he can get back to his own base. If he can succeed in this, then must the person thus touched go to the prison belonging to his base, and there remain until he is rescued by one of his own party sallying forth, and touching the prisoner, if he can manage to get to him without being himself touched by one of the opposite party. If, however, "chevy chase" gets back untouched to his own home, the pursuer in his turn is followed by another from the enemy's camp, and is liable to be touched. Thus, any player may sally forth and pursue any other of the opposite party *who has left* the base before him, with the intent to touch him before he can get back to his own base; and every one so touched must go to prison, until

51

he is released by one of his own side getting to his prison and touching him. The two leaders, who of course are the best runners, should not quit their bases except in cases of emergency, as much depends upon their generalship. When several prisoners are in prison together, they may take hold of hands; and the last only need keep his foot in the prison, the rest stretching out in a diagonal line toward their own base. This shortens the distance the rescuer has to run to release one of them. No one who quits the base for the rescue of one prisoner may attempt to rescue another, until he has first returned to his base. When all the prisoners on both sides are released, the game begins again, by a "chevy" being given in their turn by the party last challenged; and it is seldom such a challenge passes without one or more prisoners being the result. The side which manages to send all its adversaries to prison, so that none remain to rescue them, wins the game.

There is a variety of this game in which no prisoner can be rescued; once touched, he is shut out of the game, which concludes when all on one side have been thus excluded. This way of playing at "Prisoner's Base" is, of course, more expeditious than the ordinary method; but far less amusing to those players who happen to get shut out early in the campaign, and have to walk about doing nothing until the contest is decided.

KING SENIO

This sport, the name of which is probably a corruption of "King Cæsar", is rather a romp than a game, but it affords capital fun in cold weather. Two lines are drawn, at about seven or eight yards' distance from each other, on the ground. The players range themselves behind these lines, leaving the intermediate space clear. One of them, called the "king", stands in the vacant space. The object of the players is to run from one base to another, across this space, without being arrested by the king, who, on his part, must try to hold any one of them, while he taps him on the head, and repeats the following formula:

"One, two, three, I crown thee;
Now thou art in Senio's fee."

The player thus captured becomes one of the king's men, and must assist in capturing his former comrades, in their expeditions from base to base. They, on their part, may hop some way out of a base, and *hop* back again, on the approach of danger; but if they *run* out, or put both feet to the ground, they may not return, but must run to the opposite base, be the risk what it may. When more than half the players have been captured, a rush is sometimes made by the stronger party into the bases, to capture the remainder *en masse*, as ships in wartime used to be taken by boarding; at any rate, the game must end sooner or later in the triumph of the king, whose power goes on increasing with every fresh capture; for when a man has once been taken, there is no way of redeeming him.

KING OF THE CASTLE

The accompanying engraving will explain what this game is like. One of the players posts himself on "ground of vantage", and the rest try to pull him down from his elevated position. Sometimes the players divide into two parties, one for attack, and the other for defence, and a good deal of fun, not unmingled with tearing of jackets, is generally the result. In this sport, which is rather a rough one, boys should be particularly careful to "fight fairly", and to keep their tempers, though they may lose the game. Fair pulls and fair pushes only, are allowed in this game; the players must not take hold of any part of the clothes of the king, and must confine their grasps to the hand, the leg, or the arm. The player who succeeds in dethroning the king, takes his place, and is subjected to the like attacks.

FOLLOW MY LEADER

The name of this game sufficiently indicates its nature. A quick, clever lad is chosen as "leader", and the other players have to follow him wherever he goes, to take any leap he chooses, to clamber up any steep place he has climbed; in fact, they must never desert him. The game may be made very amusing, if the leader have wit enough to set his followers such tasks as they can just manage to accomplish by dint of great exertion; for instance, we have heard of a leader who made some of his followers, they being somewhat of the fat type of boys, crawl through the very narrow windows of an outhouse, at the imminent risk of sticking in the middle, in their zeal to stick to their leader. The sailors on board ship often play at this game when they are "turned up", on a fine afternoon, to "skylark" or enjoy themselves; and Captain Marryat tells a tale of an impudent fellow of a sailor leader, who, after leading his followers a wild-goose chase all over the ship, ran off to the galley-fire, and blacked his face with the soot. All the men had to do the same thing; and as they followed their leader, shouting and laughing, he led them to the end of the mainyard, and dropped off *into the sea*. Of course it was a point of honour to follow him, and sailors are not the men to hang back in such a case; but some of them, who could not swim, were nearly drowned. The sailor was called before the captain to be reprimanded; and touching his hat very respectfully, excused himself on the ground that the men were all so dirty, he thought a little washing would do them good—whereupon the captain laughed, and said no more about the matter.

MOUNT HORSE

N. ORR-OO.

This game is best played by four boys of a side; one party being the Horses, and the other the Riders. The party to be Horses are determined by tossing up, and they arrange themselves in the following manner: No. 1 stands erect with his face to the wall; No. 2 places his head against the back of No. 1, and bends his back. No. 3 does the same at the back of No. 2, and No. 4 the same at the back of No. 3. The Riders now make their leaps. The first, making a run, must endeavour to leap over Nos. 4 and 3, to the back of No. 2, and the second rider to leap over No. 4, to No. 3; the last leaping on the back of No. 4. When thus seated, it is the province of the Horses to wriggle off the Riders, or to make their feet touch the ground, without falling themselves. They must not, in wriggling, touch the ground with any part of their bodies but their feet; and if they can succeed in making the Riders touch or fall off, they become Riders; and those who touch or fall, the Horses. The leader of the Riders has no Horse to mount, the other leader standing against the wall. So he stands off, and counts twenty, or repeats the words, "Jump, little nag-tail, one, two, three," three times, adding, at the last time, "Off, off, off!" If the Riders can keep their seats while this is being done, or if any Horse gives way under the weight of the Rider, and comes to the ground, the Riders have another go. But if either of the Horses can wriggle off or throw his Rider, without himself touching the ground, except by his feet, then the Riders become Horses, and the Horses Riders. This play in England is called "Little Nag-tail". Before jumping on, the first Rider always cries out, "Warning!" or "Boot and Saddle!"

TAG

This game may be played by any number of boys. One of the players being chosen as Tag, it is his business to run about in all directions after the other players, till he can touch one, who immediately becomes Tag in his turn. Sometimes when the game is played it is held as a law that Tag shall have no power over those boys who can touch iron or wood. The players then, when out of breath, rush to the nearest iron or wood they can find, to render themselves secure. Cross-tag is sometimes played, in which, whenever another player runs between Tag and the pursued, Tag must immediately leave the one he is after to follow him. But this rather confuses, and spoils the game.

MY GRANDMOTHER'S CLOCK

In this amusing sport the players join hands, and extend their arms to their full extent. One of the outside players remains stationary, and the others run round him as fast as they can, which proceeding is called "winding the block". In this manner the straight line becomes a confused spiral, and all the players get huddled together in a most laughable manner. The winding of the clock usually leads to such disorder that it is next to impossible to unwind it without breaking the line of boys.

BUCK, BUCK, HOW MANY HORNS DO I HOLD UP?

This is a very good game for three boys. The first is called the Buck, the second the Frog, and the third the Umpire. The boy who plays the Buck is blindfolded, and gives a back with his head down, on some wall or paling in front of him, and his hands on his knees. The Frog now leaps on his back, and the Umpire stands at his side: the Frog now holds up one, two, three, five, or any number of fingers, and cries, "Buck, Buck, how many horns do I hold up?" The Buck then endeavours to guess the right number; if he succeeds, the Frog then becomes Buck, and in turn jumps on his back. The Umpire determines whether Buck has guessed the numbers rightly or not.

BATTLE FOR THE BANNER

This game is to be played from a mound, the same as in the engraving of King of the Castle, and it may consist of any number of players. Each party selects a Captain, and having done this, divide themselves into Attackers and Defenders. The defending party provide themselves with a small flag, which is fixed on a staff on the top of the mound, and then arrange themselves on its side and at its base, so as to defend it from the attacks of their opponents, who advance toward the hillock, and endeavour to throw down those that oppose them. Those that are so thrown on either side, are called "dead men", and must lie quiet till the game is finished, which is concluded either when all the attacking party are dead, or the banner is carried off by one of them. The player who carries off the banner is called the Knight, and is chosen Captain for the next game.

BULL IN THE RING

This active, merry, noisy game can be played by any number of boys, and commences by their joining hands and forming a ring, having inclosed some boy in the middle, who is the Bull. It is the Bull's part to make a rush, break through the ring, and escape, and the part of the boys who form the ring to hold their hands so fast together that he cannot break their hold. Before making a rush the Bull must cry "Boo", to give warning, so that the boys may grasp their hands more tightly. The whole ring generally replies to the Bull's challenge by crying "Boo" all together, and a pretty noise they make. When the Bull breaks through the ring, he is pursued until captured, and the boy who seizes him first is "Bull" when they return. A good "Bull" will lead them a pretty dance, clearing fences and ditches, and if he gets back and touches some mark agreed upon, near to where he broke through the ring, he is "Bull" again.

DRAWING THE OVEN

Several boys seat themselves in a row, clasping each other round the waist, thus representing a batch of loaves. Two other players then approach, representing the baker's men, who have to detach the players from each other's hold. To attain this object, they grasp the wrists of the second boy, and endeavour to pull him away from the boy in front of him. If they succeed, they pass to the third, and so on until they have drawn the entire batch. As sometimes an obstinate loaf sticks so tight to its companion that it is not torn away without bringing with it a handful of jacket or other part of the clothing, the game ought not to be played by any but little boys.

KNOCK 'EM DOWN

is made by scooping a hole in the ground, and placing in it an upright stick; on the top of it is placed a stone, or similar substance. The player then retires  to a distance, and flings at the stone with clubs or balls, the latter being preferable. If the stone falls into the hole, the player only counts one toward game, but if it falls outside the hole, he counts two. This is a capital game for the seaside, and can be played upon the sands. This is similar to a game called Baton, which is played in this wise:

A stick is fixed in a kind of cup or hole, about six inches over, in a loose moist soil, and the players consist of the Keeper and Throwers. The Keeper places on the top of the stick some article, such as an apple or orange, and the

59

Throwers endeavour to knock it off, by throwing at it short thick sticks, or batons; whoever succeeds in doing this claims the prize, whenever it falls without the hole. The Thrower will soon find, in his play, that to hit the stick is of little importance, as from the perpendicular line of gravity which the apple or orange will take in its descent, it is almost certain to fall in the hole. The aim, therefore, should be to strike the object from the stick.

THE DRILL SERGEANT

This is a game something like Follow my Leader. It consists of the Drill Sergeant and his Squad. The Drill Sergeant places himself in a central spot, and arranges his Squad before him in a line. He then commences another guard here with various odd gestures, which all the Squad are bound to imitate. He moves his head, arms, legs, hands, feet, in various directions, sometimes sneezes, coughs, weeps, laughs, and bellows, all of which the Squad are to imitate. Sometimes this is a most amusing scene, and provokes great laughter. Those who are observed to laugh, however, are immediately ordered to stand out of the line, and when half the number of players are so put out, the others are allowed to ride them three times round the playground, while the Drill Sergeant with a knotted handkerchief accelerates their motions.

WARNING

This is an excellent game for cold weather. It may be played by any number of boys. In playing it "loose bounds" are made near a wall or fence, about four feet wide and twelve long. One of the boys is selected, who is called the Cock, who takes his place within the bounds; the other players are called the Chickens, who distribute themselves in various parts of the playground. The Cock now clasps his hands together, and cries, "Warning once, warning twice, and warning three times over; a bushel of wheat, and a bushel of rye, when the Cock crows, out jump I." He then, keeping his hands still clasped before him, runs after the other players; when he touches one,

he and the player so touched immediately make for the bounds; the other players immediately try to capture them before they get there; if they succeed, they are privileged to get upon their backs and ride them home. The Cock and his Chick now come out of the bounds hand-in-hand, and try to touch some other of the players; the moment they do this they break hands, and they and the player now touched run to the bounds as before, while the other players try to overtake them, so as to secure the ride. The three now come from the bounds in the same manner, capture or touch a boy, and return. If, while trying to touch the other boys, the players when sallying from the grounds break hands before they touch any one, they may immediately be ridden, if they can be caught before they reach the bounds. Sometimes when three players have been touched the Cock is allowed to join the out party, but this is of no advantage in playing the game.

DUCK ON THE ROCK, OR DUCK-STONE

This capital game requires at least three players, but its interest is considerably increased when there are six or eight. A large stone, called "the mammy", having a tolerably flat top, is placed on the ground, and "home" is marked off about twelve feet from it. Each player being provided with a stone about double the size of a baseball, the game is commenced by pinking for "Duck"—that is, by all standing at the home and throwing their stones or ducks in succession at the mammy. The player whose duck falls or rolls farthest from it becomes Duck, and must place his stone on the top of the mammy. The other players are allowed to take up their ducks and go to the home unmolested, while Duck is placing his stone down; they then throw their ducks, one after the other, at it, and endeavour to knock it off the mammy. Duck must replace his stone whenever it is knocked off, and the throwers must pick up their ducks and endeavour to run home while he is so engaged. Should the duck remain on after four or five have thrown at it, the stones must rest where they fell, until some player more skilful than the others knocks off the duck, and so gives the throwers a chance of getting home. If Duck can touch one of the throwers as he is running home with his duck in his hand, the one so touched becomes Duck. When the duck is knocked off by any players, it must be instantly replaced, as Duck cannot touch any one while it is off the mammy. When a thrower's duck falls and lies before the mammy, Duck may touch him if he can, even before he picks up his duck. When Duck succeeds in touching a thrower, he must run to the mammy and quickly remove his duck; if he has time, he should tap the mammy twice with his duck, and call out, "Feign double-duck!" as he may then walk home without fear of being touched by the boy whom he has just made Duck. Should all the players have thrown without being able to knock the duck off, it is frequently proposed by some of them to Duck to take either a "heeler", a "sling", or a "jump" toward home, in order that they may have a chance of reaching it. Duck may refuse or assent to these proposals at his option. The "heeler" is performed by the player kicking his duck backward toward home; the "sling" by placing the duck on the middle of the right foot, and slinging it as far in the direction of home as possible; and the "jump" by placing the duck between the feet, and holding it in that manner while a jump is taken, the jumper letting the stone go as he alights, so that it may roll forward. If the duck is so far from home that one sling, jump, or heeler will not suffice, two or more of each may be taken, provided of course that Duck allows them. If the player does not get his duck home in the number of slings, jumps, or heelers, agreed on, he becomes Duck. Duck-stone is one of the liveliest of winter games, but we must caution our readers against playing roughly or carelessly at it, as they may through negligence do one another much harm, on account of the weight of the stones and the force with which they must be thrown.

CLIMBING TREES

In climbing trees both the hands and feet are to be used, but the climber should never forget that it is to the hands that he has to trust. He should carefully look upward and select the branches for his hands, and the knobs and other excrescences of the trees for his feet. He should also mark the best openings for the advance of his body. He should also be particularly cautious in laying hold of withered branches, or those that have suffered decay at their junction with the body of the tree, in consequence of the growth of moss, or through the effects of wet. In descending, he should be more cautious than in ascending, and hold fast by his hands. He should rarely slide down by a branch to the ground, as distances are very ill calculated from the branches of a tree.

MARBLES

The old-fashioned marbles were made by the attrition of pieces of stone against each other in a kind of mill, and were far better than many of those now in use, which are made of porcelain. When we were young the painted marbles, now a deal in vogue, were called "Chinese", and were not valued so much as others. They are generally too smooth to shoot well. Marbles then, and still are wherever marbles is much

63

played, divided into common marbles and "alleys". Of these last a "red alley" is equal to two common marbles, a "black alley" equal to three, and a "white alley" to four. Very large marbles called "tomtrollers", are sometimes, but not often used—never in the ring games; and the very small marbles, called "peewees", are only fit for children with very small hands.

There are three ways of shooting a marble. 1, *Trolling*, which consists in projecting the marble so that it rolls along the ground, until it strikes the marble at which it is aimed; 2, *Hoisting*, where the marble is shot from at or above the level of the knee, while the party stands; and *Knuckling down*, where the player shoots with the middle knuckle of his fore-finger touching the ground, but makes his marble describe a curve in the air on its way to the ring. A boy has to be a good player, a "dabster", as they say, to knuckle down well.

To shoot a marble properly, it must be held between the tip of the fore-finger and the first joint of the thumb, resting on the bend of the second finger, and propelled forward by suddenly forcing up the thumb-nail. Some boys place it between the bend of the first finger and the thumb-joint.

This is called "shooting cunnethumb", and not only subjects those who do it to the ridicule of their associates, but tires the thumb very much.

Marbles is a game played in different

ways. We play it in the United States different somewhat from the English, and in different parts of this country various games prevail.

TEETOTUM

is a game of marbles. A teetotum, with figures on its sides, is set spinning, and shot at. If it be hit and knocked over while spinning, the lucky shooter gets the number of marbles set down on the upper side of the teetotum.

BOUNCE-EYE

is an English game requiring no skill. Each player puts his marble in a ring, and then each in turn drops a marble on the pile. All they thus knock out they take. If a player's marble stays in the ring, it is lost and goes to the general stock.

THE PILE GAME

is similar, but requires better players. Three marbles are placed in the ring, and one set on top. The shooters get all they knock out, but forfeit their alley if they miss.

PICKING CHERRIES

(in England "Picking Plums") is played by laying the marbles of the players in a row, instead of a ring, and shooting at them under the same rules of gain and loss as in the "Pile game".

DIE-SHOT

is an English game. We have never seen it played here. A marble is rubbed nearly square—at least enough to stand firmly, and to have a flat upper surface. On this last part an ivory die is placed. The player is to strike the marble so that the die will fall off, paying first one marble for his shot. If he succeeds, whatever number is uppermost on the die indicates the number of marbles he is to receive.

THE POT GAME

is played by making three holes, or "pots", in the ground, about four feet apart. To determine who shoots first, one boy takes a marble and places his hands behind his back. He then shows his closed fists to one of the others, who guesses which hand holds the marble. If he guesses right, the other boy goes last, and the successful one tries with another. If he succeeds with him, he tries another, and so on. If he fails he is next to last, and the one who guessed right goes before him, and takes his place to try. For instance: four boys are to play. John Smith takes a marble, and puts it in one hand behind his back. He then shows both fists to Peter Brown, and asks which hand has the marble. Peter Brown touches the right hand. The hands are opened, and the marble is found to be in the left hand. Peter Brown is the last to play. John Smith now tries Andrew Jones. Andrew guesses the right hand, and it is found there. Now John Smith is next to last, and Andrew Jones tries Alfred Williams. Alfred guesses the left hand, and the marble was in the right hand. Consequently he falls back; and the players shoot in the following order: 1. Andrew Jones. 2. Alfred Williams. 3. John Smith. 4. Peter Brown. Andrew now knuckles down at a line six feet from the first hole, and shoots. If his marble gets into the hole, he shoots from there to the second; and if he gets into that, then into the third, and wins a marble from each of the others. If he misses, he puts his alley, or another instead, into the first hole; and Alfred takes his turn. So it goes in succession. If the player who wins the first hole chooses, he can make each of his opponents in turn put down their alleys for him to shoot at. If he hits them they are his. If he misses, the one whose alley he aimed at may shoot at his alley. If that be hit, he is out of the game, and his alley gone.

SPANS AND SNOPS

consists of one boy laying down his marble, and, giving a distance, his antagonist shoots at it; if he misses, the first boy shoots at the alley of the second, till one is struck, which the striker claims. He also gets it, if he can span the space between the two marbles, so that his thumb will rest on one and his forefinger on the other. Failing to do this, his companion shoots with his marble at that of his adversary, and thus the game goes on, a marble being paid each time a span or a snop occurs.

FORTIFICATIONS

may be called an elaborate version of "picking cherries". The marbles are not merely ranged along a line, but disposed on a diagram, as in the illustration, and the players try to shoot them out of the limits of the fortification, not being allowed to consider a marble as won until it is quite clear of the outworks.

If the taw of the attacking person remains within the fortress, it is considered as a prisoner of war, and must remain where it is, until shot out by another player, whose booty it becomes, according to the laws and regulations of war. This "fortification" game is much played in France, and is supposed to have been recently introduced here by some young Americans, on their return to their native country, after a residence in a French college at Paris.

KNOCK OUT, OR LAG OUT

is played by knocking marbles against a wall, or perpendicular board set up for the purpose; and the skill displayed in it

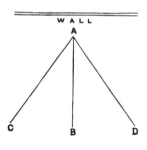

depends upon the player's attention to what is called in mechanics the resolution of forces. For instance, if an object be struck against the wall at A from the mark at B, it will return again to B in a straight line; if it be sent from C to A, it will, instead of returning to C, pass off aslant to D, and its course will form the angle C D; the angle of incidence being equal to the angle of reflection.

The game is played by any number of players; the first player throws his marble against the wall, so that it may rebound and fall about a yard distant from it; the other players then, in succession, throw their marbles against the wall, in such a way as to cause them to strike any of those already lagged out, and the marble struck is considered won by the owner of the marble that strikes it, in addition to which, the winner has another throw. When only two boys play, each successively throws out till one of the "laggers" is struck, and he who strikes takes up all.

This game may also be played by spanning the marbles, as in *Spans and Snops*.

THE RING GAME, OR RING TAW,

as they call it in England, is the great game of marbles. The English mode is as follows: Two rings are drawn upon the ground, a small one six inches in diameter, enclosed by a larger one, six feet in diameter. Into the small ring each player puts a marble, called "shot". The players then proceed to any part of the large ring, and from thence, as an offing, shoot at the marbles in the centre. If a player knocks a marble out of the ring he wins it, and he is entitled to shoot again before his companions can have a shot. When all the players have shot their marbles, they shoot from the places at which their marbles rested at the last shot. If the shooter's marble remain in the small circle, he is out, and has to drop a marble in the ring, and he must put in besides all the marbles he had previously won in that game. It is a rule, also, that, when one player shoots at and strikes another's marble, the one so struck is considered dead, and its owner must give up to the striker of the taw all the

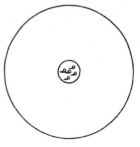

marbles he may have previously won during the game. The game is concluded when all the marbles are shot out of the ring, or all the players' marbles are killed.

In this country it is played that way in some few places. In others it is varied. The general way is as follows: instead of the outer ring, a line six feet off is drawn, and called the base. (See illustration at beginning of marbles.) From this the players knuckle down, unless someone prefers to hoist, when he must call out, "hoistings." Each player puts one alley in the ring. If the first shooter knocks any or all the marbles out they are his, and he shoots on until the ring is cleared, or he misses. If his alley remains inside of the ring, it is "fat", that is, he loses it, and is out of the game, unless it remains after shooting out the last marble. After anyone misses, the next one may, if he chooses, shoot at the alley of the other, and if he hits it, the other is killed, and is out of the game, and his alley gone. The player who has just killed one of his antagonists may then go to base, and shoot at the ring. If, however, he kills all his antagonists, he takes the ring marbles without shooting at them. And when anyone is killed, he gives to the victor all the marbles he has won during the game, whether he got them from the ring or by killing his antagonist. If his opponent's marble has got in a hole or behind any obstacle, he may cry "puts", which will give him a right to place it in an eligible position, at the same distance, or may cry "clearance", and then remove anything from between him and the marble. But if his antagonist cries "fen puts", or "fen clearance", before he cries "puts" or "clearance", he must shoot as it lies. And he must shoot from where his marble lies always. In some places, however, if he cries "roundings", before his antagonist cries "fen roundings", he can go around to some more eligible point at the same distance, and shoot from thence.

Another way, in vogue in some parts of the West: a ring is made, and one marble placed in the centre, and the others at points on the edge of the circle. The player may either hoist, troll, or knuckle down, as suits him. If he knocks out the centre marble at the first shot, it counts him one. If he hits one of the others he shoots on, till he has hit all, or misses. If he clears the ring it counts one, or if he kills all his antagonists it counts one. The players who follow the first may neglect the ring and follow him to shoot at his alley, and he do the same with them. Whoever counts three first wins the game.

In all these games the players "lag" for the first shot. That is, they troll from base to a marble placed in the centre of the ring, and whoever gets nearest, shoots first. Whoever wins a game always shoots first in the next game.

Remember that a "taw" and "marble" are the same; but in this country the word "taw" is rarely used. Strictly speaking, it only applies to the marble a player shoots with.

MAN-HUNT

This is strenuous and any number can join in. It is more exciting than a paper chase, and does not litter the country with paper.

First mark out an agreed area, say six miles by one, on the map, limited by recognisable natural features, outside which the men must not go, with your starting point on one end line and a suitable pub, as your objective, in the middle of the other end line. The hunters set off first and the two men a quarter of an hour later. The hunters may not blockade the starting point nor the objective but should stretch a cordon across the area and ambush likely points in the attempt to stop the men from passing through.

You have lunch at your objective and man-hunt home. It is unsuitable for crowded suburban areas.

FRENCH AND ENGLISH

or

PRISONERS' BASE

This game cannot be played without a sizeable lawn. Two well-matched sides are picked up or arranged, one half of the lawn being the camp or territory of the As, the other of the Bs. A given number of treasures (old shoes, red handkerchiefs and so on) are spaced along the base line of each camp, and the aim of the game is to seize the enemy's treasure. Yet if you are caught on the enemy's ground you are a prisoner and have to join the treasure on the base line until you are rescued, i.e. touched, by one of your side. Once a treasure or a rescued prisoner is in your bag (and each sortie across the enemy lines can only achieve *one* prize) you can make the return journey to your own territory unmolested. Players usually make their own subsidiary rules as the game (after all it *is* only a game) progresses. But where there are young it is better to allow the charge across the base line of the enemy camp to bring immunity and not the actual picking-up of a treasure or touching a prisoner; this can then be done at leisure while gaining breath and applying the dock leaves. N.B. It can spoil the fun if each side places a grown-up with a sadistic streak as "goalie" guarding the treasure, for it paralyses the free movement of the game.

HUMAN POLO

The biggest men are the ponies, and the girls or lighter weights mount them pick-a-back, hold on with one hand and use walking-sticks to drive a tennis-ball through goals at opposite ends of a lawn or tennis-court. Holding opponents with the hands is not allowed, nor kicking (of man or ball), but bumping, boring and hooking sticks are all part of the game. A player may remount; but may not play from the ground.

FLAT-RACING
Ponies similarly mounted race thirty yards on hands and knees; after which apply iodine to the kneecaps. Jockeys may not remount or touch the earth with their feet.

TIERCE
Or Twos-and-Threes. One player is "He", the others stand in a fairly wide circle in pairs, one in front of the other; but in one group there are three. The Behind Man in this group begins to run, and "He" has to try to catch him before or touch him before he slips into the circle and stands in front of any other pair. The moment he does so the Behind Man of that pair has to run and take his chance of being caught, as there must never be more than two people in a group. If "He" touches his prey before it saves itself by joining a new group, "He" instantly places himself in safety before one of the pairs, and the player just caught becomes "He", and chases the Third Man on the outside of the circle.

THE ROOF GAME
is played by two persons with a discarded tennis-ball and a sloping roof. The ideal roof is 60 feet long, slopes at an angle of $110°$, ends 8 feet from the ground and has a perfectly clear space in front of it. Each player in turn serves one ball from any position in this run-way and at any speed. The receiver must catch the ball before it touches the ground. If he does so, neither scores; if he fails, the server scores one point. In either event the service passes. The receiver scores one point if the server fails to reach the roof or throws the ball over the roof or so that it falls beyond the roof at the ends. In the latter event he must fetch it, as well as lose a point. A game is five points, or nine for the very strenuous. Feinting is not allowed, but a disguise of

73

direction by looking the other way is permitted. There should be no delay between receiving and serving. Given the right roof it is a great game, almost as sweaty as Squash.

A chimney is a hazard: a ball may be served against it with such force as frequently to elude the receiver; but if the server misses it he risks the penalties for throwing over the roof. This game can be played as a foursome.

WATER GAMES

Les Joûtes, or *Tilting*, between champions in boats is played by French fishermen, and is dangerous to life and limb.

The lances should be long stout bamboos, and for safety well padded at the ends, with a mop-head sewn up in canvas. The champions stand upright in the extreme stern of the boats and should wear wooden or cork breast-plates from the chin to well below the fork. Rudders should be unshipped before beginning.

Water Polo need not be played according to elaborate rules, but there must be no tackling an opponent who has not got the ball, and care should be taken not to kick one's opponent in a vital spot. It can be played with a football or any other ball or with a tenni-quoit rubber ring, but if the ball is small players must pass when tackled and not fight their way through.

Racing on rubber animals is amusing, but there are few jockeys skilled enough to complete a course of twenty yards, even in still water.

Kissing at the bottom of the sea is a strange experience and not likely to be spotted by the guardians of our morals. The lovers should stand about ten yards apart up to their necks, empty their lungs, and crawl towards each other along the bottom with their eyes open.

GAMES ON HORSEBACK

THERE are two axioms concerning all games played on horseback. The first is that the rules should be as few and as simple as possible. If the rules are complicated, the rider, even with the best of intentions, will be liable to forget them in the heat of the game, and though they may look plain enough when set out on paper, no horse has yet been taught to read.

The second axiom is that polo is far and away the best of all mounted games. Which is something of a contradiction to axiom No. 1, because the rules of polo are neither few nor simple; but in the case of polo the end justifies the means. The rules of polo are not set out here, because they are readily obtainable from a number of other sources. It may at least be said that wherever eight horsemen (or horsewomen) are gathered together, polo, if necessary in a modified form, is the best game to play. The suggestions set out here are intended for those occasions when lack of ponies, sticks or flat ground makes any sort of polo impossible.

THE HANDKERCHIEF GAME

The simplest of such games, and therefore perhaps the best according to axiom No. 1. It has no rules—the avoidance of obviously dangerous riding is not a rule, because it is a matter of ordinary common sense—and there is no limit to the number of players. One rider fixes one end of a handkerchief into his collar, through his braces, under his belt, or in any way so that it blows out behind him and is easily snatchable. The other riders try to take it away. Whoever gets it sticks it into his belt, or what you will, and becomes "he" in his (or her) turn.

Variations on the theme of pig-sticking provide a number of good games.

FOOTBALL PIG-STICKING

is one of the best. One rider draws behind him a football or bladder on a long piece of string. The other players ride in "heats" of two, three or four carrying long sticks as spears, their tips being coated with whitewash, chalk or some such substance. The first player to mark the ball or bladder secures first spear. In this game it is important that the string on which the ball is dragged is of a good length, and if the ground is rough so much the better, as it will cause the "pig" to bounce about and jink. Alternatives to the football or bladder are sacks stuffed with straw, or balloons, in which latter case first spear is won by bursting the balloon.

MUSICAL CHAIRS

is sufficiently obvious to need little description save the reminder that the players must keep in a *canter* until the music stops. To avoid congestion of horses it is a good plan to spread them out by making the players gallop away from the circle when the music stops, round a post and then back to the chairs before dismounting to sit down; an alternative is to put the chairs inside a circle, which the players must keep outside until the music stops. Overturned buckets are sturdier than chairs.

Variations on this, sometimes seen at gymkhanas, are MUSICAL STALLS, in which stalls made of hurdles are used instead of chairs, and the horses have to be ridden into them, there being as usual one stall less than the number of horses. MUSICAL HATS is a third alternative. Players ride round a row of poles which have hats on them; when the music stops each player attempts to place a hat on his or her head. This can be made more entertaining by choosing the hats half male and half female, and watching the effect when they become distributed among the riders.

GRETNA GREEN RACES

are always entertaining at gymkhanas and provide a good test of horsemanship. The race can take two forms. The "bridegroom" can ride with a led horse over two or three flights of hurdles to his "bride"; he will then dismount and pick up a ring from a table, when both "bride" and "bridegroom" mount and return hand in hand to the winning-post. Alternatively the "bridegroom" can jump one hurdle with a led horse to fetch his "bride", they will then jump to more hurdles hand in hand, dismount at a table and both sign a register (legibly), remount and return to the winning-post, hand in hand.

THE BUTTON RACE

is on a somewhat similar theme. The man must race over hurdles or similar obstacles to his partner, who is seated on a chair, bringing with him a button, a piece of cloth, a needle and thread. His partner must sew the button on to the cloth, using all the thread, before he can return to the winning-post.

THE WHISTLING RACE

The natural law that it is impossible to laugh and to whistle at the same time is the secret of the success of the Whistling Race. The men taking part are gathered at the start and each is told the name of a different popular tune. They must then race down the course to their partners, who are armed with pencil and paper, and to whom each man whistles his allotted tune. His partner writes down on the paper the name of the tune she believes it to be, and the man returns to the starting-point with the paper for verification.

CIGARETTE AND UMBRELLA RACE

Players race down the course, dismount, light a cigarette, open an umbrella, remount and return to the start with the cigarette alight and the umbrella open. This race should be reserved for gusty days.

Parlour Games for Grown-Ups

Games of Motion

FAGGOTS

THIS game consists in forming a circle and placing the parties two by two, so that a gentleman holding a lady fronting him forms what is called a *Faggot*. The players must be an even number. The Faggot being formed, two persons are chosen to chase, one running after the other. The person running first has the right to cross the circle in every direction, and for that the faggots must be wide enough apart for them to run easily around and among them. When the person who runs does not wish to be caught and made to take the place of the person running after him, he places himself before one of the faggots, in the middle of the circle, and as he pleases. Then this faggot is composed of three persons, which must not be. The one who finds himself outside of the circle must then escape to prevent being caught. If he is caught, he takes the place of the runner, who lets him run after him, or, if he prefers it, enters immediately into the circle and places himself before a faggot, which immediately provides a new runner, who is obliged to fly immediately, like the first; but he can on the instant force another to run, by placing himself before a faggot, which animates the game, if indeed the running is done with skill and agility.

This game, of which the motion and playfulness constitute all the animation, it is to be regretted, is impracticable on winter nights, when the space required would be too large.

HOT COCKLES

IS a game no less known than the first. A Penitent, chosen by chance, or by his own choice, hides his face upon a lady's lap, which lady serves as Confessor, and places herself in an armchair in the midst of the company. The Penitent places his hand behind him—not on his back, which might be dangerous if the person who is to hit it should forget the proper moderation, but on his hips. Then a lady or a gentleman hits this hand, and the owner of the hand has to guess who struck. If he succeed, the person he guessed is to take his place; if he is mistaken, he goes on till he has shown more penetration. It is very amusing to the spectators to see the impatience of the guesser, who having received several blows without guessing, hears the players coolly propose to him a *night-cap*, (a sort of reproach which they make to him), which would enable him to pass the night as he is.

But let us return to the moderation to be shown in the blows used in this game. A well-bred man will easily see that there is more propriety, as well for the striker as the stricken, in giving a light touch, or in scarce touching the hand of an amiable person, than in striking it roughly with a vigorous hit, of which the consequence will be the retreat of the guesser.

THE WOLF AND THE DOG

ALL the ladies of a party can find occupation in this game, but only one gentleman is wanted, and it is always the most active, because he has to call his courage and patience forth.

This person is called in the game the *Wolf*; the oldest lady is the *Dog*, and all the others place themselves behind her, and are called the *dog's tail*, collectively.

On the part of the Wolf, his business is to seize the player at the end of the tail; but he manifests his hostile intentions in this phrase:

"*I am the Wolf, I will eat you.*"

The Dog replies—

"*I am the Dog, and will defend myself.*"

The Wolf replies—

"*I will have a little end of your tail.*"

After this dialogue the Wolf tries to make an outbreak on the tail so much desired, but the Dog, extending her arms, defends the passage, and if he succeeds in forcing it, the young person at the end abandons her post before she can be seized, and places herself before the Dog, where she runs no risk, and so do all the others successively until the Dog is the last of the line.

Then the game stops, the unskilful player gives as many forfeits as he has suffered puppies to escape, and the players choose a successor for him.

If, on the contrary, he succeeds, before the end of the game, in seizing one of them, he does not eat her, but he has the right to kiss her, and make her give a forfeit, which promises new pleasure when the game is over.

Observe merely that this game, requiring much motion and vivacity, would be ill played in an apartment, and it offers a charming picture in a garden, a yard, or any other locality vast enough to allow young persons to show the grace and lightness of their running.

HOW DO YOU LIKE YOUR NEIGHBOURS?

THIS is a fireside game. The company are seated in a ring about the fire. One of them goes to the centre.

The man in the centre points to one of the company and says, "How do you like your neighbours?"

The reply may be, "Very well indeed", or else, "Not at all". If the reply is "Very well indeed", all change places and the man in the centre tries to find a place during the resultant confusion.

Usually the reply is "Not at all". The man in the centre

then asks, "Who would you like to change with?" "I would like to change with—"

As soon as the name is given, the two must change places, whilst the man in the centre tries to seize one of the places.

Alertness and quickness are essential if the man in the centre is to be kept out. He is not permitted to leave the centre until the name has been given, nor must he come close to the players, as is done in many other games.

One of the most attractive things about this game is that it enables you to cast out a hated rival who happens to be seated beside the lady of your heart.

WILLIAM AND MARY

ALL the company stand in a ring except two, who are blindfolded. One of these two must be a boy (William) and the other a girl (Mary).

William's object is to capture Mary, and Mary's object is to elude capture. From time to time William calls out, "Mary", and Mary must at once answer, "William". She then hurries away from the spot from which her presence was announced.

When William finally captures Mary, they kiss, the bandages are removed, and another William and Mary are appointed.

It adds to the fun if William is blindfolded before Mary is chosen by the Director, so that he is not quite sure who she is.

This is a rather dangerous game; I have known it lead to an engagement to marry.

BLIND-MAN'S BUFF, SITTING

TO play Blind-man's Buff, sitting, the party places itself in a circle on chairs drawn very near together; the person whom destiny has appointed, or who voluntarily offers himself for *Blind-Man*, receives the bandage, which is placed over his eyes by a lady if the blind-man is a gentleman, or by a gentleman if he be a lady.

When all are sure that the blind-man cannot see the

surrounding objects, all change place rapidly, in order to put his memory out. Then he approaches the circles without feeling, for that is positively forbidden him: he seats himself on the knees of the first person he meets, and, without placing his hands on the clothes, but by softly pressing the seat offered him, by listening to the smothered laughter his funny manner of reconnoitring is sure to excite, or by the rustling of the garments (the noise of which often betrays the person wearing them), he is obliged to tell the name of him or her on whose knees he is seated, and, in case he does not know the name, to designate them so they may be known.

If the blind-man guess right, the person named takes his place, receives the band, and makes the same researches. On the contrary, if he guesses wrong, the party clap hands to show him his mistake, and he goes on to another person's knees (having seen his error), without employing other means than those mentioned in the game.

It is customary for the society, to prevent the blind-man from recognising persons too soon, to execute various little stratagems, such as some of them extending to their knees the garments of their neighbours, or placing on them an armchair cushion. Ladies dressed in silk put shawls over them, each trying to disguise her individuality as much as possible.

Sometimes it is preferred to conduct the blind-man by the hand, when they wish to vary the game swiftly, and to make each take the bandage in his turn; because then the conductor can skilfully warn the blind-man of the name he should pronounce, so that each person should contribute successively to the amusement of the party.

Games which require Attention

THE TRAVELLING MONK

REQUIRES attention, but is not difficult.

He who plays the Monk relates a tour he has made for the good of his convent, and before beginning his recital he must give a name to every one of the players, so that each is called Hood, Cloak, Sandal, Cord, or some other part of his dress; and every time he speaks in his story of any one of these different articles, the person bearing its name is obliged to repeat it immediately, with this difference, that when the Monk only says it once, he is obliged to repeat it twice, and when the Monk utters it twice in succession it is to be repeated but once. When he names the *Convent* the players all together must add the name of Saint Francis to that of the article of clothing of which they bear the name; that is to say, "Cord of Saint Francis", "Sandal of Saint Francis", &c. When the monk says "My brothers", they must all reply only "Saint Francis"; when he says "Saint Francis", all repeat, "We, unworthy brothers." At every mistake they give a forfeit.

The traveller should mix up his recital with art, in order to surprise and embarrass his hearers, either by calling them, all together by the names of *Convent, my brothers*, and *Saint Francis*, or by repeating without stopping the names of the utensils and clothes they have adopted.

Attention is everything in this game, where wit is not amiss, but not absolutely necessary.

Games of Memory

CONFESSION BY DICE

THE number or the sex of the players does not matter; only they must agree beforehand upon a Confessor. He is named, and the game commences.

He takes a number of blank cards, keeps one himself, on which he writes secretly what he intends, this time, to call a *sin*, or *forbidden act*. Then, addressing the one who is on the right, nearest him, he tells him to rise, and gives him a pair of dice, which the other spins on the table, and the number which comes up indicates the number of faults of which he is to accuse himself.

The Penitent seats himself, writes his confession, and

passes it respectfully to the Confessor, who begins with the sin written first. If this last is on the paper the Penitent gives a forfeit; if not, he is declared absolved; but in either case his confession is read aloud, because the players, called upon in their turn, must not mention the same sin which the first one has, which forces the last to name the defect mentioned on the Confessor's card.

Here is an example of this game, in which the sin secretly written is Idleness.

The Confessor. "My daughter, do you feel aught upon your conscience?"

The Penitent. "Alas! yes, my father."

The Confessor. "Rise, take these dice, spin them on the table. You have turned up 4. Accuse yourself of four sins."

The Penitent writes his confession and puts it aside. The Confessor, having read her confession to himself, says—

"Then, my daughter, you are innocent, for here are your confessions:

" 'I have gone to balls.'

" 'I have gone several times to the play.'

" 'I have spoken against my neighbour.'

" 'I have eaten meat in Lent.'

"All the sins are forgiven you; go in peace, and sin not again.

"You, my son, have you aught to reproach yourself with?"

Penitent. "Only too much, father!"

The Confessor. "Rise, &c. You are guilty; give a forfeit, for you accuse yourself

" 'Of having passed yesterday in gambling,'

" 'Of drinking,'

" 'Of carefully avoiding all kinds of work,' " &c., &c.

It is only when all have confessed that the Confessor reads the names of the sins secretly inscribed on his tablets.

The turn finished, another Confessor, who also chooses a sin from which to abstain, is chosen, and the game begins again; and in this second round, as in the following ones, if they take place, it is forbidden to designate any fault before noted by the Confessor previously in power, or confessed by one of the Penitents. This it is easy to verify, since all the confessions are kept. This rule multiplies the forfeits greatly.

HIS WORSHIP THE CURATE

IN former times this game was not consistent with politeness or etiquette. It was only a succession of continual contradictions, and consisted of the use of *you* instead of *thou*. This *you*, pronounced in speaking to any but the Curate, requires a forfeit from the person who said it out of time. It was the same with the *thees* and *thous* addressed to the Curate. It is easy to see that this was not very delicate. It is now played thus:—

A Curate and a Vicar are chosen, and as many professions as there are players; and when the Curate has begun, and has said to the one he wishes to attack, "I come from your house, Mr. Optician, or Madame the Milliner, (or any other trades-person), but I did not find you in; where were you?" The person interrogated replies, "I was at—(whomever she pleases to say—Hairdresser, Tailor, Goldsmith, &c., provided one has been named.)

The person mentioned, instead of replying, "That is a falsehood," demands of him who has been questioned, "What were you doing there?" and the person must reply something suited to the trade mentioned. For instance, if he has been to the Bookseller's he replies, that it was for books. The Bookseller excuses himself, saying, "I was at the Binder's," who asks him, "*What were you doing there?*" "Getting a book bound." A forfeit must be given when something is said not suited to the trade mentioned. It is the same if the same motive be assigned for a visit as before. They have also the right to go to the Curate's, and at his question, "*What were you doing there?*" is replied, "Getting married," or any thing relating to his ministry, and the Curate is obliged to make a reply conformable to the person whose trade he mentions.

It is easy to see that, played *thus*, the play has nothing rude in it; and that it can become useful in giving general notions in arts and trades.

THE LOVE LEAF

HE who proposes the game (and no one should do that who is not sure he can lead it, unless he designates another who can),—He, I say, who proposes, distributes a hand at piquet, by three or four cards, to each member of the society, according to its number, and keeps in reserve the remainder, which he alone is free to consult when he pleases, since he takes no part in the game, except to inspect it as far as necessary. All who have received take care to keep theirs hid, so as not to give their comrades any advantage over them.

The distribution finished, the Master of the game says to the person nearest him—

"Have you the Love-Leaf?"

She replies, "I have the Love-Leaf."

"What did you see on the Love-Leaf?"

"I saw," (here the answering one names the card she pleases, provided it is different from those in her hand.)

The conductor of the game consults his cards; if the card named is found, the answering one gives a forfeit; if it is not there, each of the players examines his hand, and the one who finds it deposits it in the Master's hand.

If the person who designates the card, and the one who has it are of opposite sex, the result is a kiss to each other; if not, both give a forfeit. In either case the game continues; that is to say, the one who has replied interrogates the right-hand person, and employs the same formula, "Have you read?" &c., and so on until all the cards are given to the distributor.

By dint of naming cards it is natural that some should be repeated. Then the player so maladroit as to forget those already mentioned, is obliged to give a forfeit. Thus, and to avoid the continual researches which would render the game interminable, the distributor should carefully avoid all those named, and keep them hidden, in order to give the start, and consult them each time he calls a new one.

It is rigorously required that any card named which is in

his hands when he makes this mistake through ignorance or forgetfulness.

As the cards are exhausted, the persons who have no more leave the game. They do not give any sign, under pain of a forfeit.

THE LOVE-BOX

THIS Game, invented for forfeits, is played thus:—

The one who begins presents a box to his right-hand neighbour, and says, "I sell you my Box of Love which contains three words, *love, kiss,* and *dismiss*." The neighbour replies, "Whom do you love?" "Whom do you kiss?" "Whom do you dismiss?"

The player who has given the box names, at each question, one of the persons in the company whom she *loves, kisses,* and *dismisses*. The person she *kisses* kisses her in reality, and the one she *dismisses* gives a forfeit. One may *love, kiss,* and *dismiss* several and even all the persons present, but that is not permitted till the end, which is thus shown.

THE AVIARY

CHOOSE one of the company to act as Bird-catcher. All the rest then secretly adopt the name of some bird. The Bird-catcher has these names told him in a whisper, and if he is not sure of his memory, he takes a note of each, taking care to repeat none. He places opposite the names of the persons who have chosen them, and then opens the game in this manner:—

"Ladies and Gentlemen, I have just got together a complete Aviary. There is an Eagle, a Vulture, a Parrot, a Crow, a Pigeon, a Crane, a Fly-catcher (and any other bird the players have chosen). I wish to know now which are the objects of your affection or antipathy. You, fair lady—

"Which of my birds has your heart?

"To which will you tell your secret?

"From which will you take a feather?"

The lady replies, "I give my heart to the Eagle, my secret to the Parrot, and I take a plume from the Duck."

The Bird-catcher makes a note of these arrangements. Then he addresses the same questions to a gentleman, who says, we will suppose, "I give my heart to the Crow, my secret to the Crane, and I take a feather from the Pigeon."

When the player points out, as the keeper of his heart, a bird already on the list with the same intentions, and which does not figure on the list of the Bird-catcher, he gives a forfeit, and is obliged to make another choice. If he is again mistaken, it is a new forfeit. He must give great attention to the reading of the list and the choice of the first speakers.

When all have replied, the Bird-catcher tells the persons designated by the birds.

The one is kissed to whom a heart is given, a secret is told to the one to whom confidence was promised, and the one whose feather was stolen has a forfeit.

The heart or the secret are not given to oneself, under pain of a forfeit, and no feather is pulled from oneself under pain of two.

Games for Catching, or which are intended to mystify or tease.

"I COME FROM MARKET."

WHEN the company has formed a circle, one of them says to his right-hand neighbour, "I return from market." "What did you buy?" replies he. "A dress, a waistcoat, and flowers," is the answer—any thing the purchaser may choose, provided he can, on pronouncing the word, touch the object he mentions. The person who neglects to do so gives a forfeit.

A means of multiplying the forfeits is, in observing the above rules, to limit oneself to naming, alternately, a masculine or a feminine thing, so that the one who hears that his neighbour has bought a *cat*, says that he has bought a *horse*, or something which, or a representation of which, he can touch, &c.

No object already mentioned, must be named, under pain of a forfeit.

THE COOK WHO DOES NOT LIKE BONES

SOME ONE of the company is chosen to act as leader. He asks of his right-hand neighbour, and then of the persons present, successively, the following question:

"My cook does not like bones: what shall we give her to eat?"

If anyone says, "Carrots, peas," he answers, "She don't like them, give a forfeit."

But if the person says, "Parsnips, beans, veal, or ducks,"— "She likes them," is replied, and the player gives no forfeit.

This game is founded on a *conundrum*. It is the *letter o* in the word bones, which must be avoided. So that, not to be caught up, answers must be given of meats which do not contain in their names the letter *o*, such as *meat, bread, fruit,* &c.

THE CHERRIES

EACH of the persons composing the company take the name of a fruit, as Pear, Apricot, Peach, Plum, &c.

On the table a basket of cherries, with long stems, is placed.

Then the leader says, "Who wants cherries?" Each one says, "I," and takes one. All seat themselves except the Questioner, who remains standing in the middle of the circle, and he says, "I would give my Cherry for a Pear," or any other fruit he chooses to mention. The person named Pear replies, "I have a pear." "Well," says the Questioner, "give me your pear, and I will give you my cherry." "Which end will you take it by, the head or the tail?" The Questioner says, we suppose, "By the stem." Then the person has several modes of obeying: one is, to put the stem in his mouth, and let the fruit be taken, or to place it in his hair, his slipper, or under a lamp, &c. There is quite another way of replying to this answer, "By the head," which is to fling the fruit at the person's head who answers. Then, confused and humiliated, he says, "The *pear* is not ripe." He gives a forfeit, and begins with another fruit which he chooses to have, which sometimes ends as before.

Sometimes, instead of beginning "By the head," the Questioner answers, "By the stem." Then the person questioned hands him the stem, holding the cherry in his fingers, and lets him take it entire. By this means he is made easy, and gives, or pretends to give, his cherry to the one who takes his place.

If, instead of holding it in her fingers, the person questioned puts it in her mouth, the other takes the end, or stem, but in vain, for the fruit comes off, and then the Replier swallows it, the Questioner bearing away the tail, which tricks him, and he must give a forfeit. His only resource is to offer his cherry to another, who tries to catch him as the other did.

THE KING AND THE CLOTHES

OUR ancestors were very partial to the following game, and for this reason we must give it to our readers.

First, a King and Queen are chosen, who are placed on an elevated throne, at one end of the parlour; then a slave is pointed out, who is seated on a stool at the foot of the throne.

The King calls by name someone of the company, and says to him, "Come near, my slave."

If the person called does not know the game, she approaches, and gives a forfeit for her pains, and is obliged to take the place of the slave (which she is suffered to do without the reason being told her, so as to mislead others). If she knows the game, she says, "Sire, shall I dare?" The King replies, "Dare." She then approaches, and says, "I have obeyed, sire; what shall I do?"

The King then tells her to take off from the slave any part of his clothing he pleases to designate; but the other, under the same penalty, must not proceed without saying first, "Shall I dare, sire?" to which the King again replies, "Dare."

After the execution of this order the person says again, "I

have obeyed, sire; what must I do?" The King orders something else, or says, "Return to your place," which the player must take care to do immediately, if she wish to avoid a forfeit or becoming a slave; but she must reply, "Sire, shall I dare?" and must only return when she receives permission to "dare".

It is, of course, very rare for anyone to have several things taken off, because the person called to do so neglects, sooner or later, her formula, and becomes a slave in her turn.

Games in which Gallantry can be shown, or Wit, or Learning

THE ALPHABET; OR, I LOVE MY LOVE WITH AN A, OR A B

FORMERLY, in this game, it sufficed to say, "I love my love with an A, because he is Amiable, Alert, Ambitious, Adroit," &c., and forfeits were only given for the repetitions of qualities, or for faults of spelling, such as the person would make who said, "Because he is *A*teful, *H*artful, *A*rdy, or *A*sty, (for these words are spelled Hateful, Artful, Hardy, and Hasty), but its sameness caused additions to be made, which make it amusing and instructive.

The letter is agreed on, on which to play, because all can be successively used, and each speaker in turn carefully avoiding, according to the old rule of the game, faults of spelling or repetition, which cost forfeits.

The ladies say, "I love my love"—

The gentlemen say, "I love my sweetheart"—with an A, (we suppose), because he (or she) is *Accessible*; because he (or she) is named *Andrew*, or *Angelica*. I give her an *Amethyst*, I feed her on *Asparagus*, and I present her a bouquet of *Anemonies*.

"I love"— with a B, because he (or she) is named *Bastian*, or *Barbara*; because he is *Boisterous*, or *Babbling*. I give her a

Boat to come to meet me. I lodge her (or him) for a *Bagatelle*. I feed him (or her) on *Buckwheat cakes*. I give her a bouquet of *Bachelor's Buttons*; and so on with the letters, all except K and Q, which are too hard.

THE ACROSTIC

WHOEVER begins the game announces that he returns from market, where he bought an object, which he names, and of which the name forms as many letters as there are players present, without counting the pretended buyer. He then asks each what they will give him for one of the letters of a word which expresses the object bought. Armed with a paper and a pencil, he notes the offer made, which must always begin with the letter he wishes to sell. Then he must read aloud all these offers, and declare in a succinct manner, although impromptu, the use he intends to make of the offered objects.

Here is an example for a company composed of ten persons, without counting the speaker.

"I return from market, where I bought a Dromedary; but I wish to sell him: (*to the first person*), what will you give me for my D? A offer is made, of which the Orator takes a note, and so on with nine others. Then he says:—

"It was proposed to give me for my

D	a	Turkey,
R	a	Rattle,
O	an	Organ,
M	a	Mattrass,
A	an	Aviary,
D	a	Diligence,
A	an	Artichoke,
I	an	Ivy,
R	a	Register,
E	an	Epistle.

"I accept all, and I intend to use them thus:

92

"I propose to return without delay to my native country, and, in order to avoid fatigue, I start in the *Diligence* with the *Epistle* in my pocket. If I am attacked on the road, I shall defend myself. I will then inscribe all my effects on the *Register*, and will make also a journal of my voyage. When I have nothing else to do in the coach, I will play on the *Organ* to amuse myself. Not far from here is my stopping-place; I shall then arrive early in the morning. While waiting for my parents to rise, I will plant my *Ivy* in a garden where I remember one is wanted; and I will then play with my *Rattle*. During this time everybody rises. They come into the garden, which is raked and nicely fixed. All are surprised. They seek me, and find me at last in an arbour; they kiss me, and give me the handsomest room in the house; there I make the rest of my arrangements. I place my *Aviary* as a sentinel in a corner, and tell the birds to catch all the flies which may conspire against the freshness of my room. I eat with a good appetite, my *Artichoke* peppered. I spread out my *Mattrass*, when some hours' slumber naturally bring me to the hour of eating in the family, at which my *Turkey* will figure extensively."

This story ended, the ten other players, one after the other, make an acrostic of the same kind, remembering that there are forfeits due, first, for the choice of words which require more letters than players; secondly, for faults of spelling in the offered objects; and then again, for a repetition of the same offer.

THE BOUQUET

COMPOSING, in turn, a bouquet of three different flowers, each player names them aloud to the leader of the game.

He (the leader) writes the names of the three flowers, and adds, without communicating his addition, those of the persons in the company, at his choice. He then asks of the player what he intends doing with the flowers he has chosen. The player mentions the use, and the Master of the Game applies it to the three persons he has noted down.

EXAMPLE

The Master. "Miss Julia, choose your three flowers."

Julia. "The Marigold, the Bachelor's Button, and the Rose."

The Master. "I have taken notes. Now what will you do with the Marigold?"

Julia. "I throw it behind me."

Master. "And the Bachelor's Button?"

Julia. "I place it in my window."

Master. "And the Rose?"

Julia. "I put it on my chimney-piece."

Master. "Very well; you have cast behind you Mr. Adolphus, put in your window Miss Agatha, and put Mr. Julian on your chimney-piece."

"And you, Mr. Adolphus," &c.

THE COCK-AND-BULL STORIES

EVERY person present giving a word, while the one who is charged to put the questions holds herself off, in order not to hear.

When all the words are given, the Questioner approaches and addresses to each player a particular question, to which is abruptly answered the chosen word, which makes a funny conversation.

This game only has the difficulty of giving good questions, and varying them, so as to serve for all sorts of answers.

Suppose the persons composing a company have each chosen a word, and the Questioner (Emilius) to have made to each a remark—

Emilius. "How do you go?"

Adele. "On a chair."

Emilius. "Do you like reading?"

Emma. "With a little sauce."

Emilius. "Have you good friends?"

Adolphus. "One at a time."

Emilius. "Do you like dancing?"

Virginia. "In my boudoir," &c. &c.

THE RHYMES

GIVING an answer of which the first word rhymes with the last of the demand addressed to you, is the difficulty of this game, which makes many forfeits.

EXAMPLE

The company is ranged in a circle, intermixed with ladies and gentlemen, who interrogate their right-hand neighbours. These reply, and go on questioning to the right, and so on, thus:—

A Lady. "How is your *aunty*?"

A Gentleman. "*Jaunty* as possible. What will you do on *Sunday*?"

A Lady. "*Monday*, I have a balloon fight at Saint Cloud. Have you a good *appetite*?"

A Gentleman. "*Quite.* Do you love *company*?"

A Lady. "*Not any.* When are you at *home*?"

A Gentleman. "*Some*times. Are you not afraid of being *caught*?" &c.

If you can find a word without rhyme, give it. The player thus answered is obliged to give a forfeit, as are those who do not immediately find rhymes.

THE STOOL

BOTH memory and wit are needed in this game: the first, for the President, who is to receive secretly the accusations brought to her by the other players, who are so many Judges, and who must question on every article him whom fate or his own will has placed on the Stool; the second, wit, is necessary for the Judges, to bring fine and delicate charges, which cannot offend the self-love of the Accused.

Here is the process of the game:—

The assembly form a half circle, in the middle of which is seated the President; the Criminal is placed opposite on a stool, and the President opens the session:—

"Illustrious Judges, do you know why N—, the accused, is on the stool?"

95

"We know."

Then all the Judges approach successively the President's ear, and tell him in a whisper the reasons they choose.

The voices gathered together, each takes his place, and the President, addressing the pretended Criminal, says—

"Such a one accuses you"—of such a thing. He then details the accusations. "Do you know who is your denouncer for each of these things?"

The Accused recapitulates them, and at each one names one of the Judges. If he mistakes each, he gives a forfeit, and, remaining on the stool, must reply to new accusations: if he guesses one of his denouncers, that one takes his place, gives a forfeit, and waits till process is made against him.

This game requires great attention on the part of the Judge-Accusers. They must consider the age, the sex, and the external qualities, and those of the mind, of the Accused. When they wish to pay a compliment, they must not speak of a quality which she has not, or which is exaggerated, for it would become ironical; if they speak of a fault or a foolish defect, it is better to accuse the person of a false one than a real one, which last would appear rude. It is necessary, in general, to avoid all excess, and observe the rules of politeness rigorously; for their forgetfulness causes many quarrels, in play as well as social relations.

THE SECRETARY

THIS game can be played in two ways; for both, the company must surround a table covered with pens in sufficient number, and all materials for writing.

The Secretary (the name of the leader of the game) distributes to each player a white card or a square of paper.

When all have agreed to follow the old process of the play, all write legibly their names at the head of the paper given them, and give it to the Secretary, who carefully puts all these papers, and has one taken at hazard by each person, without his letting the others see the name fallen to him. Then each, separately and without constraint, writes beneath the name what he thinks of its bearer, folds his manuscript, and gives it again to the Secretary, who, after having collected all, mixes them again, and reads them aloud, without allowing the handwriting to be inspected. The reading finished, all the papers are burned, in order to avoid the quarrels which might arise from the mischievous things therein written, if their authors were known.

As this game often degenerates into dangerous personalities, here is a new way of playing it, which does not lead to similar results:—

When the Secretary distributes his loose leaves, each adopts a name according to his humour or the qualities he chooses to attribute to himself, and writes it at the head of his square of paper after his real name, without letting his neighbours see what he has chosen. This done, the Secretary gathers all his leaves together, and hastens to inscribe on as many squares as he takes the name *adopted* by one person, mixes all the squares, and distributes them to each player, who, torturing himself to find out whose name it is, writes a strange portrait, which he signs with his adopted name. In this manner, the eulogy of a person is made who would not have been spared if his real name had been known; and others pitilessly dealt with to whom something agreeable would have been said. The result is still more amusing discussions, when the Secretary, after reading all the papers, names the masks; and no one has any right to be angry, or to be proud of praise which was given at hazard.

WRITTEN CONFESSIONS

IN this game, the persons who amuse themselves thus must be an equal number of men and women, with a gentleman or lady besides, who is chosen for Confessor. This grave personage distributes to each of his Penitents a square of paper, on which they must write three mortal sins or venial ones, which they remember to have committed. Then they make a little discourse on the necessity of showing the greatest frankness in this act of humility. The Sinners receive respectfully the moral and the square of paper; they write their names at the top of the leaf, and place beneath the avowal demanded. Then they place it in the hands of the Confessor, who forms two different piles of the gentlemen's and ladies' confessions; he then mixes these together, and taking in each the confession chance has placed above the others, he calls the gentleman and lady to whom they belong, and reads aloud the contents; and if the two papers indicate similar faults, the Sinners are absolved and sent away, side by side, to occupy two seats in the circle. If, on the contrary, the sins are dissimilar, he announces that they must prepare to endure the punishment which the company may judge suitable to impose upon them, and places them in opposite corners of the room, to wait till the confessions are verified.

After the verification, the absolved Sinners (and, separate from or with them, the Confessor) point out the penances; and as they are executed, the guilty, re-entering the girdle of the company, join her in pronouncing the fate of the remainder.

Here are some examples of confession:—

Honorine

I accuse myself of having passed too much time at my toilet, of loving to surround myself with adorers, and of trying to depreciate the merit of my rivals.

Julian

I accuse myself of preferring the pleasures of the table to the duties of my salvation, gaming to working, and of loving the fair sex above all things.

Confessor

However natural these defects may be, I cannot excuse, because neither sympathises with the other. Go, each of you, to a corner, you here, to await the penance which our wisdom shall impose upon you.

Juliana

I accuse myself of voluntarily speaking against my neighbour, and of being subject to anger and jealousy.

Adolphus

I accuse myself of a natural inclination to find rivals in all who approach her I love, of fits of passion of which I hate the violence, and of speaking against those who displease me.

Confessor

You are both very guilty, but, as there is a conformity between your faults, you are excusable. Re-enter the circle, and try to better each other's morals, &c., &c., &c.

THE THREE KINGDOMS*

HE who proposes this game retires to a neighbouring room, while the rest of the company consent to give him some word to guess. When the choice is made, he is called back. He has the right to ask twelve questions, which first go on to Kingdom of nature to which belongs the object, which designate the object agreed on, or the actual state in which this object is, the country where it is most commonly found; finally, the metamorphoses which it can undergo, its uses,

---

* There are three Kingdoms in nature, viz:—

The Animal Kingdom, which comprises all that has life and motion, and also all which comes from a living thing (or animated being), such as Horn, Ivory, Skin, Hair, Wool, and Silk, &c., &c.

The Vegetable Kingdom, which comprises Trees, Plants, Flowers, Leaves, Fruits, Bark, and, in a word, all which the external world produces, and which has life without motion.

And the Mineral Kingdom, which comprises all which has neither life nor motion, like Stones, Diamonds, Metals, &c., &c.

An object can belong at the same time to two or three Kingdoms. A shoe, for instance, is of the Animal Kingdom, from the leather and skin it is composed of; to the Vegetable Kingdom, from the thread with which it is sewed; and to the Mineral Kingdom, if it is garnished with nails or points.

We must, then, before proposing a word, discuss the different parts which attach it to any Kingdom.

and its qualities. The players must reply in a way which shows what the object is, leaving, however, some doubts. However, those who give false ideas owe a forfeit. The Questioner who does not guess after twelve questions recognised as available by the company, must give one in his turn, and go away to shut himself up till another word is chosen, when he must try again.

EXAMPLE

The Questioner, who has heard the signal, re-enters, and asks the following questions:—

1. "To what Kingdom does the object thought of belong?"

A player replies, "To the Vegetable Kingdom," with a mixture of any other Kingdom.

2. "Is it naturally growing, or put in use?"

"Put in use."

3. "Is it a piece of furniture?"

"No."

4. "Its ordinary use?"

"Is to be, in regular places, covered with spots of a different colour from its own."

5. "In what country is it most commonly made?"

"In Auvergne, Normandy, Limoges, and Holland."

6. "Oh! oh! If it is not cloth, I do not know what Auvergne, Normandy, and Limoges are celebrated for."

"No; but cloth is in the matter."

7. "What metamorphosis does it undergo?"

"A very great one: it is thrown into water, bruised, reduced to a pulp, then brought to a solid state, as we see it now."

8. "It is, then, *Paper*."

"You have guessed."

The person whose answer causes the word to be guessed gives a forfeit, and becomes a Questioner in his turn.

Let us suppose that a word is agreed on which he seeks to

find out. He begins by asking the same question as the former:—

1. "To what Kingdom does it belong?"

"To three Kingdoms."

2. "Is it, then, put to work?"

"Yes."

3. "Is it a piece of furniture?"

"A portable piece of furniture."

4. "What is its usual use?"

"To keep off the *damp*."

Someone observes that this is not correct, and the Respondent owes a forfeit. This one replies, "The Deuse! If I were to say that it is to keep *rain* off, it would be guessed in a moment."

Questioner, quickly. "It is an *Umbrella*."

"Ah! I could not save my forfeit. How provoking!"

"Go, go hide; you must guess in your turn," &c., &c.

In effect, the Umbrella belongs to the Animal Kingdom, from its cover of taffety and its pieces of whale; to the Mineral Kingdom, from its wires and iron trimmings; and to the Vegetable Kingdom, from its handle of some kind of wood.

Paper, made of old rags, is purely of the Vegetable Kingdom, since cloth is made of flax or hemp, which are vegetables.

Penances which do not require any motion, attention, or memory.

FOR Penance, the first thing which comes into one's head can be mentioned, provided it be among possibilities; but they are very stale if they are limited to ordering the Penitent to *kiss* someone pointed out, and make him make *three little pies*, to send him to *look if I am somewhere else*, and such things, at the end of plays with birds in them, as "Pigeon Flies", "Little Old Man is still Alive", "Ox's Feet", &c.

They must present some interest, be discussed with wit, and

101

even proportioned to that of the person who is to execute them. We are going to mention a sufficient number, which are at least as amusing as the games which lead to them.

THE EXTINGUISHER

PASS rapidly before the nose of the Penitent a lighted candle, which he must blow out as it passes. This is harder than one would think.

THE PARROT

IN this, the person whom the Penance metamorphoses into a Parrot says to the players, one after the other, "If I were a Parrot, what would you teach me to say?"

Each player replies as his idea is. If a lady says, "Kiss, pretty Poll," the gentleman can profit by this circumstance to kiss; otherwise, he must repeat exactly each reply before passing to another person.

THE LITTLE PAPER

IF the same kind is another Penance, which consists in saying, "If I were a Paper, what would you do with me?"

The Replier is thanked in a serious or ironical manner, according to the use mentioned.

DOING THE MUTE

THIS is to execute, without speaking, a Penance which each person in the company inflicts, one after another, and without pronouncing a single word.

THE STATUE

THE Penitent is placed by each person successively in a ridiculous or awkward posture, which he must leave only to take another, while the round lasts.

Sometimes, this Penance has a difficult condition for the *Sculptor*, which is to employ a different hand from the last Posturer. If he forgets this formality, he becomes a Statue himself.

KISSING THE CANDLE

THIS is giving a kiss to a person who holds in his hand a lighted candle.

It is one of those little tricks which it is good to know, in order not to have a laugh at your expense.

THE DECEITFUL KISS

A LADY advances toward the Penitent, as though to kiss him, but she turns away, and lets her nearest neighbour kiss her.

THE ALMS

PENANCE to be done by a man. He kneels before a lady, and strikes her knees several times. She lets him languish there, saying, "Do you want bread? Do you want water? Do you want a cent? Do you want wine?" &c. To all these questions he does not answer, and continues to strike. At last she says, "Do you want a kiss?" At these words he rises and kisses the lady.

THE KISS WITH A HOOD

A GENTLEMAN and lady are placed back to back on their knees. Then both must turn their heads at the same time— one on the right and the other on the left, seeking to make their lips meet to give the ordered kiss. It is not forbidden for the gentleman to pass a gallant arm around the lady's waist, to spare her the fatigue and keep her from falling over.

SIGHING

HE who is condemned to this Penance goes into a corner and sighs. "For whom do you sigh?" is asked. A person of another sex is named, who is obliged to come to be kissed and to sigh in turn. Everybody, to the last, sighs then, and all range themselves in a long line. When it is complete, the first Sigher returns to his place, kissing all the persons of the opposite sex who are in the line; and all the others do so, to the last, who can kiss his own thumb, if he chooses.

THE VOYAGE TO CYTHERA

WHEN this Penance is ordered, the Penitent leads another person away, of the opposite sex, behind a screen or a door. There the gentleman presses the lady, and touches every part of her dress he chooses.

On returning from the voyage, they present themselves successively before all present, and the gentleman asks each what part of the dress he has touched. As long as they are mistaken, he kisses the place guessed. If it is guessed right, the gentleman kisses the lady, or is embraced by the gentleman, according to the sex of the guesser. If, on the contrary, no one guesses, the gentleman names aloud what he has touched, and kisses his lady again before conducting her to her place.

THE SPIRIT OF CONTRADICTION

IN order to fulfil this Penance, the contrary of the commands given by the company must be done. Happy is the man to whom the ladies say that they will *not* be kissed!

THE CLOCK

THE Clock Penitent places himself before a mantelpiece, and calls whom he pleases of the opposite sex. The person thus called asks what hour it is. The clock replies by giving any hour, and as many kisses as the number of the hours given are the result.

If he chooses, the person who has asked becomes a Pendulum in his turn, and all the company join in the Penance, imitating the two first.

THE BOWER OF LOVE

HE (or she) who receives this Penance takes a lady (or gentleman), whom he conducts to the middle of the hall, where both hold their hands enlaced and their arms raised in the form of a bower. Then the lady points out a gentleman, and the gentleman a lady, who must pass together under this

Bower of Love; but when they have entered halfway, the arms are lowered, and they are held prisoners till they have kissed each other. This done, the arms are raised, the imprisoned go their way, and stop to form another Bower; they call a third couple, who are to pay the same tribute, by passing under both, and then forming a third; and so on with all the gentlemen and ladies.

After all the company have formed Bowers, all return to their places.

Penances, more or less amusing, from the secret conditions imposed or the mystifications required.

THE KISS BY CHANCE

THE Penitent takes the four Kings and four Queens of a pack of cards, shuffles them, and distributes them, without looking at them, to four ladies and four gentlemen present. The one who has the Queen of Hearts embraces the King of Hearts, and so on.

Meanwhile, the Penitent looks at them with a piteous expression; but he can put malice into it by giving his kings to the gayest of the young men, and his queens to the oldest ladies.

THE BRIDGE OF LOVE

HERE the Penitent takes the same posture as in the Horse of Aristotle; that is to say, he gets on all fours, but remains still. Then a lady and gentleman seat themselves on his back, and kiss each other.

THE HARE'S KISS.

A NEEDLEFUL of thread separates the couple who are thus to kiss each other; but, gradually eaten up at both ends, it meets in their lips, where it is so short that they touch, and the kiss is given.

THE VOYAGE TO CORINTH

HOLDING a white handkerchief in his hands, a gentleman is conducted round the circle by the Penitent, who holds in his a lighted candle.

The man with the handkerchief kisses, turn by turn, all the ladies, and very politely wipes the lips of his leader, who is an idle spectator of this scene, so little amusing to him.

THE NUN'S KISS

THIS is given through the bars of a chair, of which the wood has generally half.

THE EXILE

THIS Penance requires, for one or more turns, that the person condemned shall go into the farther corner of the circle formed by the company, with whom he is forbidden to communicate.

It is from these that the *Exiled* orders the Penance, which requires the proprietor of the following Penance to do something, and he cannot leave his place till the time of his exile is expired.

THE HORSE OF ARISTOTLE

IN this, the Penitent carries on his back around the circle a lady, whom all the gentlemen kiss in turn.

KISSING ONE'S BELOVED WITHOUT ITS BEING KNOWN

DONE by kissing all the ladies present, one after the other.

THE TRICKS OF PUNCH

THIS is a lady's Penance. She who receives the order to execute it chooses a good friend; then she presents herself before a gentleman, kisses him, and gives the kiss to her companion. This kiss is repeated as many times as there are gentlemen present.

PARLOUR GAMES FOR GROWN-UPS

TO BE AT THE DISCRETION OF
THE COMPANY

THIS is to have to do whatever, in his turn, each of the persons present orders.

THE WILL

IN receiving the order to make his Will, the Penitent leaves to all those around him one of the physical or moral qualities he is supposed to possess. This Penance is an inexhaustible mine of compliments and epigrams, but the latter must be sparingly dealt with, or used with such address that they will not wound.

THE COMPARISON

A PENITENT is ordered to compare a person present to some object, and then to explain in what she resembles or differs from this object.

A lady compares a gentleman to a sheet of white paper.

The resemblance is in the facility with which both receive a first impression: the difference being in the facility with which the man only can receive several, which are easily effaced.

A gentleman compares a lady to a clock. Like this piece of furniture, she adorns the spot she inhabits; but she causes the hours she remembers to be forgotten by others, &c.

THE EMBLEM

DIFFERS from the Comparison, because it offers a spiritual likeness between a person and an object.

A young man gives the Salamander as an emblem of a young lady. "Why?" says this one. "Because you live tranquilly in the midst of the flames which devour those who approach you."

A lady sees in a Well the emblem of an uncommunicative literary man. "It is deep," says she, "but one must take away what it encloses."

THE COUNSELS

THE Penitent gives aloud, or in a whisper, according to the order he receives, a piece of advice to all the members or one member of the company.

THE KNIGHT OF THE RUEFUL COUNTENANCE

PLACING himself in an armchair, the Penitent receives on his knees a lady, whom another gentleman comes and kisses.

WOODEN FACE

HE who is condemned to this Penance goes and places himself, standing, with his back against a door. Thus posted, he calls a person of another sex, who places herself facing him. She calls a third, who places himself back to back with her; and so all the company, until the two last of the file are back to back. Then the leader of the game gives a signal, at which everybody must turn and kiss the person facing whom this motion leaves her. The result is, that the Penitent has before him the Wooden Face (of the door), to which he gives a kiss as tender as those the noise of which he hears.

THE THOUGHT

RESEMBLES "The Counsels", on the preceding page, very much. Instead of giving advice, some person tells one or all the company his opinion of them.

NOTE.—This amusement, like "The Counsels", exacts a great deal of circumspection, in order to wound no one.

THE SECRET WHICH TRAVELS

TO execute this Penance, an intermingled circle of gentlemen and ladies is formed. The Penitent tells a secret to his right-hand neighbour, who repeats it to the next, and so on to the last, who finally tells the Penitent; and this one must declare aloud whether the Secret returns as it was given, which seldom happens, because of the multiplicity of mouths through which it passes, and the self-love it may have wounded, thus causing someone to alter it.

THE SIMPLE CONFIDENCE

IT is to tell a secret in the ear of someone of the company.

If it is a lady who tells a gentleman, it must be amusing. If a gentleman tells it to a lady, the gallantry must be its merit.

CONFESSION

PROSTRATED at the feet of a Confessor chosen by oneself, a person must reply truly to the questions he addresses you, of which here are examples:—

"Have you given your heart? Have you never taken it again from anyone? Tell me the first letter of the name of him who possesses it. Describe him? What would you do with such or such a thing? What do you think of such a one? Tell your principal fault. Name your favourite perfection. How many friends have you?" &c.

ACROSTIC

THIS is like a continuation of the game of the Alphabet, in which it is said, "I love my love with an A," or any other letter of the alphabet.

EXAMPLES

Pleasure

Qualities	Imperfections
P olite,	P resuming,
L aborious,	L azy,
E xcellent,	E gotistical,
A ssiduous,	A bominable,
S weet-tempered,	S ulky,
U seful,	U seless,
R eady,	R emiss,
E arnest.	E mpty.

Grief

Qualities	Imperfections
G reat,	G rievous,
R ighteous,	R ambling,
I mpenetrable,	I mpertinent,
E xcellent,	E mpty,
F amous.	F astidious.

TO MAKE A VENUS

WE take the attractions of each of the ladies present to make a perfect woman.

A *moral Venus* is made by taking from each a personal quality which distinguishes every one.

A young man, charged with this Penance, made, to acquit himself, this distinguished impromptu:—

"Why for a single Venus do you ask,

When to find *ten* would be my easy task?"

There were ten ladies present.

Parlour Magic

SLEIGHT OF HAND

It is our intention, in the following pages, to lay more stress upon those tricks which require no apparatus, than upon those for which special apparatus or the assistance of a confederate is required. No one is so well pleased by a trick whose essence evidently lies in the machinery, while every one feels pleasure at seeing a sleight of hand trick neatly executed. For our own part, we despise all the numerous boxes, bottles, variegated covers, and other gimcracks which are generally seen on a conjurer's table; and we have never been so pleased with any performer as with one who did not even require a table, but pressed into his service articles borrowed from his audience, as he stood before them or walked among them. The spectators should never be able to say, "Ah! the trick lies in the box; he dares not show it to us!"

The following tricks have almost all been successfully performed by the editor, and have caused him some reputation in the magic art. Some are his own invention.

THE TRAVELLED BALLS

This is always a favourite feat, because it needs no apparatus, and is remarkably effective. You take three or four cups, whether of metal or china is of no consequence, provided that they be opaque: breakfast cups answer very well, and silver goblets better. Professional conjurers always have three highly-ornamented conical vessels, but we prefer to use cups and tankards because they can be borrowed in the house and excite no suspicion.

You place three cups upon a table, and exhibit an equal number of balls. Walnuts, potatoes, plums, &c., &c., will answer very well, but the easiest balls for work are made from cork, in the following manner. Take some champagne corks and cut them into spherical form, rubbing them smooth with a file. Then hold them in front of a bright fire, and they will begin to swell rapidly. When they have swollen as much as possible, char the outsides by holding them in the flame of a candle, rub them smooth with a rag, and polish with a little oil upon leather.

You put a cup over each ball, and cover them from sight. You then take each ball separately and fling it in the air. After the third ball has been thus flung away, you take up the cups again, and, to the surprise of the spectators, the three balls have come back again, and each is found under its respective cup. Then you take a ball out of one cup, fling it in the air, and presently find it under another cup; and, lastly, you bring all the three under the same cup.

The secret of this capital trick lies chiefly in the *fourth* ball, the existence of which the audience do not know.

Before you begin, put a fourth ball in some place where you can easily get at it—in your pocket, for example, or stuck on a little spike fastened to your own side of the table: a broken needle answers well for this purpose. Throw the three balls on the table, and while you are handling the cups with the left hand, and shifting the balls about in them, quietly get the fourth ball into the right hand, and hold it at the roots of the second and third fingers. You will now find that with the tips of those fingers you can pick the ball out of the palm of the hand. Being thus prepared you may commence the trick.

Put a ball under each cup, and be careful to get the balls close to the edge of the cup which is farthest from you. Let them stay there while you talk to the audience in some flourishing style, and, in the meantime, get the fourth ball between the *tips* of your second and third fingers; keep those fingers well doubled into the palm, take the right-hand cup between the thumb and forefinger, keeping the rest of the fingers behind it, lift it off the first ball, and as you set it down, neatly slip the fourth ball under it. As you will now have your hands quite empty, it may be as well to make some gesture, which shows that you have nothing concealed.

Take up the first ball, and say that it is going to Europe. Draw your hand quickly back, as if to throw, and while doing so drop the ball into the palm of the hand and catch it between the roots of the fingers, just as the fourth ball was held. Pretend to throw it away, opening your hand as if you did so, but taking care to hold it tightly in the finger-roots. Take up the second cup, slip the first ball under it as before, and proceed to do so with the third, pretending each time to throw the ball away. Take up the cups, and exhibit the three balls which have now come back again.

Now comes a neat little piece of legerdemain. Replace the cups over the balls, and as you do so slip the ball in your hand under the left-hand cup, so that there will be two balls in it. Take up the right-hand cup, pretend to throw the ball into the middle cup, pick it up and show the two balls there. As you replace the cup, slip the concealed ball into it, so as to bring three under one cup, and proceed as before. When you have finished the performance, by showing the three balls under one cup, get rid of the fourth ball by sticking it on the projecting needle.

PALMING COIN

This phrase involves an explanation of the first grand principles of the art, without which no feat of mere sleight of hand with coin can be successfully performed, and to accomplish which with ease and rapidity, requires considerable practice and experience. The exhibitor, before commencing, should turn back the sleeves of his coat, to avoid the appearance of passing anything down the arm, and may then prepare himself for the first illusion in the manner following:—

Place a coin, either a dime or a quarter, on the *tips* of the middle and third fingers, so that it may rest there of its own weight. By now turning the hand with the knuckles uppermost, and quickly closing the fingers into the palm, the coin may be held securely by the contraction of the thumb, and the hand still appear to contain nothing. This is *palming*, and with a little practice nearly every feat of simple legerdemain may be performed by its means. Care, of course, must be taken not to expose the coin by any reversed movement of the hand.

Securing the coin in the right hand, and simultaneously making it appear to pass into the left, the exhibitor may cause it either to disappear altogether, or, by holding a glass in the right hand, bid it fly from the left into the tumbler, where the expansion of the thumb will readily cause it to fall. This feat, when skilfully performed, never fails to elicit surprise and admiration.

The following simple trick may in many cases be employed instead of *palming*.

THE MAGIC COIN

Although a purely sleight of hand trick, it requires but little practice to perform this recreation with dexterity. Take a quarter of a dollar between the thumb and forefinger of the right hand, as represented in the engraving; then, by a rapid twist of the fingers, twirl the coin, by the same motion that you would use to spin a teetotum; at the same time rapidly close your hand, and the coin will disappear up your coat-sleeve; you can now open your hand,  and, much to the astonishment of your audience, the coin will not be there. This capital trick may be varied in a hundred ways. One good way is to take three dimes, or quarters, and concealing one in the palm of your left hand, place the other two, one each between the thumb and forefinger of each hand; then give the coin in the right hand the twirl, as already described, and, closing both hands quickly, the coin in the right hand will disappear up your sleeve, and the left hand, on being unclosed will be found to contain two quarters, whilst that which *was* in the right hand will have disappeared. Thus you will make the surprised spectators believe that you conjured the coin from the right hand into the left.

TO BRING TWO SEPARATE COINS
INTO ONE HAND

Take two cents, which must be carefully placed in each hand, as thus: the right hand with the coin on the fourth and little finger, as in the illustration.

Then place, at a short distance from each other, both hands open on the table, the left palm being level with the fingers of the right. By now suddenly turning the hands over, the cent from the right hand will fly, without being perceived, into the palm of the left, and make the transit appear most unaccountable to the bewildered eyes of the spectators. By placing the audience in front, and not at the side of the exhibitor, this illusion, if neatly performed, can never be detected.

THE MAGIC HANDKERCHIEF

You take any handkerchief and put a quarter or a dime into it. You fold it up, laying the four corners over it so that it is entirely hidden by the last one. You ask the audience to *touch and feel the coin* inside. You then unfold it, and the coin has disappeared without anybody seeing it removed. The method is as follows:—

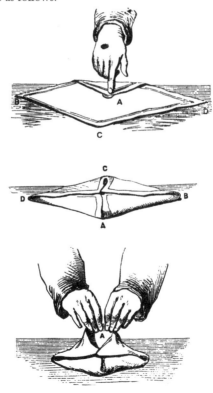

Take a dime, and privately put a piece of wax on one side of it; place it in the centre of the handkerchief, with *the waxed side up*; at the same time bring the corner of the handkerchief marked A (as represented in Fig. 1), and completely hide the coin; this must be carefully done, or the company will discover the wax on the coin.

Now press the coin very hard, so that by means of the wax it sticks to the handkerchief; then fold the corners, B, C, and D (see Fig. 1), and it will resemble Fig. 2.

Then fold the corners, B, C, and D (see Fig. 2), leaving A open. Having done this, take hold of the handkerchief with both hands, as represented in Fig. 3 at the opening, A, and sliding along your fingers at the edge of the same, the handkerchief becomes unfolded, the coin adheres to it, coming into your right hand. Detach it, shake the handkerchief out, and the coin will have disappeared. To convince the audience the coin is in the handkerchief, drop it on the table, and it will sound against the wood. This is an easy trick.

THE DOMINO ORACLE

This trick, to one not familiar with it, is certainly very surprising. Arrange twelve of the dominoes as shown in the illustration:—

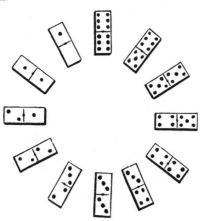

and inform anyone present, that if he will think of one of the dominoes and remember it, you will point it out to him. Now, supposing the double-deuce is the domino selected, you tell the person who has chosen it that you will count around the circle, and when you have counted twenty, *including the number of spots on the selected domino*, he must tell you to stop, and that your finger will then rest on the domino chosen. The secret is simply this—you count carelessly around, 1, 2, 3, 4, 5, 6, 7, on any of the dominoes; but at the eighth count you always manage to point to the *double-six*, and after that you continue counting around *regularly to the right*; be sure and remember this, for it is the key of the trick. For example, as we have before said, we will suppose the double-deuce to be the selected domino. We follow the above instructions, and count and point at the dominoes *promiscuously* the first seven counts; but at the eighth count we point at the double-six, and continue to the right on the six-five, double-five, and so on in succession until we arrive at the double-deuce, when we will be told to stop, because by that time we will have counted sixteen, to which if we add the spots on the domino chosen we will have twenty. This rule holds good no matter what domino happens to be selected. It is perhaps useless to inform our reader that he must not count out loud, or appear to count mentally, but let it seem as if he were only pointing at the dominoes by chance. You must let the person who selects the domino appear to do all the counting.

TO GUESS THE TWO ENDS OF
A LINE OF DOMINOES

Cause a set of dominoes to be shuffled together as much as any of the company may desire. You propose to leave the room in which the audience are assembled, and you assert that from your retreat, be it where it may, you can see, and will be able to tell, the two numbers forming the extremes of a line composed of the entire set, according to the rules established for laying one domino after another in the draw game.

All the magic consists in taking up and carrying away, unknown to everyone, one domino (not a double) taken at hazard; for the two numbers on it must be the same as those on the ends of the two outer dominoes. This experiment may be renewed, *ad infinitum*, by your taking each time a different domino, which, of course, changes the numbers to be guessed.

DOMINOES SEEN AND COUNTED
THROUGH ALL OBSTACLES

Lay a set of dominoes on their faces, one beside the other, in one black line. Then say to the company, I will go into the next room, with my eyes as closely covered as you may desire. In my absence, you may take from the line the number of dominoes you please, *provided you take them from that end which is now at my right hand*, and place them at the opposite end, so that, except for the change in the places of the pieces, the line is just the same as before.

At my return, without unbandaging my eyes, I will tell you exactly the number transported from one end to the other, for I shall have seen everything through the wall and the handkerchief which has covered my eyes. I will do more. From the midst of these dominoes, of which you have changed the position, I will draw one which, by the addition of its spots, will tell you exactly the number which you took from right to left.

To perform this trick, arrange the first thirteen dominoes, *beginning at the left*, so that the spots on the first form the number *twelve*; of the second, *eleven*; of the third, *ten*; and so on, up to a double-blank, for the thirteenth and last. You place the other dominoes afterwards, in the order in which they happen to present themselves.

If your eyes are bandaged, count with your fingers the dominoes *from left to right*, as far as the thirteenth. The spots on this thirteenth will invariably represent the number of dominoes whose position has been altered.

In performing this and many other tricks, you will

employ any ruse you can think of to puzzle those who may try to fathom them.

THE MAGICAL KNOT

A very amusing trick, consisting in simply tying one knot with two ends of a handkerchief, and, by apparently pulling the ends, untying them again.

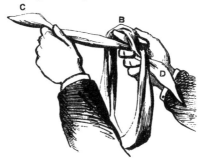

Take two ends of the handkerchief, one in each hand, the ends dropping from the inside of your hands. You simply tie a single knot, when your hands and your handkerchief will be in the position shown in the cut. Instead of pulling the ends C and D, grasp that part marked B with your thumb and forefinger, dropping the end D, and pulling upon the end C and the bend B, when, instead of really tying, you unloosen the knot.

All this should be done as quickly as possible, to prevent detection. Examine the engraving closely, and you will more readily understand the explanation.

TO CAUSE A DIME TO APPEAR IN A GLASS

Having turned up the cuffs of your coat, begin by placing a cent on your elbow and catching it in your hand.

That easy feat performed, allege that you can catch even a smaller coin in a more difficult position.

Then place a dime halfway between elbow and wrist, as in the illustration; suddenly bringing the hand down, the

coin drops into your cuff, unseen by anyone, and you express the greatest astonishment at its disappearance. Tell the audience to watch, and they will see it drop through the ceiling. Then, taking a tumbler, place it at the side of your arm, and elevating the hand for the purpose, the coin falls jingling into the tumbler, causing great marvel as to how it came there.

THE MAGNETIZED CANE

Is a very surprising little fancy, and is calculated to create much astonishment in the drawing-room. Take a piece of black silk thread, or horsehair, about two feet long, and fasten to each end of it bent hooks of a similar colour.

When unobserved, fasten the hooks in the back part of your pantaloon legs, about two inches below the bend of the knees. Then place the cane (it should be a dark one, and not too heavy) within the inner part of the thread, as represented in the engraving, and by a simple movement of the legs, you can make it dance about and perform a great variety of fantastic movements. At night your audience cannot perceive the thread, and apparently the cane will have no support whatever. The performer should inform the company, before commencing this trick, that he intends to magnetize the cane, and by moving his hands as professors of magnetism do, the motion of the legs will not be noticed.

THE OBEDIENT DIME

Lay a dime between two half-dollars, and place upon the larger coins a glass, as in the diagram. Remove the dime without displacing either of the half-dollars or the glass. After having placed the glass and coins as indicated, simply scratch the table-cloth with the nail of the forefinger in the direction you would have the dime to move, and it will answer immediately. The tablecloth is necessary; for this reason the trick is best suited to the breakfast or dinner table.

THE HAT AND QUARTER TRICK

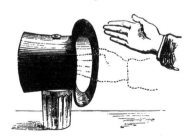

Place a hat, tumbler, and quarter, as represented in the cut; then after making several feints, as if you intended to strike the hat upon the rim, give the hat a sharp quick blow upon the *inside of the crown*, and the coin will fall into the tumbler. This is a beautiful trick, if skilfully performed.

TO MAKE A DIME PASS THROUGH A TABLE

To perform this feat you must have a *dime*, or counter, sewn in the corner of a handkerchief. Take it out of your pocket and request one of the company to lend you a dime, which you must appear to wrap carefully up in the middle of the handkerchief; instead of doing this, however, you keep it in the palm of your hand, and in its place wrap up the corner in which the other dime or counter is sewn in the midst of the handkerchief, and bid the person from whom you borrowed the dime feel that it is there. Then lay it under a hat upon the table, take a glass in the hand in which you have concealed the dime, and hold it under the table; then give three knocks upon the table, at the same time crying, "Presto! come quickly!" drop the dime into the glass, bring the glass from under the table, and exhibit the dime. Lastly, take the handkerchief from under the hat and shake it, taking care to hold it by the corner in which the counter or dime is sewn. This is a very good trick if well managed, and the dime *may be marked* previously.

THE ERRATIC EGG

Transfer the egg from one wineglass to the other, and back again to its original position, without touching the egg or glasses, or allowing any person or any thing to touch them. To perform this trick, all that you have to do is to blow smartly on one side of the egg, and it will hop into the next glass; repeat this and it will hop back again.

HOW TO TIE A TIE

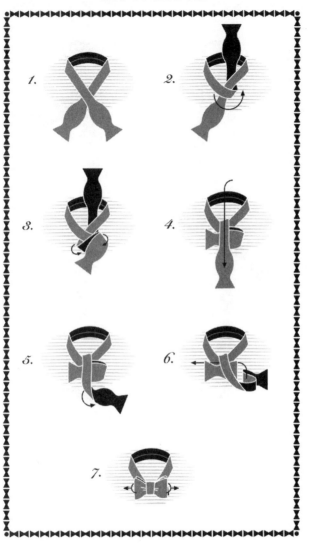

Bow tie

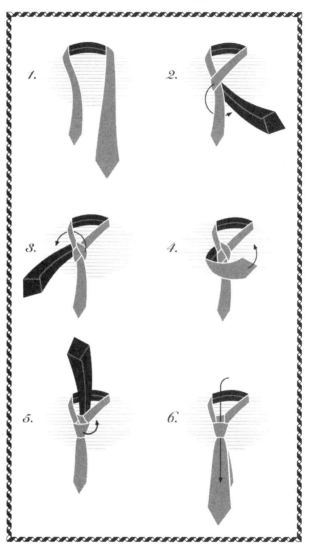

Half Windsor

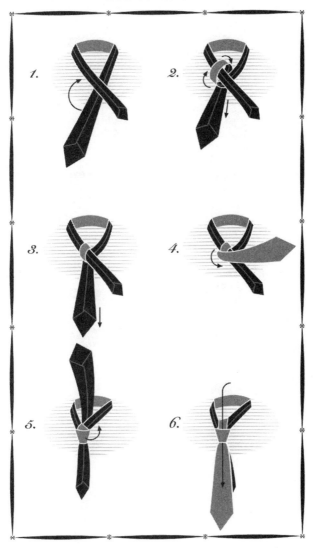

Pratt

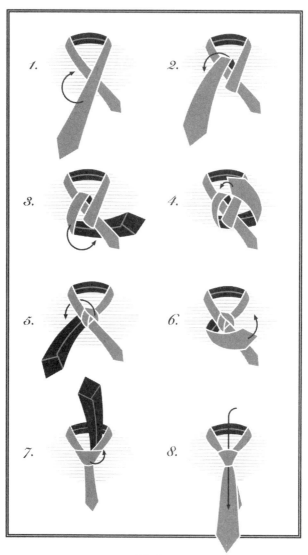

Windsor

WEEK-END WALKS

Advice on Walking

Some claim that walking is a deep, mystical, existential practise. They haven't done enough of it. I can report, after twenty-one months walking across Asia, that walking is basically a pedestrian activity. The trick is not to fall over.

There are, of course, advantages to bipedalism. Homo erectus' new posture gained us some height, allowing us to see over the hairy backs of our cousins to a more distant horizon. Our hands were freed to use tools; less surface area was exposed to the sun; only an unruly mop of hair was needed to cover our cooler and rapidly growing brain. It empowered us to forage and trade, a stride at a time, out of Africa to the Wallace Line, and in a species-slaughtering advance, over a pile of mammoths and giant rodents to Tierra del Fuego. Our success as a species is based on walking. Thus, for many early societies, walking was a sacred ritual—pacing the land, marking a trail, taking possession of every inch of soil by stroking it with our feet. Foot-falls are our earliest and most reliable music: Coleridge discovered the beat of his iambs in his echoing strides around the lakes, and dervishes unlocked their Sufi souls foot-step by foot-step across Asia.

Nevertheless, for all its glorious history, walking remains an uncomfortable activity. It is difficult to put one foot in front of the other and to balance six foot of vertical height, topped with an overweight brain, on a narrow one foot base. Our hips and knees grind and protest as we totter from heel through arch and ball and push off again from the big toe. For anyone who does a lot of it, walking is not about the interaction of landscape and mind, but about the interaction

133

of landscape and flesh. It is weight, water and blisters. And our response to this should be proportional. I have eight rules.

1. Twenty miles was the distance a Silk Road caravan moved in a day and the average daily stage for most ancient travellers. Make it your stage. Fifty miles a day, though possible, cannot be kept up for long. Reckon on a maximum of three miles an hour and twenty miles in a day, resting every couple of hours for ten minutes, and you can walk across half the world.

2. The longer the walk, the lighter the load. The day before I set off to walk from Turkey to Bangladesh, I rang Nicholas Crane, who had just walked the Pyrenees. He invited me at once to bring my pack to his house, demonstrating with the kitchen scales that two Mars Bars weighed more than all my antibiotics, and threw them out with my tent, my pots, my stove and my torch. He said it was better to eat cold food, put a plastic cover over a sleeping bag and learn to move in the dark. "Every morning," he said "you pull that pack onto your back, you will resent every hundred grams." He was right. You can walk a continent with a 10 kilo pack. The only excuses for carrying more are the Antarctic and ammunition.

3. If weight is universal, then footwear is relative. I have seen Bedu proceeding steadily, shoeless, on gravel sands that would burn a fire-walker, and walked for five hours over a glacier beside a barefoot Wakhi. Even a Scot can go barefoot on jungle mulch and pull off leeches easily. Yet although its benefits are relative, footwear is advisable. Two decades walking barefoot in Irian Jaya won't protect you against a bamboo spike. And even lions sometimes need thorns pulled from their feet. Gumboots give you blisters. Shoes are much better than sandals, for thongs bite and gravel gets under your soles. Boots are better than shoes because they hold a turned ankle. Do not be tempted into fine looking

dubbin-smeared leather, which lets in water. Army boots, if they fit, are often excellent. Two pairs of a cheap Gore-Tex boot took me 6000 miles. Wear two pairs of socks to minimise blisters. Cut your toenails. Treat blisters early.

4. Blisters are quick, intense and temporary; damage to knees is subtler, slower and more lasting. I refused to walk with twin ski-poles because I thought they looked daft and, therefore, destroyed my knees walking across the grain of the Nepali Himalayas (it was worse downhill). I was eventually forced to use twin poles. I should have used them sooner.

5. Drink deep. Each litre weighs a kilogram so drink like a camel before you start each stage—I drink a litre and a half, at least. Don't drink from a mountain burn without purifying the water—a nasty chlorine taste is better than the undetectable traces of a dead sheep upstream.

6. Even this other Eden has stinging insects, rain, bogs, loose shale, filthy water, night and fog; you can freeze to death as easily on a Scottish hillside as in the Arctic, and a fifty-foot cliff can be as fatal as a ten thousand-foot ridge. But Britain is a small island, and with map, compass, warm and dry clothing, water-purifying tablets and good boots, you should be able to walk out of any trouble.

7. Never overdress. Ten years ago, I came up Ben Vorlich on a Scottish June afternoon, barefoot and wearing a kilt, and found on the summit four men in fluorescent Gore-Tex, ice-axes casually dangling from their wrists and packs so large that I could only assume they contained oxygen tanks and small airships. Britain's hills are low, its winters mild, its wolves extinct and its tribal bandits largely under control. It is not, therefore, necessary to dress on a walk as though one is attempting to summit Cho-yu. A disproportionate amount of heat escapes from your head, so the best investment in terms of weight and warmth, is a hat. Aim to

take little more than a hat and a green coat from the hall, so that even in the Cairngorms a stranger would not know whether you had walked a thousand miles from Cornwall, or stepped out to feed the dog.

8. Be attentive to the landscape. Open your hood to feel the wind and hear the rain. Do not wear headphones, ever. Allow yourself the time to smell and saunter, register the changing light, the birdsong, the shapes of trees and the colour of leaves. Spend part of each walk silent and alone. Approach even the longest journey as a stroll, not a forced march. Focus on the present moment, not the destination. Regulate your breathing to your pace. Above all breathe.

If you can follow these eight rules: neither over-tired nor over-burdened, nor in pain from feet or knees, well-hydrated, well-prepared, understated and unharried, then you can begin to look for purpose and magic. But best of all walk with a dog.

Rory Stewart

The South Downs

A thought or two of the walks over the hills from Brighton.

Two ideals of holiday are blended in the prescriptions offered by "Dr Brighton" to all who call. One is embodied in the title of one of Richard Jefferies' essays, "Sea, Sky, and Downs", a phrase expressing what Brighton meant chiefly to him, as to so many of its truest lovers. At Brighton's near neighbour, Hove, Jefferies wrote much of "The Life of the Fields", and his philosophy is often in the minds of those who follow his steps along the chalk tracks over the downs he loved. In Dr Brighton's holiday prescription the South Down air—sea air fragrant with the scent of gorse and thyme—plays a large part; for the South Downs, just over a mile away northward, are Brighton's glory.

The other ideal is embodied in the phrase, "London-by-the-Sea". And Dr Brighton, "merry, cheerful Dr Brighton", in Thackeray's phrase, may well be proud of his town, and the five miles of unbroken sea wall and promenade, one of the sights of England, they say at Brighton; and of the sunsets over Hove. The Sun-God is very partial to Brighton. When there is a fog in London, and a white pall of mist enwraps all the weald beyond the downs, Brighton often is bathed in sunshine.

The town owes much to one, Dr Richard Russell, who discovered the virtue of sea-bathing, and in the latter days of the eighteenth century brought the fishing-village of Brighthelmstone into fashion as a watering-place. "The Brighthelmstone Guide" of 1777 tells, in doggerel verse, how the town, like London Bridge, was half broken down— it was worse than Wapping, "Not fit for souls to stop in". But Dr Russell sees to have put all right, though a word of

warning was given to all such visitors embraced by the word
"swains", and ought perhaps to be repeated here:

> Brighthelmstone was confessed by all
> To abound with females fair,
> But more so since fam'd Russell has
> Preferred the waters there.
> Then fly that dangerous town, ye swains …

Richard Jefferies said roundly, there are more handsome
women in Brighton than anywhere else in the world.

Earlier history goes back to the Brighthelmstun of
Domesday Book, the dwelling of St Brighthelm, who had a
share in founding the kingdom of the South Saxons that is
Sussex. Passing over the centuries, Charles II flits across the
stage for a moment, as we are reminded by a tomb in the
parish churchyard of a gallant sea-captain who, after
Worcester, conveyed the king oversea in his stout vessel, the
Surprise. On Dr Russell's propaganda work the Prince
Regent set his seal, and his fantastic Pavilion, believed to
have cost a million of money, keeps green the memory of
Brighton's most splendid era.

The rooks still build there, and there is an old tradition
that they always start housekeeping on St Valentine's Day.
Brighton, even apart from the downs, is like London in
having much of interest for the naturalist, as the Booth
Collection of British Birds in the Dyke Road, of peculiar
value as having been made by one man. Sussex was ever a
famed bird country, her hills are the landing-place of myriads
of migrants in the spring, and the county has been fortunate
in its chronicles of bird-life, as written by Gilbert White,
Richard Jefferies, A. E. Knox ("Ornithological Rambles in
Sussex"), William Borrer ("Birds of Sussex"), and W. H.
Hudson ("Nature in Downland"). The Booth collection is
a valuable supplement to these works.

The South Downs, described by Gilbert White as a
"chain of majestic mountains", and also as "*amusing*

mountains", stretch away from the town—the happiest of hills, with their sweet, smooth contours, steep escarpments, and flower-embroidered turf; their gorse, hawthorn, heather and wild thyme, and wild honeysuckle wreathing the old may-bushes; their romantic combes and vales, and clear-cut crest lines; ancient earthworks; music of the wind in the bents; ever-changing colours in the play of sunlight and shadow; hamlets hidden in the folds; windmills, dew-ponds, shepherds, sheep, and sheep-bells. On the springy turf, in the fine exhilarating down and sea air, you feel you could walk for ever. Like Meredith on Box Hill, as you climb some beacon-point and look out over the weald, you want to shout "Ha! ha!" to the gates of the world. But the downs are not always appreciated by those coming to them for the first time. They will bewail the bareness of these East Sussex hills, which is their charm in their lovers' eyes, perhaps echoing Dr Johnson's saying of the downs about Brighton, that it is a country so truly desolate that if one had a mind to hang oneself at being obliged to live there, it would be difficult to find a tree on which to fasten a rope. But there are rich woodlands in Stanmer Park, and some lovers of the bare, wind-swept plains sometimes lament that now there are too many trees in some of the valleys, and that there is a spreading of scrub which the shepherds of the old days would have cleared away.

Passing out of Brighton eastward through Kemp Town, you come to the high cliff-top track over the flowery turf to Newhaven, the sea on one hand, the downs on the other. Ovingdean is passed, one of the downs' hidden hamlets, with its Saxon church, and its memories of Harrison Ainsworth's "Ovingdean Grange", and his story of the flight of Charles II. Next you come shortly to Rottingdean, where Kipling wrote "Sussex", having followed Sir Edward Burne-Jones to the sweet village by the sea; there are Burne-Jones archangels in the church. Behind the village lie the downs, wide and bare to the skies, hiding several hamlets with Kipling's "little lost Down churches" that, like you, praise the Lord for making the hills. Telscombe is an example, a hamlet hidden and lost in the hills; and Falmer, on the road to Lewes. Falmer is the key to Stanmer Park, and all the wild, open downland between that road and the other one to Lewes from Ditchling, below the northern face of the downs, a lovely road rising and falling with the contours of the foothills.

Beyond Rottingdean is a phenomenon known as Peacehaven, which describes itself as the garden city of the south coast, with church, school, hotel, bungalow and golf-course in the picture, a troop of boy scouts, and a bird sanctuary. From the top of the steep chalk cliffs we look down on Newhaven, and going down thither from the south-coast road there is a fine view of Lewes in the distance. Peacehaven has a history of only some five years, but many pages of history are stamped on the old hills, including the far away story of 1264, the Battle of Lewes, when the streets of Lewes ran blood, and the vanquished fled away over the hills. Newhaven has the safest harbour between Portsmouth and the Downs (the other downs), and an old church on a hill which is an object of pilgrimage, if only to see the grave of a great Sussex character, honest Tom Tipper, who brewed a famous ale that is talked of in the town to this day. He died in 1785, and his epitaph, written by Thomas Clio Rickman, of Lewes and London (a bookseller and a verse-maker), was much admired by Charles Lamb, and considered his masterpiece. Of honest Tom the epitaph relates:

> The best old Stingo he both brewed and sold,
> Nor did one knavish act to get his gold.
> He played through life a varied comic part,
> And knew immortal Hudibras by heart.

Behind Newhaven stretches away the valley of the Ouse, with many hamlets, sheltered by a line of the hills, and looking over the marshes. There is Piddinghoe, where they shoe magpies and dig for moonshine, and where the church has one of the three round towers of the county, and a gilt dolphin (actually a salmon) for weathervane, as all the world knows from Kipling. There is Telscombe, hidden in the hills, sometimes called the capital of these downs—a very shy one; and Southease, with another of the round towers; and Rodmell, where, at the little inn, you are

> Free to sit and free to think,
> Free to pay for what you drink,

and Iford and Kingston (one of the three Sussex Kingstons). These little places are named, for the seven miles from Newhaven to Lewes are seven miles of precious quality.

Or, from Rottingdean, the explorer may strike north, dip into deep valleys and climb high hill-crests, striking the Brighton-Lewes road at the Newmarket Inn; then, still holding north, march on to the landmark of Blackcap, a miniature Chanctonbury Ring eight miles from Brighton as the crow flies—to see below a thousand square miles of the weald. This is a promontory on the crest-line of the downs running from about the hamlet of Offham, near Lewes, to the east, to Ditchling Beacon and Clayton windmills to the west—some five or six miles. There is no finer walk in Sussex than along this northern brow of the downs—or in England, perhaps. Striking eastward from Blackcap, by Mount Harry, and over the ground of the Battle of Lewes, and by Lewes race-course, the old county town is reached in about four miles, cradled by the hilld.

"Proud Lewes, Poor Brighthelmstone", runs the proverb; and there is no limit to the pride of Lewes in its encircling hills, its old castle, its seven churches, its precipitous High Street (reminiscent of Guildford) and quaint, narrow streets with gabled houses. Lewes was grey and hoary with age when Brighton was a fishing-village; Brighton's discoverer, Dr Russell, here lies buried. Brighton, in his day, was "Brighthelmstone, near Lewes". The castle tower should be climbed, for the sake of the great view of the downs and their mounts—Mount Caburn, Mount Harry, and Firle Beacon. Caburn should be climbed for the sake of what Gilbert White described as "a most engaging prospect of all the country round, besides several views of the sea".

To return to Brighton, another walk thence must be mentioned, the good line of country gained by going up the Ditchling Road to Hollingbury Camp, and on by a broad, green track past Stanmer Park. You pass on, by High Park Corner, where gipsy caravans often congregate, to Ditchling Beacon, the highest point of the East Sussex downs, six miles from Brighton as the crow flies; and as, standing below the old beacon, by the dew-pond, you look down on the weald below, you might think that all the kingdoms of the earth were stretched at your feet. Below is the royal and ancient town of Ditchling (it would be insulted if referred to as a village), proud of its associations with King Alfred, who was lord of the manor, of its Old House that belonged to Anne of Cleves, of its annual gooseberry show, held through a hundred years, and of its native charm, that brings to mind the lines about a rose-red city, half as old as time.

To return once more, one may start out again for the downs through Hove, for all that downland country lying to the north of Hove and Worthing. Hove itself is famous for three things—for being the only town on the south coast laid out on rectangular lines so that the wide streets are flooded with sunshine (Peacehaven might dispute this claim); for the great church of All Saints (which ranks with Lancing College Chapel at Shoreham nearby, and the Roman Catholic Chapel at Arundel, as having been lovingly built by slow craftsmanship in mediaeval style), and for the surf on its shore. The poet, Roden Noel, who lived at Hove, and shared Byron's and Swinburne's passion for the sea, would say, "The surf here is the finest in England." Within easy reach of Hove are many little villages and hamlets steeped in the peace of the old hills. From Hangleton the explorer is well advised to make for the Devil's Dyke (where is an inn) by an ancient track leading due north, where the

Romans may have marched, and smugglers, passing through the valleys to the weald. The story goes that the Devil was annoyed by hearing the church bells of the weald, and it was to drown their music that he cut, in one night, the great dyke, thinking to let the sea flow through the downs. This fell out "four hundred years ago or more", a ballad relates.

A Sussex ballad tells of a Brighton fisherman who once ventured as far inland as the dyke, and after beholding the view of the weald went home declaring, "He ne'er beleft, afore, that the world was half so big." His simple thought may be shared by any pilgrim who, as a new experience stands on any peak of the northern crest of the south Downs, and stares at Sussex—at the downs and the sea, southward, and the living map of the weald. He may see the Isle of Wight. He may even sense London, whither, alas, we must now go.

Marcus Woodward

FOOD ...

Country House Picnics

PILGRIMS just now in the country, at the closing of the off-season, when there is no shooting, and hunting is confined to the pedestrian chase of the wily otter, are somewhat at a "loose-end", and picnics—the gipsy parties of the early Victorian era—are popular and prominent. These *alfresco* gatherings, if well selected and managed, serve pleasantly to kill time, provided always that the scenery be sufficiently attractive and the weather auspicious. Rain is "rotten", and cold is a frost. There are absolutely requisite sunlight, calm, drought, and warmth.

The country house picnic takes many forms. We have the ducal delicacy and the lordly libation; the copious spread and the (very much) rough-it regale; the farmhouse holocaust and the crust and cheese confection, of light wares, by which the discriminating pilgrims set very light, and which, subsequently, sit very heavy. However, all these "functions" are commonly in vogue, all over rural Britain, especially wherever there are old castles, ruins, cliffs, waterfalls, woods, moors, glens, and other picturesque spots. In some cases, the tuck's the thing; in others, the entourage; in others, both. Let us regard, in retrospect, five recent picnics which recently took place in various parts of still Merrie England and vivacious Wales.

The house party at Exe Castle, in Zedshire, were treated to an out-of-doors luncheon by the Duke and Duchess. The whole party, numbering nearly fifty, with about as many servants, motored to the ruins of Quarlynch Abbey, beneath those of Abbott's Down. Happily, the weather was as Elysian as the environment. Happily, too, the temporary trippers were suitably assorted, or assorted themselves, in the matters of equal age and contrasted sexes. As for the repast, it was pretty much what it would have been at the castle, only more so. Of course, thanks to apparatus of the "Thermos" principle, there were hot soups and liquors either piping hot or icy cold, according to idiosyncrasy; and equally, of course, very prominent and profuse were lobster salad and salmon mayonnaise. There were hams and tongues and various galantined preparations; and there were quails, served hot and whole, and *not* barbarously curried and disflavoured, as some Philistines dish the luscious birds from the East. As for beverages, they ranged from champagne to claret, from burgundy to Beaune, from hock to Hermitage, from Tokay to sherry, from whisky to home-made cowslip (very breezy), from port to perry; and, being in Zedshire, there was a small cask of the wine of the country—sparkling, pure, wholesome (though intoxicating) cider. Altogether, this "outing" was a solemn success.

Number two was given from the old, ancestral manor-house of a squire on the Welsh marches. This affair was a miniature replica of the ducal one, far away. The guests were not so numerous, but they were more frolicsome, and the menu was pretty similar, save that there was introduced the toothsome novelty of lambs' tail pie, which is composed of "brushes" chopped from living animals. Cruelty-crazers and RSPCA please don't note. Here was no form of "blood sport"; only ordinary farming and butchering. Here, again, cider was present; it was secretly and seductively obtruded in the form of apple-juice, fermented, plus the admixture of plums, with the result that two maiden ladies met with an adventure. These, the Misses Smith-Smythe, being old-fashioned, were driven to and fro by their tried, trusty, sober, old coachman, who, taking but a modicum of the "faked" cider, was obliged to drive his antiquated mistresses home, kneeling on the box, between the seat and the splash-board, as though conducting (as was his wont) a prayer-meeting. Otherwise, and also thus, this picnic was greatly enjoyed by the youthful members of the party, who have now invented a cry wherewith to encourage the ancient coachman— "Ware cider, Jarvis!"

In the pretty, out-of-the-world village of Meadowsweet, in the West Midlands, there was arranged a sort of composite picnic, held on the slopes of a range of hills about half-a-dozen miles distant. There were represented the residents and visitors at the Hall, the parsonage, the Farm, Meadowsweet Villa, Meadowsweet Cottage, Meadowsweet Lodge, etc. Each contingent, driving to the Meet variously, brought a contribution, which was finally thrown into the common store; with the result that many luxuries were doubled and trebled and quadrupled, whilst several necessities were *caret*. Thus, there was a glut of ham and an utter absence of salt, mustard, and forks. However, there was "lashings" of drink, and the gathering was pretty generally voted a success. Recriminations were out of the question, as all were pretty equally involved in sins of omission and commission.

The fourth picnic was of the pedestrian and light marching order character. A dozen young people—six boys and six girls—plus two old married folk of the combined age of thirty-five, for chaperonage, assembled, by pre-arrangement, by a holy well, of the noted water of which they made no use until the time of boiling tea arrived. Each member of this party carried his or her own little store of meat and drink. There were sandwiches, pasties, biscuits, fruit, bread and cheese, and pocket flasks. Towards four o'clock a fire was made, the holy well was tapped, and tea was partaken of. But before this virtual finale, there was held a sort of impromptu gymkhana.

But the complete picnic should embrace water—not necessarily to drink, nor yet to bathe in, though, perhaps, to boat upon, or, at any rate, to gaze at. The ideal scene is laid upon the seashore, in the vicinity of rocks and caves. Failing the ocean, one craves a river; failing that, a stream; and, failing that, a lake, reservoir, or large pond or pool. If the

151

party can voyage to the rendezvous in boats, so much the better; if in sailing craft, better still, perhaps. Thus, we come to our fifth and last illustration, or mental cinema, of which the scene is laid in the lovely valley of the winding Wye.

The party assembled a little before noon by the riverside, at the foot of the park, beneath a castellated mansion. There were forty people, all told, including servants, in some half-dozen or more roomy, tubby, safe boats, which permitted larking. The flotilla paddled downstream for a mile or so, and disembarked upon a charming island, where they proceeded to lead, for a short time, a life after the manner of Robinson Crusoe, with the vast difference that they feasted daintily, copiously, and royally. After lunch most of the picnickers re-embarked, and, armed with rods and baits, angled with some little success. When the spirit lamps had boiled the water in the kettles the chef who was in attendance fried trout and troutlets in fresh water, over a fire made of dry sticks. Whoso has not thus eaten freshly caught fario knows not the delicate flavour of those toothsome fish.

.

Kitchen Folklore — Whys & Wherefores

Every day life, ordinary happenings and articles in daily use are often interwoven with superstitions and sayings which appear inexplicable; we accept much for granted or pass them by. Yet mingled with many of these superstitions are quaint fragments of history and bygone custom, and sometimes in sifting out their origin the collector of folklore not only comes across fascinating treasure-trove, but is able to throw light on matters belonging to more strictly intellectual regions.

Every housewife knows that "a watched pot never boils", that one person only should stir a boiling pot or put dough into the oven. The process of manufacture, or of transforming one substance into another, by boiling or baking, especially when any chemical process was employed, such as the "working" of dough by yeast or barm, was regarded by our ancestors as mystical and uncanny, therefore for two to share in this mystery might cause strife, so was supposed to be unlucky.

"Burn bread, and you'll go a begging", is still quoted, but to understand why it is so unlucky to burn "the staff of life" one must go back to 1800 when Great Britain was on the brink of famine owing to a succession of bad harvests and war. The Government instituted measures to conserve flour, no new bread was allowed to be eaten, and I have often wondered if the oft-repeated warning about new bread being so indigestible dates to this time. At all events, the saying that "she who drops a loaf of bread will never be a wife", probably originated at a period when caution was taken over every bit of bread.

In parts of the British Isles a cross is still marked on each loaf, as on the bunghole of every barrel of home-brewed beer; some will tell you the criss-cross on the dough brings lightness to the bread, in reality it is a hark-back to days when fear of witchcraft prevailed, and the sign kept away witches.

There is a saying, too, that if a "cottage" loaf comes apart by accident in the hand of an unmarried girl she will have no chance of marriage that year, and to a married woman that she will be a widow. Doubtless these sayings originated at the time when bread was so precious.

To spill salt is regarded as unlucky, and to this day many will take a pinch with the right thumb and toss it over the left shoulder, to avert ill luck. Why? Because salt is the emblem of eternity and immortality, so that unless one made an oblation to the gods it was believed one's very life was in danger. In the Highlands a wooden platter with a little heap of salt was always placed on the breast of a corpse, the salt being an emblem of the immortal soul. In his *Hesperides* Herrick speaks of the soul as "the salt of the body". Therefore, it is to avert any harm to the soul, we half mechanically throw salt over our shoulder.

We know, too, among the Ancients, as among Orientals of to-day, sale constituted a bond of friendship between host and guest, the Arab phrase "there is salt between us"—is another way of saying "he has eaten my salt", or partaken of hospitality, which explains an unwritten law of courtesy. Without doubt, a religious significance attached itself to salt, and quite probably this is why we still shrink from spilling it in kitchen or at table.

One must never borrow certain culinary articles, and salt is among them. Perhaps because salt is associated with sorrow accounts for this, but the superstition dates back to the days when it was believed one's Ka or spirit returned. The Egyptians said that a loan of salt should be speedily returned, lest the borrower die in the meantime, because if restitution were not made of the borrowed salt, trouble would follow. To steal salt was a crime in olden days and it was said that if a man thieved salt his soul would never know repose, signifying the high value once placed upon this everyday article of culinary use.

That one must never burn egg-shells I always believed was due to the unpleasant smell they create, but a Midland farmer's wife told me this was not the reason. She affirmed that hens cease to lay if this is done. All empty egg-shells should be collected, dried in the oven, mixed with grit and barley and scattered in the hen run. On no account must they be given without baking, or it teaches hens to eat their eggs. But this superstition, as well as many more relating to eggs, originates in the belief that an egg is the emblem of life, therefore to burn an egg-shell and destroy life is a bad omen. It is supposed to be unlucky to let eggs go out of the house after sunset.

When an egg has been eaten many people poke a hole in the bottom, probably because in nursery days they were taught to do this. Why? If this is not done "the witch will set to sea to wreck ships." Witches were supposed to sail the sea in egg-shells just as they rode the air on broomsticks. In North Devon and Cornwall, as well as in Holland this saying is still met with.

In apparently silly beliefs there are hidden grains of truth, and truly

"Men may construe things, after their fashion,
Clean from the purpose of the things themselves;"

but there is yet plenty of scope for scholarship and imagination even with simple everyday things of kitchen and household use.

Mrs. Stanley Wrench

When Foods are in Season

By being in season it is understood to mean it can be procured.

FISH

BASS. In season from May to December.

BLOATERS. All the year round.

BRILL. In season from May to January; can be procured all the year round, but inferior in February, March and April.

COD. In season from September till April.

CRABS. Obtainable all the year round.

DORIES. In season from April to September.

EELS. Can be obtained all the year round; best from September till May.

SCALLOPS. In season from October till May.

FLOUNDERS. In season all the year except May, June and July.

GURNETS. Can be obtained all the year round; inferior in October and November.

HADDOCKS. In season all the year round.

HAKE. In season from May to December.

HALIBUT. In season all the year round, but inferior in February, March and April.

HERRINGS. Obtainable from end of July till February.

LOBSTERS. Can be obtained all the year round; best in May and June.

MACKEREL. In season for nine months in the year; November, December and January they are scarce.

RED MULLET. In season July, August, September, and October.

OYSTERS. Native oysters in season from 1 September till 30 April. Cooking oysters can be procured all the year round.

PERCH AND PIKE. Out of season from 15 March to 15 June.

PLAICE. Can be obtained all the year round; inferior in February, March and April.

PRAWNS. In season from April till August.

SALMON. In season from February till 7 September; then Dutch and Norwegian salmon can be obtained.

SHRIMPS. In season from March till September, but can be procured all the year round.

SKATE. In season from October to May.

SMELTS. In season from October to May.

SEA BREAM. In season July, August, September and October.

SOLES. Can be obtained all the year round; considered out of season in April and May.

SPRATS. In season from September till April.

TENCH. In season all the year except from 15 March to 15 June.

TROUT. In season from beginning of February till 7 September.

TURBOT. Can be procured all the year round, but at its best in May.

WHITEBAIT. In season from February till August, but can be procured all the year round.

WHITING. Best from May to January; can be obtained all the year round.

MEAT

BEEF. In season all the year round.

MUTTON. In season all the year round.

LAMB. English lamb in season from January till August; best from April to June. Foreign lamb can be obtained all the year round.

VEAL can be obtained all the year round; in full season March to July.

PORK. In season from September till April.

VENISON. Buck venison in season from June to September; doe venison, November to February.

GAME AND POULTRY

BLACKCOCK. English birds are in season from 2 August to 10 December; foreign birds can be obtained till the end of June.

CAPERCAILZIE. English birds from 20 August to 10 December.

CHICKENS. In season all the year round.

CHICKENS (Spring). From March to May.

DUCKS. In season from August till February.

DUCKLINGS. In season from March till August.

DUCKS (Wild). In season 1 August to 15 March.

FOWLS. In season all the year round.

GEESE. In season from September till February.

GOSLINGS. In season from February till September.

GROUSE. The shooting season commences 12 August ends 10 December.

GUINES FOWLS. In season in March, April and May.

HARES. 1 August to 1 March.

LARKS. In season from November to March.

ORTOLANS. In season from March to May.

PARTRIDGES. The season commences on 1 September and closes on 1 February. Poulterers are allowed fourteen days after to dispose of their stock.

PIGEONS. In season all the year round.

PLOVERS. In season from 1 August till 1 March.

PTARMIGAN. English birds in season from 20 August to 10 December, then foreign birds till June.

QUAILS. In season all months.

RABBITS. In season all the year round.

SNIPE. In season from 1 August to 1 March.

TEAL. In season from 1 August to 1 March.

TURKEYS. At their best from September till March.

WIDGEON AND WOODCOCK. In season from 1 August to 1

March. These, with Teal and Snipe, can be obtained for fifteen days after, as poulterers are allowed fifteen days grace after the close time to dispose of their stock.

VEGETABLES

ARTICHOKES (Globe). Can be obtained all the year round.

ARTICHOKES (Jerusalem). October till June.

ASPARAGUS. In season from April till end of July.

BEETROOT. Obtainable all the year round.

BRUSSELS SPROUTS. In season from September till the end of March.

CABBAGES. From April till the end of October.

CARROTS. Obtainable all the year round; new Carrots in May.

CAULIFLOWERS. In season from May to November.

CELERY. In season from beginning of September till February.

CHERVIL. Can be procured all the year round.

CUCUMBERS. Can be obtained nearly all the year; best in May, June, July and August.

FRENCH BEANS. In season from July till end of October.

GARLIC. Best in winter months.

GREENS. In season from October to February.

HORSE-RADISH. Obtainable all the year round.

KALE. In season in winter months.

LEEKS. In season all the year round.

LETTUCE. English lettuces from April to November, but can be procured all months.

MUSHROOMS. Cultivated mushrooms from December to March, outdoor in August, September and October.

ONIONS. In season all the year round.

ONIONS (Spanish). From October till May.

ONIONS (Pickling). September, October and November.

PARSNIPS. In season September till April.

PEAS. English Green Peas in season from June till September. Foreign can be obtained in May.

POTATOES. All the year round. New in May; Jersey new in March.

SALSIFY. In season from December till March.

SAVOYS. In season from December till March.

SCARLET RUNNERS. From July till end of October.

SEA-KALE. In season from February till May.

SHALLOTS. Are best in winter months.

SPINACH. In season from March till December.

TOMATOES. In season all the year round.

TURNIPS. In season all the year round.

VEGETABLE MARROWS. In season from the end of August till October.

WATERCRESS. Obtainable all the year round.

FRUIT

APPLES. In season all the year except June, July and August.

APRICOTS. In season in August and September; can be procured in June, July and October.

BANANAS. In season all months.

BLACKBERRIES. In season in September and October.

CHERRIES. From June till September.

CHESTNUTS. In season from November till February.

COBNUTS. From September till February.

CRANBERRIES. In season in October, November and December.

CURRANTS (Red, Black and White). From June till end of August.

DAMSONS. September and October.

FIGS. In season all the year round. Green Figs, July, August and September.

FILBERTS. In season August, September and October.

GOOSEBERRIES (Green). Commence in May; the ripe fruit begin in June and last till August.

GRAPES. Obtainable all the year round. English of various kinds are best in July, August and September.

GREENGAGES. English fruit from middle of August till September. Foreign fruit obtainable in July.

LEMONS. Can be procured all the year round; dearest in summer months.

MEDLARS. In season from September till end of October.

MELONS (Hothouse and Rock). In August and September.

MELONS (Spanish Water). From October till Christmas.

NECTARINES. In season in September; can be procured in August and October.

ORANGES. Obtainable all the year round.

ORANGES (Seville). February and March.

ORANGES (Tangerines). November till April.

PEACHES. In season in September; obtainable in August and October.

PEARS. From August till January.

PINEAPPLES (English and St Michael). Can be obtained nearly all the year, but very dear in winter months.

PLUMS. From August till end of September.

QUINCES. In season middle of September to end of October.

RASPBERRIES. In season June, July and August.

RHUBARB. Forced is in season from January till May.

STRAWBERRIES. In season in June and July.

WALNUTS. In season September till Christmas.

NOTE. – Californian fruits, greengages, nectarines, peaches, plums, etc., arrive in February and last about a month.

Marketing Hints

ECONOMY should be studied when marketing. The real meaning of the word in this case is getting full value for the money spent. To exercise this always buy provisions when in season, and in exactly suitable quantities for the day's consumption only; dry and tinned goods according to the available storage. Flour, grains, sugar and dried fruits are cheaper bought in large quantities, and do not spoil if kept in a cool dry place. It is advisable to buy from a shop that has a quick sale and so constantly renewing the stock. In small and country shops stores often remain a long time on hand and deteriorate.

Store-rooms, whether for dry or fresh goods, must always be cool, dry, well-ventilated and lighted, and not near any open drain or pipes. There should be a good supply of shelves and cupboards, so as not to be overcrowded. Jars and boxes must be covered and plainly labelled. Goods when purchased should be compared with the invoices and occasionally weighed. Stock should always be renewed before it is exhausted. This prevents great inconvenience. In buying fresh goods a rule to remember is that they are best when in season. The flavour is fullest then. They are most plentiful, wholesome and nutritious, as well as cheapest; but now most things can be purchased all the year round if one can afford to pay the price for them.

MEAT.—Good meat is firm and not flabby: when pressed the mark quickly disappears. There is no disagreeable smell. It should be free from moisture. To test meat put in a skewer close to the bone and if it comes out clean and smells sweet the meat is in good condition.

BEEF.—The flesh should be deep red in colour, smooth grained, the lean and fat intermixed. The fat should be of a pale straw colour and somewhat soft. If very yellow it generally denotes the animal was fed on oil-cake. It is rich and greasy and wastes in cooking, but is quite wholesome.

Prices:	per lb.
Sirloin	1s. 10d. to 1s. 11½d.
Silverside	1s. 5d. to 1s. 6d.
Topside	1s. 8d. to 1s. 10½d.
Ribs	1s. 3d. to 1s. 11½d.
Brisket	10d. to 11d.
Beef Steak	1s. 6d. to 1s. 10d.
Rump Steak	2s. 7d. to 2s. 8d.

Foreign meat is 5d. to 10d. per lb. cheaper.

MUTTON.—The flesh of mutton should be fine grained and firm, paler in colour than beef; the fat white and firm. Mutton is finest when it is between four and five years old; but it is seldom met with. Sheep are generally killed when between two and three years old. Mutton should be moderately fat. If very lean it will be poor in flavour and tough.

Prices:	per lb.
Leg	1s. 10d. to 1s. 11d.
Shoulder	1s. 6d. to 1s. 8d.
Neck	1s. 2d. to 2s. 6d.
Loin	1s. 9d. to 2s. 5d.
Hindquarters	2s. to 2s. 1d.
Saddle	2s. 3d. to 2s. 4d.
Chops .	2s. 7d. to 2s. 8d.

LAMB:—Lamb is judged as mutton, but the flesh is paler in colour. It is best when about twelve weeks old. The price varies, according to the season, from 2s. to 2s. 2d. per lb. hindquarters, 1s. 7d. to 1s. 9d. per lb. forequarters.

VEAL:—Veal should always be chosen from a small animal; if large it is coarse and tough. The flesh should be fine in grain and dry; it is not fit for food if moist and clammy. The lean should be pale pink and firm in the fibre; the fat firm and white. When buying veal, two useful tests as to the condition are the state of the liver and the fat round the kidneys. The former must be clear and free from spots, and the latter firm, sweet and dry.

Prices:	per lb.
Fillet	2*s*. 5*d*. to 2*s*. 7*d*.
Loin	1*s*. 5*d*. to 2*s*. 1*d*.
Shoulder	1*s*. 5*d*. to 1*s*. 9*d*.
Breast	1*s*. 2*d*. to 1*s*. 4*d*.
Cutlets	2*s*. 7*d*. to 2*s*. 9*d*.
Calves' Heads	9*d*. to 11*d*.

PORK.—Pork must be more carefully chosen than any other butcher-meat, and should never be bought in warm weather. It is only wholesome in the winter. The lean of good pork is pale pink and firm; the fat white and clear; the skin thin and smooth and cool to the touch. Any signs of knots or kernels in the flesh indicate disease, and it should be rejected as unwholesome.

Prices:	per lb.
Leg	1*s*. 4½*d*. to 1*s*. 6*d*.
Loin .	1*s*. 3*d*. to 1*s*. 10*d*.

HAM AND BACON.—The fat of ham and bacon should have a clear pinky appearance; the lean firm; the rind, like the skin of good pork, should be thin. If it looks yellow and the salt is crusted on it, it should be rejected, as it will be rancid and unpalatable.

To test a ham, insert a bright steel skewer near the bone. If it comes out clean and free from any unpleasant smell it proves the ham is in good condition. On the other hand if the skewer is not clean and smells unpleasant, the ham should be rejected.

Prices:		per lb.
Hams:	English	1s. 5d. to 2s.
	Irish	1s. 9d. to 1s. 11d.
	American	2s. 8d. to 2s. 10d.

Bacon varies in price according to where it is cut.

Irish	8½d. to 2s. 1d.
Wiltshire	9d. to 2s. 3d.
Danish	7d. to 1s. 11d.

POULTRY.—Always buy poultry when young, except for soup and stock. If young the breast-bone and the tips of the pinions will be soft, the beak brittle, the spurs short, legs smooth; the feathers downy and an absence of long coarse hairs. If in good condition the flesh should be firm, the breast plump, and there should be some fat. If too fat the flavour is rank and the flesh greasy. Poultry should always be cooked while fresh, staleness being very objectionable and easily detected by a faint unpleasant odour. When freshly killed there is no smell, the feet are limp and moist, and the eyes full.

When the flesh is discoloured or has begun to turn green it should be rejected, and it is not advisable to purchase fowls with the skin torn in plucking or the breast-bone broken. This spoils the appearance when served.

White-legged fowls should be chosen for boiling, as they have the whitest flesh. Those with black or yellow legs are suitable for roasting, as the flavour is richer. When buying poultry already trussed from a poulterer it is advisable to wipe the birds carefully, pick them over and retruss them, replacing steel skewers or using a trussing needle and string for the wooden skewers used by the poulterer. These often impart a flavour to the flesh and are difficult to remove when the birds are cooked.

GAME.—Most of the tests for the age of poultry can be applied to game; but game should always be bought in its feathers, never after it is plucked. Game is greatly improved in tenderness and flavour by hanging; it is not considered worth eating while fresh. The length of time for hanging depends on the weather and the larder. In cold dry windy weather it will keep for some weeks, according to the taste of the consumer; but if the atmosphere is moist and warm, it decomposes quickly and becomes unwholesome and unfit to eat. Birds should be hung by the neck and sprinkled with pepper to keep away the flies and hung in a safe in the open air if possible.

Waterfowl, such as wild duck, snipe, teal, etc., should not hang more than a day or two. Pheasant are in season from 1 October to 1 February; Partridge, 1 September to 1 February; Grouse, 12 August to 10 December; Blackcock, 20 August to 10 December; Ptarmigan, 12 August to 10 December; Hares, 1 September to 1 March; Wild Duck, Teal, Snipe, Widgeon, 1 August to 1 March; Buck Venison, June to September; Doe Venison, November to February.

FISH.—It is most essential that fish should be fresh and in full season; it decomposes more quickly than any food. It is in best condition, most plentiful and cheapest when in season. When fish is kept on ice it is difficult to detect if it is stale; but after it has been removed it quickly loses its apparent freshness and can be judged by its smell and appearance. No one can mistake the smell of stale fish. If in good condition the flesh should be firm and plump, of a good even colour, eyes bright, gills and spots red. There are a few kinds that can be kept for a short time, such as turbot, cod and halibut; but it must be kept in a cool place in a current of air, and not in water. Fish may need soaking before cooking, but must not lie long in water, as this impoverishes the flavour and the fish becomes flabby. If fish is slimy, especially fresh-water fish, rub it with dry salt, as well as thoroughly wash it. Mackerel is unfit for food unless quite fresh. Salmon is best cooked as soon as possible after it is caught. The price varies with the supply and the season.

VEGETABLES.—The same rule applies as to fish and other foods. Vegetables are always best and cheapest when in season. The flavour is never so good when they are forced and are out of season.

Vegetables can never be too fresh; when stale they become unwholesome and indigestible. Absolute freshness cannot be obtained unless they are procured straight from the garden. This is impossible to those living in towns, so it is advisable to buy from a shop that has a good constant supply. Cabbage and green vegetables of all kinds should be bright in colour and crisp; a leaf or pod should break with a sharp crack when bent. If soft, flabby and a faded yellow colour they are stale.

Certain vegetables, such as cucumbers, vegetable marrows, and asparagus keep fresh for a day or two if the stalks are put in water. Root vegetables are stored for winter use; but the flavour is not so good as when fresh. They must not be stored until fully ripe, and must be carefully arranged in a cool dry place and protected from the frost.

Proper Proportions

Milk Puddings:

> 2 *oz.* cereals to 1 pint milk.
> 1 *oz.* semolina to 1 pint milk.

Moulds:

> 3 *oz.* whole cereals to 1 pint milk.
> 2 *oz.* ground cereals to 1 pint milk.

Sauces:

1. Foundation Sauces:
> 2 *oz.* butter, 2 *oz.* flour to 1 pint liquid.
2. Thickened Gravies:
> 1 *oz.* butter, 1 *oz.* flour to 1 pint liquid.
3. Stiff Binding Mixtures (Panada):
> 1 *oz.* butter, 1 *oz.* flour to 1 gill liquid.

Soups:

1. Stock:
> 1 lb. bones or bones and meat to 1 quart cold water and 1 quart over for evaporation.
2. Thick Soups:
> 1 *oz.* flour to 1 quart soup.
> 1 *oz.* sago, rice, etc., to 1 quart soup.
3. Purées:
> 2 *oz.* butter and 2 *oz.* flour to 1 quart purée.

Creams:

1. Whole Creams:
> ½ *oz.* gelatine to 1 pint cream.
2. Custard and Fruit Creams:

¾ *oz.* gelatine to 1 pint cream.

Jellies:

2 *oz.* gelatine to 1 quart liquid.

Aspic Jelly: 2½ *oz.* gelatine to 1 quart liquid.

Increase the proportion in hot weather.

Custard:

1. Plain:

2 yolks of eggs and 1 *oz.* cornflour to 1 pint milk.

2. Rich:

4 yolks of eggs to ¾ pint milk.

Bread:

1. Fermented:

½ *oz.* yeast to 1 lb. flour.

1 *oz.* yeast to 3½ lb. flour.

2. Baking Powder Bread (unfermented):

2 teaspoonfuls baking powder to 1 lb. flour.

Pastry:

1. Suet Crust:

8 *oz.* suet to 1 lb. flour (good).

6 *oz.* suet to 1 lb. flour and 1 teastpoonful baking powder (cheaper).

2. Short Crust:

8 *oz.* fat to 1 lb. flour.

6 *oz.* fat to 1 lb. flour and 1 teaspoonful baking powder.

3. Flaky:

10 *oz.* shortening to 1 lb. flour.

4. Puff Pastry:

1 lb. shortening to 1 lb. flour.

Batter:

Pancake Batter:

8 *oz.* flour, 1 pint milk, 2 eggs.

More eggs and less milk for richer batter.

169

Various Dishes & Their Usual Accompaniments

FISH

BOILED COD. Oyster, Egg, or Parsley Sauce.

BOILED SALT COD. Egg Sauce and Parsnips.

COD'S ROE. Italian or Piquante Sauce.

BOILED EELS. Parsley Sauce and Lemon.

FRIED EELS. Tartare Sauce.

BOILED HADDOCK. Anchovy or Egg Sauce and Lemon.

GRILLED HERRINGS. Mustard Sauce.

BOILED MACKEREL. Fennel, Parsley or Gooseberry Sauce.

OYSTERS. Cut Brown Bread and Butter and Lemon.

PLAICE. Any suitable sauce, Cut Lemon and Parsley.

BOILED SALMON. Dressed Cucumber, Lobster, Caper, Hollandaise, Shrimps or Melted Butter Sauce.

COLD SALMON. Mayonnaise, Tartare, or Anchovy Cream Sauce, Salad, Cucumber.

GRILLED SALMON. Tartare, Italienne, Maître d'Hôtel, Piquante, Tomato or Bearnaise Sauce.

SMELTS. Tomato or Anchovy Sauce.

SOLES. Any Suitable Sauce, Cut Lemon.

BOILED TURBOT. Shrimp, Lobster or Hollandaise Sauce, Garnish Lobster Coral and Cut Lemon.

WHITING. Anchovy, Parsley or Caper Sauce, Lemon.

WHITEBAIT. Lemon, Cut Brown Bread and Butter.

MEAT

ROAST BEEF. Yorkshire Pudding, Roast Potatoes, Scraped Horse-radish and Horse-radish Sauce.

BOILED BEEF. Suet Dumplings, Carrots, Turnips, Parsnips.

COLD BEEF. Salad, Pickles, Beetroot, Mashed Potatoes.

GRILLED STEAK. Oysters, Maître d'Hôtel Butter, Horse-radish Sauce, Potato Chips.

CALF'S HEAD. Parsley Sauce, Bacon, Lemon, Garnish with Brains and Tongue (sliced).

BOILED MUTTON. Carrots and Turnips, Caper or Parsley Sauce.

ROAST MUTTON (Shoulder). Onion Sauce.

ROAST MUTTON (Saddle and Haunch). Baked Potatoes, Gravy, Red Currant Jelly.

ROAST PORK. Sage and Onion Stuffing, Apple Sauce, Gravy.

BOILED PORK. Pease Pudding, Boiled Green Vegetables.

ROAST VEAL. Veal Forcemeat, Bacon or Pork, Melted Butter Sauce and Gravy.

VENISON. Red Currant Jelly, Port Wine Sauce.

VEGETABLES

ARTICHOKES. White Sauce.

ASPARAGUS. Toast underneath and Melted Butter.

BROAD BEANS. Parsley Sauce.

CAULIFLOWER. White Sauce or Cheese Sauce.

CELERY. White or Brown Sauce.

HARICOT BEANS. Butter and Chopped Parsley or Parsley Sauce.

ONIONS. Butter, White or Brown Sauce.

NEW POTATOES. Butter and Chopped Parsley.

SEA-KALE AND SALSIFY. White Sauce.

SPINACH. Hard-boiled Egg and Fried Bread.

VEGETABLE MARROW. White Sauce.

POULTRY AND GAME

BLACKCOCK. Toast, Good Gravy, Bread Sauce, Watercress.

WILD DUCK. Orange Sauce or Good Gravy and Orange Salad, Watercress.

GROUSE. Toast, Bread Sauce, Gravy, Browned Crumbs, Salad, Potato Chips.

ROAST HARE. Forcemeat Balls, Good Gravy, Red Currant Jelly.

ROAST PARTRIDGE. Bread Sauce, Gravy, Browned Crumbs, Salad, Potato Chips.

ROAST PHEASANT. Bread Sauce, Gravy, Browned Crumbs, Salad.

TEAL, ETC. Orange Sauce or Salad, Lemon Quarters, Watercress.

QUAILS, SNIPE, PLOVERS, ETC. Toast spread with Trail, Good Brown Gravy.

BOILED FOWL. Parsley, Egg, Celery, or White Sauce, Lemon.

ROAST FOWL. Bread Sauce, Bacon, Gravy, Watercress.

ROAST DUCK. Sage and Onion Stuffing, Gravy, Apple Sauce, Green Peas.

ROAST GOOSE. Sage and Onion Stuffing, Gravy, Apple Sauce.

GUINEA FOWL. Bread Sauce, Good Brown Gravy.

PIGEONS. Bread or Piquante Sauce.

BOILED RABBIT. Onion or Parsley Sauce.

ROAST RABBIT. Bread Sauce and Gravy, or Brown Sauce and Red Currant Jelly.

BOILED TURKEY. Celery, Chestnut or Oyster Sauce, Boiled Ham or Tongue.

ROAST TURKEY. Veal and Sausage or Chestnut Stuffing, Bread Sauce, Gravy, Sausages.

Digestion Table of Different Foods

Food	How cooked	Time in Stomach. Hours
Apples	Raw	1 ½ to 2
Apple Dumpling	Boiled	3
Beans	Boiled	2 ½
Beef	Boiled	2 ¾
Beef	Roasted	3 ½
Beef	Fried	4
Beefsteak	Broiled	3
Brains	Boiled	1 ¾
Bread	Baked	3 ½
Butter	Melted	3 ½
Cabbage	Boiled	4 ½
Carrots	Boiled	3 ¼
Cheese	Raw	3 ½
Chicken	Fricassée	2 ¾
Custard	Baked	2 ¾
Duck	Roasted	4
Eggs	Raw	1 ½
Eggs	Boiled (soft)	3
Eggs	Boiled (hard)	3 ½
Eggs	Fried	3 ½
Fowl	Boiled	4
Fowl	Roasted	4

Hash, with meat and vegetables	Warmed	2 ½
Lamb (fresh)	Broiled	2 ½
Milk	Boiled	2
Milk	Raw	2 ¼
Mutton	Boiled	3
Mutton	Roasted	3 ½
Oysters	Raw	2.55
Pork (salt)	Boiled	4 ½
Pork	Roasted	5 ¼
Potatoes	Baked	2 ½
Potatoes	Boiled	3 ½
Rice	Boiled	1
Sago	Boiled	1 ¾
Salmon	Boiled	4
Sponge Cake	Baked	2 ½
Suet (Beef)	Boiled	5.3
Suet (Mutton)	Boiled	4 ½
Tapioca	Boiled	2
Tripe	Boiled	1
Turkey	Boiled	2.25
Turkey	Roasted	2 ½
Turnips	Boiled	3 ½
Veal	Broiled	4

Recipes

SOUPS

Kidney Soup

1 ox kidney.	1 *oz*. dripping.
1 carrot.	3 pints water.
½ turnip.	1 teaspoonful vinegar.
1 onion.	½ tablespoonful ketchup.
3 small potatoes.	salt.
1 *oz*. flour.	pepper.

(Enough for five or six people.)

Wash and cut up the kidney into pieces, prepare and slice the vegetables, melt the dripping in the saucepan and fry the onion, dip the pieces of kidney in the flour and fry lightly, add the water and vegetables, simmer for three hours, rub all through a sieve and reheat and add the seasoning and flavourings, some of the pieces of kidney may be kept back before sieving and served in the soup as a garnish.

Mock Turtle Soup

4 quarts water.	½ lb. ham (raw).
½ calf's head.	bunch of herbs.
1 shallot.	blade of mace.
1 onion.	6 cloves.
1 carrot.	3 *oz*. butter.
1 turnip.	3 *oz*. flour.
2 sticks celery.	2 wineglasses sherry.
6 mushrooms.	salt and pepper.

(Enough for twelve or fourteen people.)

Wash the head thoroughly, cut the flesh from the bones and tie in a cloth, place in a stewpan with the bones and simmer gently for three and a half hours, take out the head, strain the stock, and when it is cold remove the fat. Melt the butter in a stewpan and fry the vegetables and ham, add the flour and brown it carefully, add all the flavourings, pour in the stock and simmer for two hours, removing the fat as it rises, strain, return to the stewpan, add some of the calf's head cut into neat pieces, with the sherry; season well, and serve with small force-meat balls made with veal stuffing and previously fried, or with egg balls.

Egg Balls

2 hard-boiled eggs.	½ an egg.
salt.	cayenne.

Pound the hard-boiled eggs and mix to a paste with the raw egg, add salt and cayenne, form into small balls using some flour, poach in boiling water for five or six minutes.

Oyster Soup

1 quart white stock (made from chicken, veal or cod's head and shoulders).	blade of mace.
	½ pint cream.
	few peppercorns.
2 doz. Oysters.	3 or 4 sprigs parsley.
1 small whiting.	1 *oz.* butter.
1 onion.	1 *oz.* flour.
2 sticks of celery.	1 yolk of egg.
salt and cayenne.	

(Enough for five or six people.)

Put into a saucepan the stock, whiting (cut in pieces, not skinned), mace, parsley, onion, peppercorns and oyster beards, simmer for one hour, strain through a hair sieve, cook butter and flour together, add the strained stock and boil, season and add oyster liquor, yolk of egg mixed with the cream and the oysters cut into three or four pieces, reheat and serve.

French Cheese Soup

1 pint white stock.	1 *oz*. butter.
½ pint milk.	1 *oz*. flour.
1 onion.	3 *oz*. Gruyère cheese.
1 bay leaf.	salt and pepper.

(Enough for three people.)

Chop the onion, fry lightly in the butter, add the milk and boil up, add the bay leaf and the flour mixed smoothly with a little milk, allow it to boil for fifteen minutes, stirring well; then add the grated cheese and season, boil again and serve.

Lobster Soup

1 lobster.	1 strip lemon rind.
1 quart stock.	½ pint milk.
1 onion.	bunch of herbs.
2 *oz*. butter.	mace, salt and pepper.
1 *oz*. flour.	little cream.

(Enough for four or five people.)

Take the meat from the shell of the lobster, put in a pan with the stock, herbs, mace and lemon rind, simmer from one and a half to two hours till all the flavour has been extracted, strain through a sieve, melt the butter in a saucepan, add the flour, cook together, then add the milk and the soup, and stir till it boils, season well and colour if necessary, drop in a few neat pieces of lobster meat and add a little cream just before serving.

FISH

Sole à la Turque

1 sole.	1 shallot.
1 tablespoonful bread crumbs.	½ teaspoonful herbs.
½ *oz*. suet.	1 teaspoonful chopped parsley.
1 gill picked shrimps.	¼ *oz*. butter.
1 egg.	few brown bread crumbs.
grated rind of ½ lemon.	pepper and salt.
½ pint stock.	

(*Enough for four people.*)

Skin the sole, remove head, tail and fins, wash thoroughly, make an incision down the fish on one side and raise the fillets, chop the shrimps, make a stuffing with the other ingredients, moisten with the beaten egg, place it in the fish, put in some small bits of butter, bake in a fireproof dish with the stock round for twenty minutes. Add a little sherry to the liquor; if liked sprinkle over a few brown crumbs and garnish with cut lemon and parsley.

Lobster Cutlets

1 lobster or small tin.	lemon juice.
1 *oz*. flour.	salt and pepper.
1 *oz*. butter.	egg and bread crumbs.
1 gill milk.	parsley.

(*Enough for six people.*)

Cut open lobster, crack the claws, take out the meat and chop it finely, make a roux with the flour and butter, add the milk in which the shells have been simmered, add the lobster meat, lemon juice, salt and pepper, put the mixture on a wet plate, divide it into equal portions and allow to cool, form into cutlet shapes, coat with egg and bread crumbs, fry a golden brown in hot fat, place a small piece of claw in each cutlet as a bone, place the head in the centre of the dish on a bed of fried parsley and place the cutlets round; if tinned lobster is used a croûton of fried bread can take the place of the head, to support the cutlets.

Lobster au Gratin

1 lobster or ½ a tin.	1 egg.
2 small shallots.	1 tablespoonful chopped parsley.
1 oz. butter.	little anchovy essence.
1 oz. flour.	salt, cayenne.
½ pint milk.	

(*Enough for four people.*)

Chop lobster into small pieces, lightly fry the chopped shallot in the butter, add the flour and cook, then the milk, simmer for five minutes, put in lobster, parsley, anchovy essence, salt and cayenne, stir till it boils, cool and add the well-beaten egg, grease some scallop shells, fill with the mixture, sprinkle over some bread crumbs and pour over a little melted butter, brown in the oven and serve very hot.

Stewed Eels

1 eel.	little lemon juice.
1 gill stock.	½ oz. flour.
2 tablespoonfuls port wine.	1 dessertspoonful mushroom ketchup.
blade of mace.	pepper and salt.
2 cloves.	½ oz. butter.
1 shallot.	

(*Enough for three or four people.*)

Thoroughly cleanse the eel and cut in pieces three inches long, cook them in a stewpan in the stock and port wine, adding the mace, cloves, chopped shallot and lemon juice, simmer for about an hour, strain and thicken the gravy with the butter and flour, boil up and add ketchup and salt and pepper, dish the eel in a circle and pour the sauce over.

Salmon Darioles en Belle-Vue

½ lb. cooked salmon.	1 gill tomato sauce.
aspic jelly.	1 tablespoonful anchovy paste.
mayonnaise sauce.	truffle.
2 sheets gelatine.	cucumber.

(*Enough for four or five people.*)

Line six oval moulds with aspic jelly, decorate with fancy shapes of truffle and cucumber rind. When set pour in a layer of mayonnaise and aspic mixed in equal quantities with some cream added. Remove the skin and bone from the salmon and pound, add some mayonnaise cream, anchovy paste and gelatine dissolved in the tomato sauce and seasoning. Fill the moulds with this and put on ice to set. Turn out on a silver dish and garnish with chopped aspic and slices of cucumber.

Sole Rouennaise

1 sole.	½ tin lobster.
½ *oz*. butter.	lemon juice.
½ *oz*. flour.	salt, cayenne.
½ gill fish stock or milk.	white sauce.

(*Enough for two or three people.*)

Skin and fillet the sole. Make a sauce with the butter, flour and fish stock or milk, season with salt and cayenne, chop the lobster finely and add to the sauce with a little lemon juice. Lay some of the mixture on the fillets, fold over in half, place on a greased tin, sprinkle with salt and lemon juice, cover with greased paper and bake for ten minutes. Place on a hot dish, coat with a well-flavoured white sauce, garnish with cut lemon and parsley.

Fillets of Sole à l'Americaine

2 soles.	1 shallot.
3 tomatoes.	½ pint Béchamel sauce.
2 *oz*. butter.	1 gill white wine.
1 *oz*. bread crumbs.	salt and pepper.

(*Enough for four people.*)

Make a purée with 1 *oz*. of butter and the tomatoes sliced, rub through a sieve. Boil up the Béchamel sauce and add the tomato purée, fillet the soles, fold the fillets in half, place in a buttered gratin dish, sprinkle with chopped shallot, pour over the wine, cover with a buttered paper. Cook in a moderate oven from ten to fifteen minutes. Add the liquor from the fish to the prepared sauce, pour over the fillets. Sprinkle the bread crumbs on the top with the butter in small pieces, brown nicely in a quick oven.

Scallops en Coquilles

some scallops.	lemon juice.
white sauce.	bread crumbs.
butter.	salt and pepper.

Trim the scallops, removing the black portion, wash them in vinegar, cut them up, place in some buttered shells mixed with some thick white sauce and some of the bread crumbs. Season and squeeze over some lemon juice, sprinkle over some more bread crumbs, put some small bits of butter on top, brown nicely in a quick oven.

MEAT DISHES

Liver and Kidney Pudding

½ lb. ox kidney.	½ lb. calf's liver.
2 *oz.* bacon.	2 *oz.* dripping.
½ pint water or stock.	1 *oz.* flour.

For Pastry

6 *oz.* flour.	3 *oz.* suet.
1 *oz.* bread crumbs.	water.
1 *oz.* flour.	salt and pepper.

(Enough for five or six people.)

Cut the bacon small and fry it in the dripping, cut up the liver and kidney, season with salt and pepper, fry lightly, mix in bacon, flour, and add the stock or water, make a suet crust, line a basin with it, put in the liver and kidney, cover with pastry, steam from one and a half to two hours.

Tripe and Onions

1 lb. tripe.	½ pint milk.
2 onions.	salt and pepper.
1 *oz.* flour.	

(Enough for four people.)

Wash the tripe, place it in a stewpan, cover with cold water and bring to the boil, put it on a board, scrape it if necessary, cut into neat pieces, return it to the pan with about three-quarters of a pint of water and the onions finely chopped, simmer till the tripe is tender, mix the flour smoothly with the milk, add it, stir till it boils, season well and serve.

Beef Olives

1 lb. steak.	1 ½ *oz*. butter.
1 carrot.	1 *oz*. flour.
1 turnip.	¾ pint stock.
1 onion.	salt and pepper.
2 cloves.	

Forcemeat

2 *oz*. bread crumbs.	little grated lemon peel.
1 *oz*. suet.	½ teaspoonful herbs.
1 teaspoonful chopped parsley.	1 egg.
	salt and pepper.

(*Enough for five or six people.*)

Cut the beef into thin slices, make a stuffing with the crumbs, suet and seasonings, bind with egg, place a little stuffing on each slice, roll up and secure with a piece of thread or a match, melt the butter, fry the olives brown with the onion stuck with cloves, remove the meat and onion, add the flour and brown it, taking care not to let it burn, add the stock gradually, stir till it boils, add the vegetables and put back the olives, simmer gently till the olives are tender, place them in the centre of a hot dish, removing the thread, strain the gravy round, having carefully seasoned it.

Boiled Ox Tongue

1 ox tongue.	2 sticks celery.
1 carrot.	bunch of herbs.
1 turnip.	brown or piquante sauce.
1 onion.	

(*Enough for eight or nine people.*)

Wash the tongue in cold water, if it is pickled let it soak for some hours, put it in a saucepan with tepid water to cover, bring it to the boil, remove the scum, add the prepared vegetables and simmer gently from three to four hours.

When tender remove the skin, brush over with glaze and put it in the oven for a few minutes, serve with a good brown or piquante sauce. Spinach is a suitable vegetable to serve with the tongue, and can be used to garnish the dish. If the tongue is to be served cold it must be trimmed and fastened on a board in an upright position with skewers. When cold and firm glaze it and decorate with butter, put through a forcing bag with a fancy tube and aspic jelly.

Fillet of Beef à la Pompadour

1 lb. beef fillet.	vegetables for garnish.
3 tomatoes.	mashed potatoes.
½ *oz*. butter.	½ pint brown or tomato sauce.
1 teaspoonful chopped parsley.	salt and pepper.

(*Enough for four or five people.*)

Cut the fillet into neat rounds and fry in butter in a sauté pan, cut the tomatoes in slices and bake on a greased tin with some small pieces of fat of the beef. When cooked, dish the fillets on a border of mashed potato with a small piece of fat on each, put on a slice of tomato. Pile a suitable vegetable in the centre, such as peas, beans, spinach, and just before serving pour the brown or tomato sauce round and place a small square of maître d'hôtel butter on each fillet.

Beef Galantine

½ lb. lean beef.	1 shallot.
½ lb. raw ham.	chopped parsley.
½ lb. sausages.	¼ lb. mushrooms.
½ lb. bread crumbs.	salt and pepper.
2 or 3 eggs.	little glaze.

Put the beef and ham through a mincing machine separately, then both together, mix with skinned sausages, bread crumbs, chopped mushrooms, shallot, parsley and plenty of salt and pepper, bind with raw eggs, form the mixture into a smooth roll like a sausage, tie securely in a pudding cloth and boil it gently for two and a half hours; when it is cold brush over with a little glaze made with dissolved gelatine flavoured and coloured with Liebig's extract.

Roast Sheep's Heart

1 sheep's heart.	1 small onion.
2 *oz*. bread crumbs.	½ teaspoonful herbs.
1 *oz*. chopped suet.	1 egg or little milk.
1 teaspoonful parsley.	salt and pepper.

(*Enough for one or two people.*)

Thoroughly cleanse the heart in salt and water, cut off the muscle, mix the stuffing, fill the heart with it, skewer or sew up the openings. Bake in the oven, basting frequently, dish on a hot dish, pour off the fat, put a little flour in the tin, brown it, add water, boil up, season it and pour round the heart. The heart can be cooked in a saucepan if more convenient.

Mutton Cutlets à la Reforme

best end of neck of mutton.	2 *oz*. tongue.
1 carrot.	mashed potatoes.
2 truffles.	salt and pepper.
2 gherkins.	reform sauce.
cooked white of egg.	

(*Enough to make six or seven cutlets.*)

Cut and trim the cutlets, dip in a mixture of trimmings of truffles, tongue and gherkins seasoned, then coat with egg and bread crumbs, fry a nice brown in a sauté pan, dish on a border of mashed potatoes, make a garnish with shreds of carrot, gherkin, truffles, tongue and white of egg, shake in butter and season, pile it in the centre and pour reform sauce round the cutlets.

Calf's Feet Fritters

3 or 4 calf's feet.   tomato sauce.
egg and bread crumbs.
(Enough for four or five people.)

Stew the calf's feet till tender, cut open and remove the bones, put the meat aside until cold, then cut it in neat pieces, coat with egg and bread crumbs, fry to a golden brown in hot fat, drain and serve on a hot dish with tomato sauce.

Fried Calves' Brains

2 sets of brains.   1 tablespoonful vinegar.
1 shallot.   pepper and salt.
chopped parsley.   frying batter.
1 tablespoonful salad oil.   tomato sauce.
(Enough for three or four people.)

Cleanse the brains thoroughly and remove the skin, place in a stewpan with cold water and salt, boil up and simmer for ten minutes, remove the brains, rinse them in cold water and allow them to get cold, and then cut into neat pieces, soak the brains for an hour in a deep dish with the oil, vinegar, chopped parsley and shallot, take the brains out, dry them, dip in flour lightly and then in frying batter, and fry a golden brown in deep fat, drain carefully and dish on a fancy paper or folded serviette, garnish with fried parsley and serve with tomato sauce.

Dresden Patties

thick slices of bread.   gravy.
cold meat.   salt and pepper.

Cut the thick slices of bread into small rounds, mark with a smaller cutter and hollow out the centre; fry the cases in hot fat, also a small round for a top. Mince the cold meat, add some good gravy or brown sauce, season well, make hot, fill the bread cases, put on the top and serve on a fancy paper, garnish with fried parsley.

POULTRY AND GAME

Poulet à la Sefton

remains of cold fowl.	little butter.
2 tablespoonfuls Harvey sauce.	2 tablespoonfuls mustard.
1 tablespoonful mushroom ketchup.	1 tablespoonful Bengal chutney.
1 tablespoonful curry powder.	

Cut up fowl into neat joints—remains of a plainly-boiled fowl are best—mix all the ingredients well together, brush over each joint, put in the oven a few minutes to set, then grill over a clear fire for ten minutes. Just before serving brush over with butter, and serve hot with mustard sauce if liked.

Galantine of Chicken

1 chicken.	12 pistachio nuts.
1 lb. sausage meat.	3 truffles.
¼ lb. tongue.	1 teaspoonful chopped parsley.
¼ lb. ham.	
2 hard-boiled eggs.	salt and pepper.
	aspic jelly.

(*Enough for nine or ten people.*)

Bone the fowl, cut the egg into slices, the ham and tongue in strips, place in half of the sausage meat, then the tongue, ham, slices of egg, blanched pistachio nuts, chopped truffles and seasoning in layers, then the rest of the sausage meat. Roll in a cloth and tie tightly for boiling, simmer gently in well-flavoured stock from two to two and a half hours. Take it out, untie the cloth and roll it up again firmly, place it between two dishes with a weight on top. When cold take off the cloth, wipe the galantine with a hot cloth, glaze with aspic and serve with salad, and garnish with chopped aspic jelly.

Chaudfroid of Chicken

1 boiled chicken.	aspic jelly.
1 pint Béchamel sauce.	salad.
truffles.	ham.

(Enough for six or seven people.)

Cut the chicken into neat joints, remove the skin and trim them, place on a cake rack with a dish underneath, warm the Béchamel sauce, add about two tablespoonfuls of liquid aspic, coat the joints with it, decorate the joints with little fancy shapes of truffle and coat again with aspic. When cold and set arrange round a high croûte of fried bread, using fancy skewers to keep them in place; place some dressed salad round the dish and garnish with chopped aspic and chopped ham.

Pigeon Pie

3 or 4 pigeons.	2 *oz.* ham.
1 lb. beef steak.	stock.
3 hard-boiled eggs.	salt and pepper.
flour.	flaky or puff pastry.

(Enough for seven or eight people.)

Prepare, singe and draw the pigeons, cut them in halves or quarters. Cut the steak in small pieces, dip them into seasoned flour, put the steak, pigeons, ham and slices of hard-boiled eggs in a pie dish in layers, pour over enough good gravy or stock to half fill the dish, cover with pastry, trim edges, glaze and decorate in the usual way. Bake from two to two and a half hours, scald and skin the feet and put in the centre when the pie is cooked, to show what the pie is made of. If the pie is to be eaten cold, when it is cooked pour in some more good gravy or stock to which some gelatine has been added.

Roast Partridge

1 brace of partridges.	watercress.
a little fat bacon	fried crumbs.
gravy.	croutons of toast.
bread sauce.	

(Enough for three or four people.)

Pluck, singe and draw the birds, truss firmly, making them look plump, roast for thirty minutes, basting frequently. A slice of fat bacon can be tied on the breast to keep them moist; remove it and flour and froth them well a few minutes before dishing. Dish on crouton of toast, garnish with watercress, serve with bread sauce and fried bread crumbs.

Jugged Hare

1 hare.	3 *oz*. butter.
1 ½ lb. beef steak.	3 *oz*. flour.
2 onions.	2 glasses of port wine.
2 or 3 cloves.	red–currant jelly.
bunch of herbs.	salt and pepper.
strip of lemon rind.	forcemeat balls.
stock or water.	

(Enough for nine or ten people.)

Skin the hare, do not wash it, let the blood from the upper part of the body run into a basin and put it aside, then wipe it carefully. Cut into neat joints, dip them in well seasoned flour and fry a nice brown in butter, put the joints into a large stewing jar with the steak cut in pieces, herbs, onions, cloves, lemon rind. Cover with stock or water, cover the jar closely, cook gently in the oven for three or four hours. When ready to serve take out the joints, onion and herbs, mix the flour with some water. Add it to the gravy and boil, then add the wine and the forcemeat balls, lastly the seasoning and blood. Do not boil after the blood is added.

Put back the joints to reheat. Dish with joints piled in centre, gravy poured round, garnish with forcemeat balls and serve with red-currant jelly.

To make Forcemeat Balls: To some veal stuffing, well seasoned, add the parboiled and chopped liver of hare, fry in butter.

Stewed Partridges

2 partridges.	beans.
onions.	2 *oz*. butter.
carrots.	gravy browning.
turnip.	sherry.
chopped parsley.	salt and pepper.
bunch of herbs.	

(Enough for four people.)

Prepare the partridges, cut them in halves, put them in a stewpan with the butter and seasoning and prepared vegetables, cover and cook over a moderate fire for five or six minutes, then place the stewpan in the oven and leave it there for three-quarters of an hour, dish the partridges on a hot dish with the vegetables round, add some gravy browning to the liquid, boil up, season, add chopped parsley, pour over the partridges and serve with potato chips.

Grouse Pie

2 or 3 grouse.	hard-boiled eggs.
1 lb. beef steak.	butter.
mushrooms.	gravy.
2 shallots.	salt and pepper.
mace.	puff pastry.

Pluck, singe and draw the grouse, cut each neatly into four pieces, fry them till half cooked in butter seasoned with salt pepper and mace, cut the beef into pieces and fry with some mushrooms and shallots chopped, arrange both neatly in a pie dish with some hard-boiled eggs cut in quarters and some good gravy, cover the dish with puff pastry, decorate with leaves, brush over with egg and cook from one and a half to two hours in a quick oven; some more gravy should be added when the pie is taken from the oven.

Zephires of Game

½ lb. cooked game.	1 tablespoonful white sauce.
2 *oz.* cooked ham.	½ pint aspic jelly.
2 truffles.	seasoning.
2 yolks of hard-boiled eggs.	salad.
	2 tablespoonfuls cream

(*Enough for five or six people.*)

Line six or seven dariole moulds with aspic jelly, decorate with truffle cut in fancy shapes, mix nearly a gill of aspic with the cream, line the mould with it and put on ice to set. Pound the game in a mortar with the yolks of eggs, sauce, chopped truffle and seasoning, and a little melted aspic, fill the moulds with this and allow to set, turn out when required on to a silver entrée dish with some dressed salad and garnish with chopped aspic.

SAVOURY DISHES

Chicken Kromeskies

4 *oz.* cooked chicken.	1 gill white sauce.
2 *oz.* cooked ham.	1 yolk of egg.
1 or 2 mushrooms.	salt and pepper.
6 rashers of bacon.	frying batter.

(*Enough to make twelve kromeskies.*)

Remove all skin, gristle and bone from the chicken, chop the meat finely, add to it the ham and mushrooms chopped. Heat the white sauce, stir in the chicken and ham, etc., season well, add the yolk of egg, allow it to get thoroughly hot, put the mixture on a plate and set aside to cool, form up

191

into small rolls. Wrap each in a very thin rasher of bacon, dip in frying batter and fry a golden brown in hot fat, drain well, serve on a hot dish with fancy paper.

Kidney Omelet

4 eggs.	1 shallot.
1 ½ *oz.* butter.	1 teaspoonful parsley.
1 kidney.	salt and pepper.

Skin the kidney and chop finely, put half an ounce of butter into a small saucepan, add the finely-chopped shallot and fry for a few minutes, then add the kidney and cook for three or four minutes, season well with salt and pepper. Beat the eggs, melt the remainder of the butter in an omelette pan, pour in the eggs and stir till the mixture begins to set. When cooked sufficiently put the kidney in the centre and fold over in the usual way, serve on a hot dish with a little gravy poured round if liked.

Sardine Cigarettes

3 or 4 sardines.	egg.
short pastry.	bread crumbs.

(*Enough for two or three people.*)

Remove skin and bones from sardines, roll out pastry *very thinly*, cut into small squares, lay a sardine on each, fold up, dip in egg and bread crumbs, fry about eight minutes in hot fat, dish on a fancy paper and serve hot.

SWEET DISHES

Plum Duff

8 *oz.* flour.	6 *oz.* raisins.
4 *oz.* suet.	1 egg.
1 *oz.* sugar.	little milk.
pinch of salt.	½ teaspoonful baking powder.

(*Enough for six or seven people.*)

Add the chopped suet and stoned raisins to the flour, with sugar, salt and baking powder, mix with the egg and milk, tie in a cloth and boil for two or three hours. Serve with Demerara sugar.

Boiled Batter Pudding

½ lb. flour.	pinch of salt.
1 pint of milk.	marmalade.
2 eggs.	

(Enough for four or five people.)

Add the salt to the flour, make a well in the centre, drop in the eggs, mix smoothly with a little of the milk, beat till it bubbles, add the remainder of the milk and if possible allow the batter to stand, well grease the mould or basin, line with marmalade, pour in the batter, Boil for two hours, serve with marmalade sauce.

Note.—Currants may be used instead of marmalade, they sink and form a black cap—called Black Cap Pudding. Serve with a sweet sauce.

Half-Pay Pudding.

½ lb. flour.	2 *oz.* candied peel.
½ lb. suet.	1 teaspoonful spice.
½ lb. raisins.	pinch of salt.
½ lb. currants.	½ a cup of treacle.
½ lb. bread crumbs.	1 cup of milk.

(Enough for eight or ten people.)

Chop the suet finely, stone and chop raisins, mix all the ingredients well together and boil for at least four hours.

Ambrosia

2 *oz.* cornflour.	1 pint milk.
2 *oz.* butter.	1 wineglass sherry.
2 *oz.* sugar.	

(Enough for four or five people.)

Mix the cornflour with a little of the milk, put the remainder on to boil with the butter. When boiling pour on to the cornflour and return it to the saucepan and cook thoroughly, add the sherry and sugar, pour into a wet mould, turn out when set.

Crystal Palace Pudding

8 sponge cakes.	2 eggs.
1 ½ pints milk.	flavouring.
½ *oz*. gelatine.	glacé cherries.
sugar to taste.	cream.

(Enough for five or six people.)

Cut the sponge cakes into dice. Dissolve the gelatine in the milk, strain on to the beaten eggs, add sugar to taste and flavouring (essence of vanilla or almonds), cook till it thickens. Put the sponge cakes in a mould decorated with the glacé cherries, pour over the custard. When set turn out and serve with cream.

Rhenish Cream

6 yolks of eggs.	1 *oz*. gelatine.
½ pint of sherry.	rind and juice of 2 lemons.
1 pint of boiling water.	sugar to taste.

(Enough for five or six people.)

Dissolve the gelatine in the boiling water, allow it to cool, add to the beaten yolks, cook in a double saucepan until it thickens, add the grated lemon rind, juice, sherry and sugar to taste. Pour into a wet mould.

Bachelor's Pudding

2 *oz.* bread crumbs.	½ teaspoonful ground ginger.
2 *oz.* flour.	1 egg and little milk.
2 *oz.* suet.	½ teaspoonful baking powder.
2 *oz.* raisins.	pinch of salt.
2 *oz.* sugar.	

(Enough for five or six people.)

Chop the suet finely, stone and cut the raisins across, put all the dry ingredients together, beat the egg with a little milk, stir well, put mixture into a greased mould sprinkled with brown sugar, cover with greased paper and steam for 1 ½ hours, and serve with a sweet sauce.

Sauce

1 *oz.* butter.	1 gill water.
¾ *oz.* flour.	1 gill milk.
1 dessertspoonful sugar.	

Cook the flour in the butter, add water and milk, boil, add sugar.

Leche Cream

1 ½ pints milk.	2 eggs.
4 *oz.* flour.	rind of ½ lemon.
2 *oz.* castor sugar.	cinnamon.
2 *oz.* ratafias.	little jam.

(Enough for five or six people.)

Mix the flour and sugar smoothly with some of the cold milk, put the remainder on to boil with the lemon rind. Spread the bottom of a dish with jam, sprinkle over half of the ratafias crushed. Strain the boiling milk over the flour, return to the saucepan and stir till it boils and thickens, add the eggs well beaten, pour over the jam, sprinkle the top with cinnamon and decorate with whole ratafias.

St Cloud Puddings

3 *oz*. cake crumbs.	1 *oz*. almonds.
3 *oz*. chopped cherries.	½ *oz*. gelatine.
½ pint milk.	coffee essence and sugar to taste.
2 eggs.	coffee butter icing.

(*Enough for five or six people.*)

Make a custard with the milk and eggs. When thickened pour over the cake crumbs, add sugar and coffee essence to taste and allow to cool. Dissolve the gelatine in a little water and strain into the other ingredients, pour into small dariole moulds. When set turn out, pipe over with coffee butter icing, sprinkle with pistachio nuts and browned chopped almonds.

Liquid Refreshment

A year or two ago Paris, home of the word bizarre and of much that it conveys, was amused by the story of an intoxicated horse in the Villette quarter. The animal had been dosed with wine by its groom, and subsequently learnt its way to the cellar, where it finally lay helplessly inebriated among the glassy *débris* of its debauch. Yet, on the whole, and under perfectly natural conditions, intoxication is confined to the highest existing mammal, and the lower animals may, with a few admissible exceptions, be broadly defined as "brutes that never get drunk". Some little investigation, however, of the phenomenon of drinking in the animal world, tends to sweep away the barrier between the human aristocracy and its poor relations, and we learn that many Indian bats and humming-birds sip without restraint of the palm-juice collected in cocoanut-shells by the natives, and are, after their wanton indulgence, picked up at the foot of the seductive tree in a helpless state that may fairly be compared with that which is vulgarly known as drunk. Bears and monkeys approach still more closely the human ideal, and trainers and showmen know well their readiness to drink from a bottle. An amusing story, by the way, was once told me by the superintendent of Barnum's Menagerie, to the effect that a favourite bear in his charge stole on one occasion a bottle of whisky and clambered with it into a tree. Bruin then assimilated the contents of the bottle at a gulp and promptly fell to the ground, and bruised himself so badly that never again could he be persuaded to drink from a bottle. A similar case of profiting by adverse experience was once told in the *Field*, a cat having impounded some brandy

199

and milk prescribed for its mistress who lay sick. So ill was the cat, however, that it never again touched the compound, and even fought shy of its milk for a day or two. And here I am prompted to digress for a moment in quest of a reminiscence of remarkable intelligence, not unmixed with the reverse, exhibited by a lurcher that belongs to a friend of mine. It has nothing to do with drink, but as an instance of perverted memory, if I may so term it, is too good to be forgotten, and I know for a fact that the incident has not been recorded. This particular dog had engaged in a fight with a neighbour, a mere friendly bout that removed part of its nose and left the muzzle very much torn. To make matters worse, it persistently worried the sores with its paw, and, as a brilliant inspiration, my friend bound a piece of rag round the limb, and anointed it generously with mustard. This brought the desired rest to the healing nose, but the dog was now firmly convinced that his leg must be broken, and hobbled on the perfectly sound leg until the bandage was removed. On enquiry I found that the leg had really been hurt at Oxford *three years earlier*, on which occasion a similar bandage had been applied, minus, of course, the condiment. I must apologise for setting down this irrelevant incident of dog memory, only a better opportunity may not be given me, and I am loth to let it go unpublished.

The newest recruits to the great intemperate are the ants and butterflies. There is nothing incongruous in the notion of a butterfly, symbol of giddiness, sipping immoderately of nectar, but the steady, workaday ant gave promise of better things. In mitigation of its failing, however, it must be admitted that the only authentic cases of intoxicated ants are the result of human agency, and Sir John Lubbock's interesting experiments with the creatures artificially induced into this state are too well known to need more than a passing mention. To these I venture to add wasps, though the evidence on this subject is not, so far as I am concerned, quite first hand. Let me explain. I spent a good many hours last August in a model Cornish orchard, wherein there grew magnificent apples that would presently be converted into cider for the refection of honest yokels in the district. The gardener who used to show me round on these occasions assured me that the wasps were so stupefied by deep potions of apple juice as to be for the time absolutely innocuous. He permitted them to wander unrebuked over his face and to caress his sun-scorched arms, and, knowing my curiosity in matters of natural history, implored me to afford these gentle insects the same accommodation. A suspicion, however, forced itself on me that exposure had left its mark on the honest fellow's skin, and that some at any rate of the reticence of his visitors might be due to an excusable delusion on their part that they were perambulating a brickfield. I therefore, with a shameless indifference to so interesting an experiment in insect forbearance, forbade the alighting of trespassers, and the wasps either kept clear of me or died.

There is another aspect of drinking in the animal world, and, in contradistinction to the tipplers, a word must be said of the equally limited number of total abstainers. In using the expression I include water, as of course the total abstainers in respect of anything more insidious embrace nearly the entire assemblage of living creatures. There appeared not long since in several of the London papers a paragraph purporting to enumerate a number of creatures that never drink. That most of these would drink greedily whenever occasion offered I happened to know at the time, but there was some uncertainty in my mind as to the concluding sentence, which declared that the famous Roquefort cheese is made of the milk of cows and goats that "almost never drink". "Almost never" was indeed a delightful and ingenious piece of trimming, reminding one of the "well, hardly ever" in a still popular comic opera. Even this qualification, however, did not set my doubts at rest, and I learnt from the National School of Agriculture at Grignon, to the principal of which institution I applied for information, that the milk for Roquefort cheese is taken from ewes only, and that they drink as freely as other beasts of the farm. The accuracy of the paragraph in question in this particular is probably a fair criterion of its claim on the reader's attention throughout.

In segregating those animals which drink from those which do not, it is not unimportant to arrive at a broad view of the meaning of drink. If you swallow, for instance, a glass of water, you are unquestionably drinking; but surely you are also, for all practical purposes, drinking when you eat an orange. It is therefore abusing the word to say that desert-dwelling gazelles and antelopes never drink when, as is well known to travellers, they perform without demur journeys of hundreds of miles to partake, at the season of their ripening, of water-melons and other juicy fruits and bulbs. That a certain proportion of moisture is necessary to the well-being of every bird and beast is, I fancy, incontrovertible. True, the moisture may be taken very indirectly. Thus, captive hawks, and presumably, too, those at large, rarely take water. But they may, all the same, derive the requisite moisture from raw flesh. In like manner, the Norwegian elk, unable to get the necessary salt, an indispensable article of consumption with all herbivorous animals, adopts the extraordinary plan of turning carnivorous, and eats an occasional lemming, a small rodent not unlike a rabbit without ears, by way of finding salt in its bones. Salt and moisture may, in fact, be placed on the same basis. All creatures must, directly or indirectly, get both. The herbivorous beasts drink regularly, usually in the evening, and frequent "salt licks" wherever they can find them. The same applies to grain-feeding birds. They resort with unfailing regularity to water of an evening, and they in like manner take salt whenever occasion offers. Both tastes are scrupulously ministered to in menageries, and the pigeons and bustards are given a generous supply of water and have salt mixed with the grit in their cage. The carnivorous beasts, on the other hand, and the birds of prey get their salt, and much of their moisture, at second hand. Thus the sportsman who lies in ambush at the water's edge for a shot at antelope as the moon is rising, stands an equal chance of encountering any of the local carnivora which come to the trysting-place of weary nature not alone to drink, but rather to pounce on thirsty deer or other pilgrims to the brink. The story of a wild boar quenching its thirst between two tigers in an Indian nullah is, I believe, authentic, and indeed the courage of a boar, above all of a thirsty boar, knows no limit.

In general, then, the insectivorous and raptorial birds drink with far less regularity than those which find their sustenance in grain and fruit. I have somewhere seen that bee-eaters never drink, but I have observed these beautiful birds assembled on the edge of lagoons in Morocco, and they looked very like drinking, though I would not for a moment, on such shadowy evidence as that given by the naked eye at fifty paces, insist on the fact.

Among misjudged abstainers, the ostrich and camel are prominent. Both, it is true, are inured by the severe apprenticeship of a desert life to survive several days of drought, but both will with equal certainty wander far in search of water, and the camel has an internal storage system that has been the theme of much fable and speculation.

It has also been said that snakes drink little or nothing. All that I can, in conclusion, say is that a large python, which I brought from Australia and presented to the Zoological Gardens, drank regularly every night, a performance that was plainly audible to myself, seeing that the reptile occupied a comfortable box beneath my bunk. But for this nightly drinking bout, to the peaceful accompaniment of much contented hissing and rustling against the baize lining of its prison, I would never ask a quieter cabin companion.

F. G. *Aflalo*

Cocktails &
How To Mix Them

How the dictionaries define a cocktail, I do not know; but, were I asked, I should say that it was a delicate combination of ingredients, all of which contribute their share in building up a unique beverage, possessing an individualism of its own.

Whether the reader agrees with me or not hardly matters. What does matter is that he should appreciate that the ingredients of a cocktail have been thought out and selected by a mastermind who has blended them together to obtain a definite flavour. Thus, to alter them, in substance or quantity, will surely alter the resulting effect—and, generally, an alteration means an inferior result.

Having stressed the need for keeping faithfully to the recipes, as printed, the next point to note is that it is advisable to put the ingredients together in the order they figure in the recipes. Sometimes it is essential and, if the habit is formed, there will never be any mistakes. For your cocktail bar, a certain number of implements are, more or less, necessary. They may be enumerated as follows:

1. *A Shaker.* This consists of two metal plated containers which fit one in the other. The contrivance is held in both hands and shaken up and down until the ingredients are thoroughly mixed.

Other types of shakers, for which it was claimed no ice was needed have appeared on the market, but presumably were not successful, since they are no longer attainable.

2. *A Strainer.* This is composed of a metal ring, covered with gauze, and a handle attached. After the ingredients have been shaken or stirred, the mixture is poured through it to strain out the chips of ice, fruit pulp, etc.

3. *A Mixing Glass.* This is merely a large tumbler or bar-glass, into which the ingredients are put when they are to be stirred. Note, here, that some liquids, such as champagne, must not be shaken or they will lose their natural effervescence. Such liquids are stirred in the mixing glass.

4. *A Mixing Spoon.* This is a spoon holding about the same amount as a teaspoon, but with a very long handle. It makes stirring easy.

5. *A Gill Measure.* It should be graded to permit of the measuring of such fractions as ½, ¼, $\frac{1}{6}$, etc., gills.

6. *A Bundle of Cherry Sticks* to permit of the simple manipulation of cherries, olives, etc., which are often served with cocktails.

7. *A Supply of Drinking Straws.*

8. *A Corkscrew and Bottle Opener.*

Though the above outfit is required for any cocktail bar, there are certain things needed far more, and they are the drinks themselves. A well-appointed bar should stock the following:—

Absinthe	*Grenadine Syrup*
Angostura Bitters	*Italian Vermouth*
Brandy	*Maraschino*
Brown Curaçao	*Orange Bitters*
Calvados	*Plain Syrup*
Canadian Club Whisky	*Red Port*
Champagne	*Rum*

Dubonnet	*Scotch Whisky*
French Vermouth	*Sherry*
Gin	

With the above ingredients on hand, ninety per cent of the alcoholic recipes in this book can be compounded, if such oddments as sprigs of mint and cherries are not counted.

Now a word about the glasses in which the drinks should be served:—

1. *A Cocktail Glass* holds about ½ gill of liquid.

2. *A Small Wine Glass* holds about ¾ gill.

3. *A Large Wine Glass* holds about 1 gill.

4. *A Tumbler* holds about ½ pint, which is 2 gills.

5. *A Sherbet Glass* is like a small tumbler.

6. *A Liqueur Glass* holds about ¼ gill.

7. *A Sundae Glass* is bowl-shaped and is useful when serving fruit cocktails.

And, while mentioning gills and things, it may be useful to add, in case you have forgotten, that

> 4 *gills* make 1 *pint*
> 2 *pints* " 1 *quart*
> 4 *quarts* " 1 *gallon*.

ABSINTHE COCKTAIL

¼ *gill of Absinthe.*
1 *dash of Angostura Bitters.*
2 *dashes of Anisette (or Plain Syrup).*
1 *dash of Lemon Peel Juice.*
$^1/_6$ *gill of Water.*
1 *Cherry.*
¾ *tumbler of broken Ice.*

Three-quarters fill a tumbler with broken ice and add the Angostura Bitters. Then put in the Absinthe, the Anisette, and the Water. Shake well and pass through a strainer into a cocktail glass. Serve with a dash of lemon peel juice on top and with a cherry.

For anyone who knows little of cocktails, this is an excellent one to try at the outset.

APPLEJACK COCKTAIL

$\frac{1}{3}$ gill of Calvados.
1 dash of Angostura Bitters.
1 teaspoonful of Brown Curaçao.
$\frac{1}{2}$ tumblerful of broken Ice.
1 Cherry.
1 dash of Lemon Peel Juice.

Half fill the tumbler with broken ice and add the Angostura Bitters. Then add the Calvados and the Brown Curaçao. Stir up and pass through a strainer into a cocktail glass. Serve with a cherry and a dash of lemon peel juice on top.

Orange Bitters can be used instead of Angostura Bitters, if preferred.

Calvados is the continental name for Applejack Brandy.

BAMBOO COCKTAIL

$\frac{1}{4}$ gill of Dry Sherry.
$\frac{1}{4}$ gill of French Vermouth.
$\frac{1}{2}$ teaspoonful of Orange Bitters.
1 dash of Lemon Peel Juice.
$\frac{1}{2}$ tumblerful of broken Ice.

Half fill a tumbler with broken ice and add the Orange Bitters. Then add the Dry Sherry and the French Vermouth. Stir well, strain and serve in a cocktail glass with a dash of lemon peel juice on top.

BAMBOO COCKTAIL—2

$\frac{1}{3}$ gill of Dry Sherry.
$\frac{1}{6}$ gill of Italian Vermouth.
$\frac{1}{2}$ teaspoonful of Orange Bitters.
1 dash of Lemon Peel Juice.
$\frac{1}{2}$ tumblerful of broken Ice.

This cocktail is made up in exactly the same way as the previous one; but Italian Vermouth is used instead of French

Vermouth. This makes the flavour much sweeter and, in out experience, it is preferred by women-folk.

BEVERLY HILLS COCKTAIL

½ *gill of Calvados.*
2 *dashes of Angostura Bitters.*
1 *dash of Lemon Peel Juice.*
1 *Cherry.*
½ *tumblerful of broken Ice.*

The tumbler is half filled with broken ice and the Angostura Bitters added. Then add the Calvados. Stir well and pass through a strainer into a cocktail glass. Serve with a cherry and a dash of lemon peel juice on top.

This cocktail is named after the famous town near Hollywood, California.

BIG BOY COCKTAIL

⅛ *gill of French Vermouth.*
⅛ *gill of Italian Vermouth.*
¼ *gill of Gin.*
1 *teaspoonful of Angostura Bitters.*
1 *teaspoonful of Absinthe.*
1 *Cherry.*
½ *tumblerful of broken Ice.*

Half fill the tumbler with broken ice and add the Angostura Bitters. Then add the French Vermouth, the Italian Vermouth, the Gin and the Absinthe. Stir up and pass through a strainer into a cocktail glass. Serve with a cherry and a dash of lemon peel juice on top.

A very pleasant cocktail which is, also, fairly strong.

BROADWAY COCKTAIL

A few drops of Orange Bitters.
¼ *gill of Italian Vermouth.*
½ *gill of Dry Gin.*
1 *dash of Orange Peel Juice.*
½ *shakerful of broken Ice.*

Half fill the shaker with broken ice and add the Orange Bitters. Then put in the Italian Vermouth and the Dry Gin. Shake well and pass through a strainer into a small wine glass. Serve with a dash of orange peel juice on top.

This cocktail is very popular in New York.

BRONX COCKTAIL
$1/_{12}$gill of Italian Vermouth.
$1/_{12}$ gill of French Vermouth.
$1/_{6}$ gill of Dry Gin.
1 *dash of Orange Bitters.*
1 *tablespoonful of Orange Juice.*
½ *shakerful of broken Ice.*

Half fill the shaker with broken ice and then, in the following order, put in the Dry Gin, the Italian Vermouth, the French Vermouth, the Orange Juice and the Orange Bitters. Shake well and pass through a strainer into a cocktail glass.

Some connoisseurs prefer the above without the Orange Bitters. They say that it gives a smoother flavour.

BUZZER COCKTAIL
¼ *gill of Dry Gin.*
¼ *gill of Italian Vermouth.*
1 *teaspoonful of Crème de Menthe.*
2 *dashes of Angostura Bitters.*
1 *Cherry.*
½ *shakerful of broken Ice.*

The shaker is half filled with broken ice and the Angostura Bitters added. Then add the Dry Gin, the Italian Vermouth and the Crème de Menthe. Shake well and pass through a strainer into a cocktail glass. Serve with a cherry.

A pleasant and fairly strong cocktail.

CHOCOLATE COCKTAIL
¼ gill of Red Port.
The yolk of a fresh Egg.
1 teaspoonful of Chocolate Powder.
½ tumblerful of broken Ice.

Half fill a tumbler with broken ice and add the yolk of an egg. Then add the Red Port and the chocolate powder. Stir well and pass through a strainer into a wine glass.

Some people like to add 1 or 2 dashes of Yellow Chartreuse as well; but this is entirely optional.

CLOVER CLUB COCKTAIL
½ gill of Dry Gin.
1 teaspoonful of Grenadine Syrup.
The juice of a Lemon.
The white of an Egg.
1 dash of Nutmeg.
½ shakerful of broken Ice.

Half fill the shaker with broken ice and add the white of an egg. Then add the lemon juice, the Grenadine Syrup and the Dry Gin. Shake well and pass through a strainer into a cocktail glass containing a dash of nutmeg.

Raspberry Syrup can be used instead of Grenadine Syrup, if desired. Be careful not to overdo the nutmeg.

DEVIL'S COCKTAIL
⅙ gill of Peppermint.
⅓ gill of Old Brandy.
½ shakerful of broken Ice.

Half fill the shaker with broken ice and add the Peppermint. Then add the Brandy. Shake up and pass through a strainer into a cocktail glass.

This cocktail is quite strong. Not for beginners.

FIRE DEVIL COCKTAIL

¼ *gill of Sloe Gin.*
⅑ *gill of French Vermouth.*
⅑ *gill of Italian Vermouth.*
2 *dashes of Angostura Bitters.*
1 *dash of Lemon Peel Juice.*
½ *tumblerful of broken Ice.*

The tumbler is half filled with broken ice and the Angostura Bitters added. Now put in the Sloe Gin, the French Vermouth and the Italian Vermouth. Stir up and pass through a strainer into a cocktail glass. Serve with a dash of lemon peel juice on top.

Using Peach or Orange Bitters makes a pleasant variation.

GANGSTER COCKTAIL

¼ *gill of Brandy.*
¼ *gill of Brown Curaçao.*
1 *dash of Lemon Peel Juice.*
1 *Cherry.*
½ *shakerful of broken Ice.*

Half fill the shaker with broken ice. Then put in the Brandy and the Brown Curaçao. Shake well and pass through a strainer into a cocktail glass. Serve with a cherry and a dash of lemon peel juice.

This is quite a strong cocktail and should not be drunk on an empty stomach.

HOLLYWOOD COCKTAIL

⅛ *gill of French Vermouth.*
⅛ *gill of Italian Vermouth.*
¼ *gill of Dry Gin.*
2 *dashes of Brown Curaçao.*
1 *dash of Lemon Peel Juice.*
1 *Cherry.*
½ *tumblerful of broken Ice.*

Half fill the tumbler with broken ice and add the French Vermouth. Then put in the Italian Vermouth, the Dry Gin and the Brown Curaçao. Stir well and pass through a strainer into a cocktail glass. Serve with a cherry and a dash of lemon peel juice on top.

This cocktail is very popular in America.

If required dry, double the quantity of French Vermouth and leave out the Italian.

INCA COCKTAIL

$1/_8$ *gill of Gin.*
$1/_8$ *gill of French Vermouth.*
$1/_8$ *gill of Dry Sherry.*
1 *teaspoonful of Orange Bitters.*
1 *teaspoonful of Plain Syrup.*
1 *dash of Orange Peel Juice.*
1 *Cherry.*
½ *tumblerful of broken Ice.*

The tumbler is half filled with broken ice and the Orange Bitters is added. Next add the Gin, the French Vermouth, the Pale Sherry and the Plain Syrup. Stir well and pass through a strainer into a cocktail glass. Serve with a cherry and a dash of orange peel juice on top.

INDIAN COCKTAIL

$1/_8$ *gill of Canadian Club Whisky.*
$1/_8$ *gill of Italian Vermouth.*
$1/_8$ *gill of Gin.*
1 *teaspoonful of Triple Sec Cointreau.*
1 *teaspoonful of Orange Bitters.*
1 *teaspoonful of Brown Curaçao.*
1 *dash of Lemon Peel Juice.*
½ *tumblerful of broken Ice.*

Half fill the tumbler with broken ice and add the Orange Bitters. Then add the Canadian Club Whisky, the Italian Vermouth, the Gin, the Cointreau and the Brown Curaçao. Stir well and pass through a strainer into a cocktail glass. Serve with a dash of lemon peel juice on top.

This is a fairly strong cocktail, not advised in hot weather.

LONDON COCKTAIL

1/3 *gill of Dry Gin.*
1 *teaspoonful of Absinthe.*
1 *teaspoonful of Orange Bitters.*
2 *teaspoonfuls of Plain Syrup.*
1 *dash of Orange Peel Juice.*
½ *tumblerful of broken Ice.*

Half fill a tumbler with broken ice and add the Orange Bitters. Then add the Dry Gin, the Absinthe and the Plain Syrup. Stir well and pass through a strainer into a cocktail glass. Serve with a dash of orange peel juice on top.

If this is sweeter than desired, reduce the quantity of Plain Syrup.

MILLIONAIRE COCKTAIL

1 *dash of Absinthe.*
1/3 *gill of Canadian Club Whisky.*
1 *teaspoonful of Grenadine Syrup.*
1 *teaspoonful of Brown Curaçao.*
1 *dash of Orange Bitters.*
The white of a fresh Egg.
½ *shakerful of broken Ice.*

Half fill the shaker with broken ice and add the Orange Bitters. Then put in the Canadian Club Whisky, the Brown Curaçao, the Absinthe and the Grenadine Syrup. Shake well and pass through a strainer into a cocktail glass. Serve with a cherry.

The Absinthe improves the flavour of this cocktail, but it can be omitted if desired.

MONKEY GLAND COCKTAIL

1/3 *gill of Gin.*
1/3 *gill of Orange Juice.*
4 or 5 *dashes of Absinthe.*
6 or 7 *dashes of Grenadine Syrup.*
1 *dash of Orange Peel Juice.*
½ *shakerful of broken Ice.*

The shaker is half filled with broken ice and the Grenadine added. Then add the Absinthe, the Gin and the Orange juice. Shake well and pass through a strainer into a wine glass. Serve with a dash of orange peel juice on top.

Raspberry Syrup may be used instead of Grenadine Syrup, if desired. Both are rather sweet and some may prefer to reduce the quantity of the Syrup.

PING PONG COCKTAIL

¼ *gill of Sloe Gin.*
¼ *gill of Italian Vermouth.*
1 *dash of Angostura Bitters.*
1 *Cherry.*
½ *tumblerful of broken Ice.*

Half fill the tumbler with broken ice and add the Angostura Bitters. Then add the Sloe Gin and the Italian Vermouth. Stir well and pass through a strainer into a cocktail glass. Serve with a cherry.

Another way of making up this cocktail is to use French Vermouth in place of Italian.

YOKOHAMA COCKTAIL

$\frac{1}{6}$ *gill of Gin.*
$\frac{1}{6}$ *gill of Italian Vermouth.*
$\frac{1}{6}$ *gill of Crème de Menthe.*
1 *dash of Lemon Peel Juice.*
1 *Olive.*
½ *shakerful of broken Ice.*

Half fill the shaker with broken ice and add the Gin. Then add the Italian Vermouth and the Crème de Menthe. Shake well and pass through a strainer into a cocktail glass. Serve with an olive and a dash of lemon peel juice on top.

If required not quite so sweet, use French Vermouth in place of Italian.

ZA ZA COCKTAIL

¼ *gill of Dubonnet.*
¼ *gill of Dry Gin.*
2 *dashes of Angostura Bitters.*
½ *shakerful of broken Ice.*

Half fill the shaker with broken ice and add the Angostura Bitters. Then add the Dry Gin and the Dubonnet. Shake well and pass through a strainer into a cocktail glass.

This cocktail is an excellent *apéritif.*

ZERO HOUR COCKTAIL

2 *dashes of Absinthe.*
3 *dashes of Crème de Menthe.*
¼ *gill of Brandy.*
⅛ *gill of Apricot Brandy.*
1 *Olive.*
½ *shakerful of broken Ice.*

The shaker is half filled with broken ice and the Brandy added. Then the Apricot Brandy and the Crème de Menthe are added. Shake well and pass through a strainer into a cocktail glass. Serve with an olive and two dashes of Absinthe on top.

The following are not true Cocktails: but very much like them.

ABSINTHE COOLER

½ *gill of Whisky.*
2 or 3 *dashes of Absinthe.*
⅛ *gill of Lemon Juice.*
2 *dashes of Angostura Bitters.*
½ *pint of Ginger Ale.*
1 *lump of Ice.*

Put the lump of ice in a tall glass and add the Angostura Bitters. Then add the Whisky, the Lemon Juice and the Ginger Ale. Stir well. Serve with two or three dashes of Absinthe on top.

A pleasant drink.

ANGOSTURA FIZZ
¼ *gill of Angostura Bitters.*
½ *gill of Lemon Juice.*
⅛ *gill of Plain Syrup.*
The white of an Egg.
Soda Water.
½ *shakerful of broken Ice.*

Half fill the shaker with broken ice and add the Plain Syrup. Then add the Angostura Bitters, the Lemon juice and the white of an egg. Shake well and pass through a strainer into a tumbler. To serve, fill up with Soda Water.

BADMINTON CUP
1 *bottle of Claret.*
2 *bottles of Soda Water.*
The juice and rind of 1 *Lemon.*
3 *slices of Cucumber.*
3 *oz. of Icing Sugar.*
¾ *gill of Brown Curaçao.*
Ice Chips.

Put the Claret into a large bowl and add the sugar. Then add the Lemon juice and the Brown Curaçao. Stir well. Surround the bowl with the ice and leave for half an hour; then strain the mixture and add the Soda water. Serve in a large tumbler with the lemon rind and the slices of cucumber on top.

BRANDY CRUSTA
⅓ *gill of Brandy.*
⅙ *gill of Lemon Juice.*
1 *teaspoonful of Plain Syrup.*
1 *teaspoonful of Maraschino.*
1 *dash of Orange Bitters.*
1 *dash of Angostura Bitters.*
The peel of a Lemon cut in a spiral.
Slices of fresh Fruit.

½ teaspoonful of powdered Sugar.
½ shakerful of broken Ice.

Half fill the shaker with broken ice and add the Orange
Bitters. Then add the Angostura Bitters, the Lemon juice,
the Plain Syrup, the Brandy and the Maraschino. Shake well
and strain. Now moisten the inside of a wine glass with
Lemon juice and sprinkle with sugar. Then put in the lemon
peel, cut spiral fashion, and add the mixture. Serve with
slices of fruit.

BRANDY DAISY

½ gill of Brandy.
½ gill of Lime Juice.
½ gill of Lemon Juice.
¼ gill of Grenadine Syrup.
Slices of fresh Fruit.
Soda Water.
½ shakerful of broken Ice.

Half fill the shaker with broken ice and add the Brandy.
Then put in the Lime juice, the Lemon juice, and the
Grenadine Syrup. Shake well, pass through a strainer into a
large tumbler and fill up with Soda Water. Serve with slices
of fresh fruit on top and with a spoon.

If you prefer it, you can halve the quantities of the above
ingredients and serve in a large wine glass without adding
the Soda Water.

BULLDOG COOLER

½ gill of Dry Gin.
1 or 2 dashes of Orange Peel Juice.
The juice of half an Orange.
1 or 2 dashes of Plain Syrup.
⅓ pint of Ginger Ale.
1 lump of Ice.

Put the lump of ice in a tall glass. Then add the Dry Gin,
the Orange juice, the Plain syrup and the Ginger Ale. Stir
well and serve with a dash of orange peel juice on top.

If this is sweeter than required, reduce the quantity of Plain Syrup.

BURGUNDY CUP

1 *bottle of Burgundy.*
½ *gill of Brandy.*
½ *gill of Maraschino.*
¼ *gill of Brown Curaçao.*
2 or 3 *dashes of Bénédictine.*
2 or 3 *slices of Lemon.*
1 or 2 *slices of Orange.*
Slices of fresh Fruit.
1 *bottle of Soda Water.*
1 *big lump of Ice.*

Put the piece of ice into a large bowl and add the Burgundy. Then put in the Brandy, the Maraschino, the Brown Curaçao, the Bénédictine and the Soda Water. Stir well and strain the mixture. Serve in a large tumbler with the slices of lemon, orange and the fresh fruit on top.

CIDER CUP

1 *large bottle of Cider.*
⅓ *gill of Brown Curaçao.*
¼ *gill of Maraschino.*
½ *gill of Brandy.*
¾ *gill of Pale Sherry.*
1 *teaspoonful of Lemon Juice.*
2 or 3 *slices of Lemon.*
2 or 3 *slices of Orange.*
Slices of fresh Fruit.
2 *sprigs of Mint.*
1 *big lump of Ice.*

Put the piece of ice into a large bowl and add the Cider. Then put in the Brown Curaçao, the Maraschino, the Brandy, the Pale Sherry and the Lemon Juice. Stir well and strain the mixture. Serve in a large tumbler with the slices of lemon, orange, fresh fruit and the sprigs of mint on top.

GIN HIGHBALL

1 *gill of Dry Gin.*
1 *slice of Lemon.*
1 *gill of Soda Water.*
1 *lump of Ice.*

Put the lump of ice in a tumbler and add the Dry Gin. Then fill up with Soda Water. Serve with a slice of Lemon.

This recipe can be varied by using Brandy, French Vermouth, Italian Vermouth, Port, Rum, Sherry or Whisky in place of Gin.

MINT COOLER

1 *dash of Crème de Menthe.*
½ *pint of Ginger Ale.*
2 or 3 *sprigs of Mint.*
1 *lump of Ice.*

Put the sprigs of mint in a tall glass and squash with a spoon. Then add the lump of ice, the Crème de Menthe and the Ginger Ale. Stir well and serve with a sprig of mint.

A very refreshing drink.

NEW YORK COOLER

½ *gill of Canadian Club Whisky.*
¼ *gill of Lemon Squash.*
1 *dash of Lemon Peel Juice.*
3 *dashes of Grenadine Syrup.*
1 *slice of Lemon.*
1 *lump of Ice.*
Fill up with Soda Water.

Put the lump of ice in a tall glass and add the Canadian Club Whisky. Then add the Lemon Squash and the Grenadine Syrup. Fill up with Soda Water and stir well. Serve with a dash of lemon peel juice and a slice of lemon.

If this is sweeter than required reduce the quantity of Grenadine syrup.

RYE FIZZ

½ *gill of Canadian Club Whisky.*
¾ *gill of Lemon Juice.*
⅑ *gill of Grenadine Syrup.*
1 *teaspoonful of Brown Curaçao.*
The white of an egg.
Soda Water.
½ *shakerful of broken Ice.*

Half fill the shaker with broken ice and add the Lemon juice. Then add the Grenadine Syrup, the white of an egg, the Brandy and the Brown Curaçao. Shake well and pass through a strainer into a tumbler. To serve, fill up the tumbler with Soda Water.

A very pleasing drink of medium strength.

SAUTERNE CUP

1 *bottle of Sauterne.*
½ *gill of Lemon Juice.*
⅛ *gill of Grenadine Syrup.*
½ *gill of Maraschino.*
⅓ *gill of Yellow Chartreuse.*
¼ *gill of Bénédictine.*
½ *gill of Brandy.*
¼ *gill of Brown Curaçao.*
4 *slices of Lemon.*
1 *slice of Cucumber.*
Slices of fresh Fruit.
1 *pint of Soda Water.*
1 *big lump of Ice.*

Put the lump of ice into a large bowl and add the Sauterne. Then put in the Lemon juice, the Grenadine Syrup, the Brown Curaçao, the Maraschino, the Yellow Chartreuse, the Bénédictine, the Brandy and the Soda Water. Stir well and strain the mixture. Serve with the slices of lemon, cucumber, and fresh fruit on top.

If desired you can omit the Yellow Chartreuse and the Bénédictine.

WHITE HORSE DAISY

½ *gill of Scotch Whisky.*
½ *gill of Lemon Juice.*
2 *dashes of Grenadine Syrup.*
1 *teaspoonful of Absinthe.*
The white of an Egg.
Slices of fresh Fruit.
Soda Water.
½ *shakerful of broken Ice.*

Half fill the shaker with broken ice and add the white of an egg. Then put in the Lemon juice, the Grenadine Syrup, the Whisky and the Absinthe. Shake well and pass through a strainer into a large tumbler. Fill up with Soda Water. Serve with slices of fresh fruit and a spoon.

If desired, a dash of Anisette may be added to the above. This improves the flavour.

WHIZBANG COOLER

½ *gill of Dry Gin.*
1 or 2 *sprigs of Mint.*
1 *dash of Peppermint.*
½ *pint of Ginger Ale.*
1 *lump of Ice.*

Put the lump of ice in a tall glass. Then add the Dry Gin and the Ginger Ale. Stir well and serve with a dash of Peppermint and the sprigs of mint on top.

This drink is very delicious and refreshing.

Some Toasts

Then to this Flowing Bowl did I adjourn,
My lips the secret well of life to learn;
And lip to lip it murmur'd "While you live,
Drink! For once dead, you never shall return."
—Omar Khayyam

Happy Days.

Set them up again.

Here's looking at you.

Drink hearty.

Here's to your health.

Let's have a nip.

May we never want a friend or a bottle to share it with him.

Here's to those I love,
Here's to those who love me,
Here's to those who love those I love,
And here's to those who love those who love me.

Here's a toast to all who are here,
No matter where you are from;
May the best day you have ever seen
Be worse than your worst to come.

Happy are we met, happy have we been, happy may we part,
and happy meet again.

To-morrow can wait;
Let us have wine and women, mirth and laughter,
Sermons and soda water the day after.

Drink while you can

Drink to-day and drown all sorrow,
You shall perhaps not do it to-morrow.
Best while you have it use you breath,
There is no drinking after death.

Laugh at all things,
Great and small things,
Sick or well, on sea or shore,
While we are quaffing
Let's have some laughing.
Who the devil cares for more?

While we live let's live in clover.
For when we're dead we're dead all over.

Let her role.

Be glad and your friends are many,
          Be sad and you lose them all;
They do not decline your nectared wine,
          But alone you must drink life's gall.
                    Let's have a smile.

To my enemies here's my toast;
          I hope each shall be a ghost,
                    And that the devil
                    Will ne'er be a day well
          Till all have been given a roast.
          Sing, and the hills will answer
                         Sigh, it is lost on the air;
          The echoes bound to a joyous sound,
          And good wine banishes care.

Champagne for our real friends and real pain for our sham
friends.

                    Here's to a chaperone.
            May she learn from Cupid
            Just enough blindness to be sweetly stupid.

May Dame Fortune ever smile on you, but never here
daughter, Miss Fortune.

To the hardware trade: although they profess to honesty, they sell iron and steel for a living.

Drink to a fair woman who I think is most entitled to it, for if anything ever can drive me to drink, she certainly can do it.

Here's to a long life, and may you live a thousand years and I a thousand years less one day, for I would not care to live after you had passed away.

> Friend of my soul, this goblet sip,
> 'Twill chase the pensive tear.
> 'Tis not so sweet as woman's lip,
> But oh, 'Tis more sincere.

Drink, for you know not whence you came nor why.
Drink, for you know not why you go nor whence.

Here's to you, my dear, and to the dear who's not here, my dear; but if the dear who's not here, my dear, were here, my dear, I'd not be drinking to you, dear, that's clear.
Here's to a long life and a merry one,
A quick death and a happy one,
A good girl and a pretty one,
A cold bottle and another one.

Wine is good,
    Love is better,
    False morals spin a spider's fetter.
        So fill up the bowl,
        Be a jolly old soul,
    And you'll be loved by your girl when you get her.
Oh, fill the wine-cup high,

    The sparkling liquor pour,
For we will care and grief defy,
        They ne'er shall plague us no more.

Say, why did Time his glass sublime
        Fill up with sand unsightly
When wine, he knew, runs brisker through,
        And sparkles far more brightly?

Here's to the moneyless man crushed with sorrow and pain.
May he think of the barman when his star rises again.

    Here's to you, as good as you are;
    And here's to me, as bad as I am.
    But as good as you are, and as bad as I am;
    I'm as good as you are, as bad as I am.

May the hinges of friendship never rust or the wings
of love lose a feather.

    To sum up all, be merry I advise;
    As we're merry may we still be wise.

    This is a good world to live in,
    To lend, to spend, to give in,
    But to get, to borrow, or to keep what's one's own,
    'Tis the very worst world that ever was known.

HOLIDAYS & ADVENTURES

The Seaside

SOUTHEND-ON-SEA is not everybody's money. One man's holiday resort is another man's bugbear, and people have been heard to wonder why anybody ever goes to Southend-on-Sea. Yet crowds do go there regularly year after year. I am told this is not out of affection for the place (nobody could be so guilty as that), but because these people cannot afford to go anywhere else.

City men have suddenly made a suburb of Southend-on-Sea. It is really necessary to always write the name of the place in full, otherwise people might wonder. They have taken their "little house" there, not because they are fond of the place. They have the happiness of seeing it only on Sundays. But the accelerated train service is useful.

Expert prevaricators say that what strikes the nose with impressive effect is the scent of ozone. This may or may not be so, but there is certainly something unmistakable in the atmosphere when the tide is out. It goes out a long way (about a mile and a quarter), and I have been told that it has not quite enough courage to come all the way back again. However, it is carefully affirmed that it really is possible to see the sea from the promenade—if the weather is clear and you carry binoculars—and know how to use them.

Frinton is another waterside resort that ostentatiously labels itself "on-Sea", as if to say, "and don't you forget it". You cannot forget it when at Frinton, for there is nothing else to think of. All you can do at Frinton is bathe, and I do not suppose that even Mr Holbein cares about bathing all day long. It is true you may play golf, but you can do that at Wimbledon. I object to Frinton because it consists of nothing but bathing-huts, except that part of it which consists of bathing-tents. There is no pier and no band-stand, and if you want enjoyment at Frinton you have to go to Clacton for it.

Yet even a pier palls. When I was at Yarmouth there were two piers, and there may be half-a-dozen now, for they seem to be always building a new pier at Yarmouth. When you realise that each pier harbours about four bands and three orchestras, while the whole sea-front is studded with band-stands, concert rings, and pierrot pitches, the reflection is borne in upon you that entertainment may be too lavishly offered. There is too much jam for the bread. I went to Yarmouth one day with the intention of staying a fortnight, but I came away next morning, nor did I find an hour of happiness till I was back again in London.

Then I tried Hastings, recommended thither because it is so lively. When I had a little talk with the manager of the hotel and told him that I found it a bit gay, he raised his eyebrows and said I had come at the wrong time of the year. It seems that I should have gone to Hastings in the winter, which is its season—dull enough for anybody. I saw he felt for me, so I wondered if I should find St Leonards more agreeable just then. All he said was, "St Leonards!" But I could tell what he meant. There was enough sarcasm in the three syllables to blister the whole seafront from Warrior Square to Bo-Peep.

Hastings and St Leonards, though they join, touch, and march with each other, are, like Brighton and Hove, as far as the Poles are asunder. The inhabitants turn up their noses to one another, and visitors take sides according to the situation.

These things apart, I am still at a loss to explain how and why it is people do not have a good time at Broadstairs. Perhaps they do. I do not know why.

Thackeray Bunyan

Many Ways to Take a Holiday

One of the chief uses of a doctor is to insist on a holiday: the practitioner who takes this part of his duty seriously is likely to have a full waiting-room and grateful patients. But, why pay a doctor to insist? Why not make it at least as much a part of the annual routine as the doubtfully welcomed "spring cleaning"? Quite often it is the will that is as lacking as the cash, for do we not find that among our friends surprising people set their minds in this direction and achieve what others feel would be a sheer extravagance. Yet nothing very dreadful happens and it may well be that these "extravagant" ones are those that push ahead and have that extra competence, extra vitality that lifts them just the little bit above their neighbours. "Why do you always feel better if you have a talk with Mrs. A.?" asked a harassed mother. "Because she's got something to tell you about her last holiday," was the reply; "she's fresh herself and it radiates to you too." Clearly Mrs. A. had the secret and used it for the benefit of her neighbours as for herself.

The housewife, of all others, needs some degree of change and leisure: the everlastingness of household chores settles on her spirit like the fine dust that she battles with so constantly. If it stays, a dimness comes, unrecognized probably, but showing itself in a lessened desire to attack the problems and opportunities that surround her. "The reasonable undertaking of hard things" is allowed to pass to someone no more capable, but with just that extra bit of

231

energy that has been grown in a period of freedom from the usual round.

The country woman's need is no whit the less than that of her town neighbours. "You can't live on a view," snapped an overdriven Women's Institute secretary to a speaker from a town who thought one could never get tired in such a glorious spot. One can hunger for gas-lamps, as Robert Louis Stevenson did, and find refreshment of spirit in the meanest streets. Those who live in the wilds may need the "close-up" for their tonic; the rattle of street sounds may be their sedative. To the modern child the railway train may be far more romantic than the touring car: perhaps as the bath-chair age approaches we shall find even that method of progression will give us time to observe things as we pass that we should miss if we travelled by aeroplane.

A most delightful and accessible holiday may be the one little recognised as such—the day in bed. Even the most copiously flowing cold in the head need not drown the uplifting spirit that has time to revel for twelve hours in a new world. It may be a detective story or a crossword puzzle that brings release, or again a mixed grill of poetry, the newspaper and the box of old letters to sort; but it is one's very own opportunity; the thing that does not happen on ordinary days—the treasure that one holds but rarely.

A tiny child in a sanatorium ward was listening gravely to its neighbours repeating the Lord's Prayer at bedtime. "I can say that," she remarked to the nurse approaching to tuck her up, and, with the four-year-old's imitative facility, she recited the whole with but one slip, "Give us this day our *day in bed*."

Truly, out of the mouth of babes comes truth: the child had the cardinal point of the sanatorium system in the altered petition, and beyond that a lesson for many another bearing the burden and heat of the day and beginning to flag a little under it.

The individual character of the holiday is a factor of principal value: the husband who wants his games is ill served by the deckchair on the promenade; the walker who likes to take a rest at the end only is bored by the companion who desires to poke about for wildflowers or gaze at the view at every turn. Have the courage to separate, to make the brief holiday time really one's own. The pleasure of renewal of family life becomes something saved up for the return and may lead to the discovery that "the best part of going away is coming home."

The form of holiday luxury that is increasingly hard to come by is silence. But how well worth while to seek it out. Even one hour under a tree or stretched on a greensward alone, with birds, or bees, or distant bells can make a memory that will clear a winter day of mists and fog. If friends should be grappled to the soul with hooks of steel, so also should absence from them be cultivated on occasion. Best of all perhaps is the company of *one* like-minded; otherwise, seek peace in solitude as food for the days to come.

The word food brings a good common-sense thought to finish with: let food come into the holiday plan along with scenery, books and companions. Have it different, sample the unknown, educate the palate as the eye or ear. "I suppose Father always fell back on an omelette," wrote the daughter, commenting on the parental tour abroad. Well, so he did, but Mother had read *Country Fare in Many Lands*, and was consequently more adventurous.

Even in one's own country there may be local dishes that can be tried with advantage. Give the jaded stomach a change as you give the tired head or the weary feet. Why not snails or frogs, if it is the custom of the country to consume them? If unpleasant, there is always the joyful prospect of the return to the familiar fare at home: if accepted, there is the sense of acquisition, of adventure. "You can't have both comfort and adventure together," was the dictum of a wise holiday maker. Very well, then choose the one or the other; but whichever it is, determine it shall help you on your way—and it will.

Housekeeping On a Great Liner of To-Day

An ocean liner of to-day, such as the "Bremen," is more self-contained and self-sufficient than the largest hotel. None of the ancient tinned beef and sea biscuits for one of her round trips. The storage capacity is arranged to accommodate everything from mussels and whipped cream, to crude ice.

Quality is, of course, important, and only the best of everything is shipped; nevertheless quantity does not seem far behind.

We all like to see the machinery go round. Being a woman and therefore interested in the organisation of the food question I asked, when travelling in the "Bremen", to be allowed to go through the kitchens.

Cleanliness and Tidiness

The first thing I noticed was the cleanliness and tidiness. The Chefs (who had a list of diplomas in every language that would make one's brain reel) and their assistants were dressed in snowy starched coats and cap and aprons.

Among the things that impressed me most was the potato peeler which automatically peels the three tons of potatoes that are needed a day with a simple turn of the wrist. Three tons of potatoes is enough for a family of four for a year!

Then there was the automatic cream whipping machine, the bread cutter that always cuts straight slices of bread, and the dough mixer which can deal with 5 cwt. of flour at a time. The latter is especially necessary when it is learned that 12,000 rolls are baked and eaten every day on board ship, besides the countless cakes, pastries and specialities from all countries to tempt the passengers' appetite.

There were tier on tier of ovens and stoves of every description; shining time-saving machines lined that cupboards and walls. Time is of great importance when one remembers that there are 1,950 passengers and 900 crew to be fed at least three times a day.

Have you ever heard a steward of the dining-room say, "So sorry, Madam, the caviar is off, will you have smoked salmon?" No, all requests are granted with lightning speed and with the steady frequency of a conjuror producing rabbits out of a hat.

A Tour of Inspection

From the kitchens, I was taken through the storage rooms where the vegetables, fish, flour, butter, &c., are stored. The stock of milk on the start of a trip from Bremerhaven to New York and back is 2,641 gallons or more than a herd of 40 cows produce in a week.

The stock of flour, of 44,092 lbs., is treated as though it were worth its weight in gold. Did you know that flour was temperamental? The temperature of the storage room must be just so and remain just so no matter what the climate outside does. Added to this, the flour is placed carefully on its back to start the journey and then at specified intervals put on its side. Quite a business turning 44,092 lbs. of flour every now and then.

As for yeast—if it is not treated like the most important passenger it promptly ferments; no warning—just ferments. In order to avoid this, yeast is kept at a temperature of 3 to 5 degrees centigrade, and when the ship approaches such climatic changes as the Gulf Stream, it is always with one eye on the yeast. Otherwise the effect is disastrous.

Provisions required for a round voyage of an Express Liner—Bremerhaven-New York and back.

Passengers:	1,950
Crew:	900
Total:	2,850

38,580 lb.	meat, sausage, &c.
6,614 lb.	ham, bacon, preserved meat, &c.
17,637 lb.	poultry (Christmas Dinner for 2,500 families)
2,205 lb.	game
11,023 lb.	fresh fish
4,410 lb.	shell fish
15,000	mussels
772 lb.	delicatessen—caviare, olives, potted fish, sauces, spices, &c.
2,500	tins and glasses of delicatessen
1,323 lb.	smoked fish
22,046 lb.	dry groceries—preserved vegetables and fruit, jam, jellies, marmalade, fruit syrups, edible oils, dried fruit, nuts, etc.
44,092 lb.	flour
165 lb.	yeast
5,512 lb.	salted and dried vegetables
4,410 lb.	milling products
1,433 lb.	baked goods and cereals ready for table
11,023 lb.	coffee, malted coffee, chocolate, tea and sugar
14,330 lb.	butter and margarine
2,641 gall.	milk, cream and whipped cream
3,307 lb.	cheese
70,000	eggs
110 gall.	vinegar
110 lb.	spices
110,230 lb.	potatoes
52,910 lb.	fresh vegetables
50,000	items fresh fruit—oranges, lemons, grapefruit, &c.
26,455 lb.	fresh fruit—apples, pears, grapes, &c.
70,547 lb.	ice
3,200	glasses of ice cream

Each class in the "Bremen", cabin, tourist and third class, has its own kitchens and cooks, although the food supply is all from the same store.

An express liner carries 45,000 passengers a year, which is as though the total population of Folkestone, man, woman and child, went on 14-day cruises in relays.

A desert island stocked with a population of 45,000 people, and the total contents of the "Bremen", would bear no resemblance to the one inhabited by the Swiss Family Robinson!

Mary E. Morrell

How To Camp Out Without a Tent

The next best thing to really living in the woods is talking over such an experience. A thousand little incidents, scarcely thought of at the time, crowd upon my mind, and bring back with them the feeling of freedom and adventure so dear to the heart of every boy. Shall I ever enjoy any flavour earth can afford as we did our coffee's aroma? The flapjacks—how good and appetising! the fish—how delicate and sweet! And the wonderful cottage of boughs, thatched with the tassels of the pine—was there ever a cottage out of a fairy tale that could compare with it?

In fancy I can see it now. There stands the little cot, flooded with the light of the setting sun; those who built it and use it for a habitation are off exploring, hunting, fishing, and foraging for their evening meal, and the small, shy creatures of the wood take the opportunity to satisfy the curiosity with which they have, from a safe distance, viewed the erection of so large and singular a nest.

The boys will soon return, each with his contribution to the larder—a fish, a squirrel, a bird, or a rabbit, which will be cooked and eaten with better appetite and enjoyment than the most elaborate viands that home could afford. And although such joys are denied to me now, I can, at least, in remembering them, give others an opportunity to possess similar pleasures. It shall be my object to describe how these houses may be built and these dinners cooked, and that, too, where there are neither planks, nor nails, nor stoves. To boys

Fig. 1 Frame of Cottage.

well informed in woodcraft, only a few hints need be given; but for the benefit of amateurs we will go more into detail.

Four persons make a good camping-party. Before arriving at their destination these persons should choose one of their number as captain.

The captain gives directions and superintends the pitching of the tent or the building of the rustic cottage. The site for the camp should be upon a knoll, mound, or rising ground, so as to afford a good drainage. If the forest abounds in pine trees, the young cottage-builder's task is an easy one. It often happens that two or three trees already standing can be made to serve for the corners of the proposed edifice, though trees for corners are not absolutely necessary.

Fig. 1 represents part of the framework of one of the simplest forms of rustic cottage. In this case, two trees serve for the two posts of the rear wall. The front posts are young trees that have been cut down and firmly planted at about four or five paces in front of the trees, as shown in the illustration. Enough of the branches have been left adhering to the trunks of the upright posts to serve as rests for the

239

cross bars. To prevent complication in the diagram, the roof is not shown. To make this, fasten on an additional cross bar or two to the rear wall, then put a pole at each side, slanting down from the rear to the front, and cover these poles with cross sticks. When the framework is finished, the security and durability of the structure will be improved by fastening all the loose joints, tying them together with withes of willow, grass, or reeds. The next step is to cover the frame. This is done after the method shown in Fig. 2. From among some boughs, saved for this purpose, take one and hang it upon the third cross bar, counting from the ground up; bring the bough down, passing it inside the second bar and resting the end on the ground outside the first bar; repeat this with other boughs until the row is finished. Then begin at the fourth bar, passing the boughs down inside the third and outside the second bar, so that they will overlap the first row.

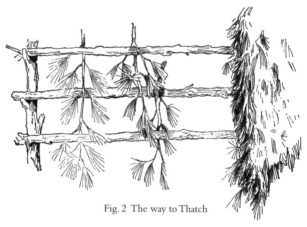

Fig. 2 The way to Thatch

Continue in this manner until the four walls are closed in, leaving spaces open where windows or doors are wanted. The roof is thatched after the same method, beginning at the front and working upward and backward to the rear wall, each row overlapping the preceding row of thatch. The more closely and compactly you thatch the roof and walls, the better protection will they afford from any passing shower. This completed, the house is finished, and you will be astonished to see what a lovely little green cot you have built.

A cottage may be built differing from the one we have just described by having the roof extended so as to form a sort of verandah, or porch, in front; the floor of the porch may be covered with a layer of pine-needles. Should you find your house too small to accommodate your party, you can, by erecting a duplicate cottage four or five paces at one side, and roofing over the intervening space, have a house of two rooms with an open hallway between.

Before going to housekeeping, some furniture will be necessary; and for this we propose to do our shopping right in the neighbourhood of our cottage. Here is our cabinet and upholstery shop, in the wholesome fragrance of the pines.

After the labour of building, your thoughts will naturally turn to a place for sleeping. Cut four forked sticks, sharpen the ends, and drive them firmly into the ground at the spot where you wish the bed to stand in your room. Two strong poles, long enough to reach lengthwise from fork to fork, will serve for side boards; a number of short sticks will answer for slats; after these are fastened in place you have the rustic bedstead shown in Fig. 3.

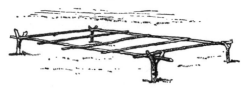

Fig. 3 Bedstead

A good spring mattress is very desirable, and not difficult to obtain. Gather a lot of small green branches, or brush, and cover your bedstead with a layer of it about one foot thick; this you will find a capital substitute for springs. For your mattress proper, go to your upholstery shop under the pine tree and gather several armfuls of the dry pine-needles;

cover the elastic brush *springs* with a thick layer of these needles; over this spread your India-rubber blanket, with the rubber side under, so that any moisture or dampness there may be in your mattress may be prevented from coming through. You may now make up your bed with what wraps or blankets you have with you, and you have (Fig. 4) as complete and comfortable a bed as any forester need wish for. In the place of pine-needles, hay or grass may be used. I have slept very comfortably upon a brush mattress covered with iron-weed.*

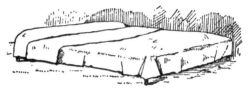

Fig. 4 Bed made up

I would suggest to any boy who means to try this rustic cabinet-making, to select carefully for the bed-posts sticks strong enough to support the weight he intends them to bear, otherwise his slumbers may be interrupted in an abrupt and disagreeable manner. My first experiment in this line proved disastrous. I spent the greater part of one day in building and neatly finishing a bed like the one described. After it was made up, with an army blanket for a coverlid, it looked so soft, comfortable, and inviting that I scarcely could wait for bedtime to try it.

When the evening meal was over and the last story told around the blazing campfire, I took off hat, coat, and boots and snuggled down in my new and original couch, curiously watched by my companions, who lay, rolled in their blankets, upon the hard ground. It does not take a boy long to fall asleep, particularly after a hard day's work in the open air, but it takes longer, after being aroused from a sound nap, for him

★ Iron-weed; flat top (*Vernonia noveboracensis*); a common Kentucky weed, with beautiful purple blossoms.

to get his wits together—especially when suddenly dumped upon the ground with a crash, amid a heap of broken sticks and dry brush, as I happened to be on that eventful night. Loud and long were the shouts of laughter of my companions when they discovered my misfortune. Theoretically, the bed was well planned, but practically it was a failure, because it had rotten sticks for bed-posts.

Having provided bed and shelter, it is high time to look after the inner boy; and while the foragers are off in search of provisions, it will be the cook's duty to provide some method of cooking the food that will be brought in.

One of the simplest and most practical forms of bake-oven can be made of clay and an old barrel. Remove one head of the barrel, scoop out a space in the nearest bank, and fit the barrel in (Fig. 5).

Fig. 5 Barrel in Bank

If the mud or clay is not damp enough, moisten it and plaster it over the barrel to the depth of a foot or more, leaving a place for a chimney at the back end, where part of a stave has been cut away; around this place build a chimney of sticks arranged log-cabin fashion and plastered with mud (Fig. 6). After this, make a good, rousing fire in the barrel, and keep adding fuel until all the staves are burned out and the surrounding clay is baked hard. This makes an oven that will bake as well, if not better, than any new patented stove or range at home. To use it, build a fire inside and let it burn until the oven is thoroughly heated, then rake out all the coal and embers, put your dinner in and close up the front with the head of the barrel preserved for this purpose. The clay will remain hot for several hours and keep the inside of the oven hot enough to roast meat or bake bread.

Fig. 6 Heating the Oven

If there be no bank convenient, or if you have no barrel with which to build this style of oven, there are other methods that will answer for all the cooking necessary to a party of boys camping out. Many rare fish have I eaten in my time. The delicious pompano at New Orleans, the brook-trout and grayling, fresh from the cold water of Northern Michigan, but never have I had fish taste better than did a certain large cat-fish that we boys once caught on a set-line in Kentucky. We built a fireplace of flat stones, a picture of

Fig. 7 A Stone Stove.

which you have in Fig. 7, covered it with a thin piece of slate, cleaned the fish and with its skin still on, placed it upon the slate. When it was brown upon one side we turned it over until it was thoroughly cooked. With green sticks we lifted off the fish and placed it upon a piece of clean bark; the skin adhered to the stone, and the meat came off in smoking, snowy pieces, which we ate with the aid of our pocket-knives and rustic forks made of small green twigs with the forked ends sharpened.

Fig. 8 A Butter-Knife

If stones cannot be had to answer for this stove, there still remains the old, primitive campfire and pot-hook. The very sight of this iron pot swinging over a blazing fire suggests soup, to eat which with any comfort spoons are necessary. These are quickly and easily made by thrusting clam or mussel shells into splits made in the ends of sticks. A splendid butter-knife can be made from the shell of a razor-oyster with a little care in a similar manner (see Fig. 8).

245

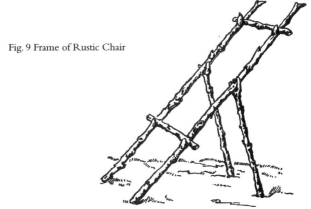

Fig. 9 Frame of Rustic Chair

If you stay any time in your forest home you can, by a little ingenuity, add many comforts and conveniences. I have drawn some diagrams, as hints, in this direction. For instance, Fig. 9 shows the manner of making an excellent rustic chair of two stout poles and two cross poles, to which are fastened the ends of a piece of canvas, carpet or leather (Fig. 10), which swinging loose, fits itself exactly to your form, making a most comfortable easy-chair in which to rest or take a nap after a hard day's tramp. It often happens that the peculiar formation

Fig. 10 The Rustic Chair Finished

246

Fig. 11 A Camp Table

of some stump or branch suggests new styles of seats. A table can be very readily made by driving four forked sticks into the ground for legs, and covering the cross sticks upon the top with pieces of birch or other smooth bark. Fig. 11 shows a table made in this manner, with one piece of bark removed to reveal its construction.

As a general rule, what is taught in boys' books, though correct in theory, when tried proves impracticable. This brings to mind an incident that happened to a party of young hunters camping out in Ohio. Early one morning one of the boys procured from a distant farmhouse a dozen pretty little white bantam eggs. Having no game, and only one small fish in the way of fresh meat, the party congratulated themselves upon the elegant breakfast they would make of fresh eggs, toasted crackers, and coffee. How to cook the eggs was the question. One of the party proposed his plan.

"I have just read a book," said he, "which tells how some travellers cooked fowls and fish by rolling them up in clay and tossing them into the fire. Shall we try that plan with the eggs?"

The rest of the party assented, and soon all were busy rolling rather large balls of blue clay, in the centre of each of which was an egg. A dozen were placed in the midst of the hottest embers, and the boys seated themselves around the fire, impatiently waiting for the eggs to cook. They did cook—with a vengeance! Zip, bang! went one, then another and another, until, in less time than it takes to tell it, not an

247

egg remained unexploded; and the hot embers and bits of clay that stuck to the boys' hair and clothes were all that was left to remind them of those nice, fresh bantam eggs. It was all very funny, but ever after the boys of that party showed the greatest caution in trying new schemes, no matter how well they might seem to be endorsed.

Hints to Amateur Campers

From time immemorial it has been the custom of the city fellows to laugh at their country cousins, and to poke all manner of fun at them on account of their verdancy in regard to city manners and customs. This is hardly fair, for if a real city fellow be placed on a farm, or in the woods, his ignorance is just as laughable and absurd. It was only the other day I saw a young New York artist refuse to drink from a spring because something *was bubbling up at the bottom*. Experience is a great teacher. Even the artist just mentioned, after making himself sick upon stagnant water, would, no doubt, learn to select bubbling springs in the future. A few timely hints may, however, prevent many mishaps and unpleasant accidents.

Provisions

It is always desirable to take as large a stock of provisions as can be conveniently transported. In these days of canned meats, soups, vegetables, and fruits, a large amount of provisions may be stored in a small space. Do not fail to take a plentiful supply of salt, pepper, and sugar; also bacon, flour, meal, grits, or hominy, tea, coffee, and condensed milk. If you have any sort of luck with your rod, gun, or traps, the forest and stream ought to supply fresh meat, and with the appetite only enjoyed by people who live outdoors you can "live like a king".

Shelter

Because I have described but one sort of shelter my readers must not suppose that it is absolutely necessary to build a cottage like the one described. On the contrary, there are a thousand different plans that will suggest themselves to fellows who are accustomed to camping out. The huts, or sheds, built of "slabs" by some of the Adirondack hunters are very convenient, but unless the open ends are protected, in time of a storm, the rain is apt to drive in and soak the inmates. The two sheds face each other, and in the middle of the space between the campfire blazes, throwing a ruddy light at night into both compartments.

By taking advantage of a rock, a fallen or uprooted tree, the work of building a hut is often materially lessened.

Tents, of course, are very handy and comfortable, and if obtainable should be all means be used. At least one or two good sharp hatchets should form a part of the equipment of every camp; it is astonishing, with their aid and a little practice, what a comfortable house may be built in a very short time.

Choosing Companions

Never join a camping party that has among its members a single peevish, irritable, or selfish person, or a "shirk". Although the company of such a boy may be only slightly annoying at school or upon the playground, in camp the companionship of a fellow of this description becomes unbearable. Even if the game fill the woods and the waters are alive with fish, an irritable or selfish companion will spoil all the fun and take the sunshine out of the brightest day. The whole party should be composed of fellows who are willing to take things as they come and make the best of everything. With such companions there is no such thing as "bad luck"; rain or shine everything is always jolly, and when you return from the woods, strengthened in mind and body, you will always remember with pleasure your camping experience.

On Weights & Measures

IN the days when I was a child in sailor-suits, I used to learn my tables out of a small book compiled by a gentleman of whose surname all I can remember is an initial W. I can remember quite vividly, however, that his little book was bound in paper covers of a peculiar orange tint that fascinated and allured me—against my will, for in those early days I detested arithmetic as heartily as, later on, I came to detest mathematics. I had already fairly mastered the principles of addition, when the orange-tinted Mr. W. came into my life, and I knew instinctively that nine more was one less in the next ten, and eight more two less. Seven more, however, still demanded physical exertion, and I used to do it on my fingers till my governess exercised her veto, when I resorted craftily to my toes. It was by the aid of my toes, then, that I climbed to the dizzy heights from which Mr. W. was ever seeking to eject me. Many and stern were the struggles in which we engaged. The primer was full of insidious traps for the unwary. It opened, for example, with a sheep in wolf's clothing—a pompous statement concerning the times, which I regarded bitterly as nothing but an underhand attempt to throw dust in my eyes. It ended with a bewildering and superfluously comprehensive "ready reckoner", which informed me how much I would have to pay a servant per annum if I engaged her at (say) the nicely adjusted wage of 5s. 0¾d. per week. But what I objected to above everything else, what I loathed with all the might of my soul, were the tables of weights and measures that occurred in the middle of the volume and had to be learnt off by heart. I still abhor them, still chafe against the laborious hours I spent over them when I might have been looking at the pictures in the B.O.P. or playing tip-and-run under the cherry-tree in the garden. For of what service (I ask myself) has it been to me in all my life to know that ten chains make one furlong, that 30¼ sq. ft. make one rod, pole, or perch, or that five quarters make one wey or load? These tables, of which nine-tenths help nobody but the specialists in liquor or drugs or mangel-wurzels, are crammed into our minds with merciless vigour. Yet there are innumerable terms of weight and measure, employed by ordinary men and women every day of their lives, which not only are never taught in schools, but have never even been standardised by the authorities at all. I do not want to know, and it would not help me to know, how large a rood is or how heavy a hogshead; but I do want to know, and it would often help me to know, how long "half-a-jiffy" is and how far "a step". Then when people told me that they wouldn't be half a jiffy or that it wasn't a step—things they are telling me every day, whereas they never speak to me in terms of degrees and perches—I should be a wiser man and could regulate my arrangements accordingly.

* * *

Let me take the unexplored question of time first. We all know how long it takes to say "knife" and how long it takes to say "Jack Robinson"; but we do not know how many Jack Robinsons there are in a brace of shakes or how many brace of shakes it takes to make two twos. For myself, I am not even certain whether a brace of shakes lasts longer or not so long as two twos, with the result that I am often hopelessly at sea. It may be objected that all these are slang phrases; but are they not the measures of time most commonly used among the plebs today, and do they not, on that ground alone, demand immediate standardisation? Is it not a fact that people are every day taking advantage of the prevailing slovenliness and lack of system by expanding the elastic interpretation of these terms to their own advantage? Would not the greengrocers cheat you if there were no standard dry measure, and the price cards ran: "3*d*. for a few grapes" or "A lot of strawberries for 6*d*." ? And do not our friends cheat us now out of valuable time by saying that they won't be two twos when, in reality, they are probably at least sixteen? Something has got to be done. We must decide, once and for all, exactly how many trices there are in a day, how many ticks in a lunar month. The officials make no stir. In desperation, then, I have taken the matter into my own hands. I may have attained only an approximation to accuracy. But the whole system of weights and measures is, after all, based on convention—it is simply a matter of agreeing that things shall be so—and my figures may, therefore, be allowed to stand. Here, then, for the benefit of the schoolmasters, is the new timetable, as nearly as I am able to gauge it.

3 knives make 1 Jack Robinson.
3 Jack Robinsons make 1 trice.
2 trices make 1 twinkling.
5 twinklings make 2 twos or 1 brace of shakes.
4 twos or 2 brace of shakes make 1 shake, tick, or jiffy.
4 shakes, ticks, or jiffies make ½ a mo.
3 half-a-mo's make 1 mo.
4 ¼ half-a-mo's make 1 instant.
2 instants make 1 sec.

It will be observed that a brace of shakes is shorter than a shake, and that it takes 1 ½ mo's to make a mo. These apparent absurdities are based on a close observation of the current acceptation of the terms. It is worth noting that there are 1,020 twinklings in a sea, and that you can say "knife" 180 times a jiffy.

★ ★ ★

Then there is the question of distance. When I am told that it is only "a step" to such-and-such a place, how am I to know just what this means? How far is a stone's throw? How far a "tidy stretch"? The table should run something after this fashion:

12 steps make 1 stone's throw.

12 stones' throws make 1 goodish way.

2 goodish ways make 1 tidy stretch.

12 tidy stretches make 1 easy walking distance of sea.

With these two tables accepted in all the schools, we should begin to find education of some practical value. I picture the examination paper of the future:

Q. Turn 12 easy walking distances of sea, 10 tidy stretches, and 3 goodish ways into steps.

Or:—

Q. If a man can walk 10 stones' throws 7 steps in 2 secs. 3 ticks and a brace of shakes, how far will he walk before you can say "Jack Robinson"?

* * *

Of course, all this is merely an indication of the line I should like to see developed. We ought all to know how many sips there are in a gulp, how many tipsies in a drunk, how many dashes in a damn, how many licks and promises in a wash, how many snores in a nap and naps in a trance. Before we can remedy the pest of mutual misunderstandings with which our conversation is beset, it is imperative that all these questions should be satisfactorily answered; and I sincerely trust that when the next General Election comes on—and the other side says (I understand) that it will come on very soon—everybody who has read this paper will insist upon his candidate making the Rationalisation of our Weights and Measures Tables an essential element of his platform.

H. F.

253

How to Rig & Sail Small Boats

To have the tiller in one's own hands and feel competent, under all ordinary circumstances, to bring a boat safely into port, gives the same zest and excitement to a sail (only in a far greater degree) that the handling of the whip and reins over a lively trotter does to a drive.

Knowing and feeling this, it was my intention to devote a couple of chapters to telling how to sail a boat; but through the kind courtesy of the editor of *The American Canoeist*, I am able to do much better by giving my readers a talk on this subject by one whose theoretical knowledge and practical experience renders him pre-eminently fit to give reliable advice and counsel. The following is what Mr Charles Ledyard Norton, editor of the above-mentioned journal, says:

"Very many persons seem to ignore the fact that a boy who knows how to manage a gun is, upon the whole, less likely to be shot than one who is a bungler through ignorance, or that a good swimmer is less likely to be drowned than a poor one. Such, however, is the truth beyond question. If a skilled sportsman is now and then shot, or an expert swimmer drowned, the fault is not apt to be his own, and if the one who is really to blame had received proper training, it is not likely that the accident would have occurred at all. The same argument holds good with regard to the management of boats, and the author is confident that he merits the thanks of mothers, whether he receives them or not, for giving their boys a few hints as to practical rigging and sailing.

"In general, there are three ways of learning how to sail boats. First, from the light of nature, which is a poor way; second, from books, which is better; and third, from another fellow who knows how, which is best of all. I will try to make this article as much like the other fellow and as little bookish as possible.

"Of course, what I shall say in these few paragraphs will be of small use to those who live within reach of the sea or some big lake, and have always been used to boats; but there are thousands and thousands of boys and men who never saw the sea, nor even set eyes on a sail, and who have not the least idea how to make the wind take them where they want to go. I once knew some young men from the interior who went down to the seaside and hired a boat, with the idea that they had nothing to do but hoist the sail and be blown wherever they liked. The result was that they performed a remarkable set of manoeuvres within sight of the boathouse, and at last went helplessly out to sea and had to be sent after and brought back, when they were well laughed at for their performances, and had reason to consider themselves lucky for having gotten off so cheaply.

"The general principles of sailing are as simple as the national game of 'one ole cat'. That is to say, if the wind always blew moderately and steadily, it would be as easy and as safe to sail a boat as it is to drive a steady old family horse of good and regular habits. The fact, however, is that winds and currents are variable in their moods, and as capable of unexpected freaks as the most fiery of unbroken colts; but when properly watched and humoured they are tractable and fascinating playmates and servants.

"Now, let us come right down to first principles. Take a bit of pine board, sharpen it at one end, set up a mast about a quarter of the length of the whole piece from the bow, fit on a square piece of stiff paper or card for a sail, and you are ready for action. Put this in the water, with the sail set squarely across (A, Fig. 1), and she will run off before the wind—which is supposed to be blowing as indicated by the

255

arrow—at a good rate of speed. If she does not steer herself, put a small weight near the stern, or square end; or, if you like, arrange a thin bit of wood for a rudder.

Fig. 1

"Probably the first primeval man who was born with nautical instincts discovered this fact, and, using a bush for a sail, greatly astonished his fellow primevals by winning some prehistoric regatta. But that was all he could do. He was as helpless as a balloonist is in mid-air. He could go, but he could not get back, and we may be sure that ages passed away before the possibility of sailing to windward was discovered.

"Now, put up, or 'step', another mast and sail like the first, about as far from the stern as the first is from the bow. Turn the two sails at an angle of forty-five degrees across the boat (B or C, Fig. 1), and set her adrift. She will make considerable progress across the course of the wind, although she will at the same time drift with it. If she wholly refuses to go in the right direction, place a light weight on her bow, so that she will be a little 'down by the head', or move the aftermost mast and sail a little nearer to the stern.

"The little rude affair thus used for experiment will not actually make any progress to windward, because she is so light that she moves sidewise almost as easily as she does forward. With a larger, deeper boat, and with sails which can be set at any angle, the effect will be different. So long as the wind presses against the after side of the sail, the boat will move through the water in the direction of the least resistance, which is forward. A square sail, having the mast in the middle, was easiest to begin with for purposes of explanation; but now we will change to a 'fore-and-aft' rig—that is, one with the mast at the forward edge or 'luff' of the sail, as in Fig. 2.

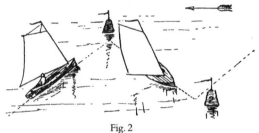

Fig. 2

Suppose the sail to be set at the angle shown, and the wind blowing as the arrow points. The boat cannot readily move sidewise, because of the broadside resistance; she does not move backward, because the wind is pressing on the aftermost side of the sail. So she very naturally moves forward. When she nears buoy No. 1, the helmsman moves the 'tiller', or handle of the rudder, toward the sail. This causes the boat to turn her head toward buoy No. 2, the sail swings across to the other side of the boat and fills on that side, which now in turn becomes the aftermost, and she moves toward buoy No. 2 nearly at right angles to her former course. Thus, through a series of zigzags, the wind is made to work against itself. This operation is called 'tacking', or 'working to windward', and the act of turning, as at the buoys No.1 and No. 2, is called 'going about'.

"It will be seen, then, that the science of sailing lies in being able to manage a boat with her head pointing at any possible angle to or from the wind. Nothing but experience can teach one all the niceties of the art, but a little aptitude and address will do to start with, keeping near shore and carrying little sail.

Simplest Rig Possible

"I will suppose that the reader has the use of a broad, flat-bottomed boat without any rudder. (See Fig. 3.) She cannot be made to work like a racing yacht under canvas, but lots of fun can be had out of her.

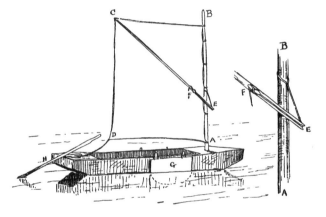

Fig. 3

"Do not go to any considerable expense at the outset. Procure an old sheet, or an old hay-cover, six or eight feet square, and experiment with that before spending your money on new material. If it is a sheet, and somewhat weakly in its texture, turn all the edges in and sew them, so that it shall not give way at the hems. At each corner sew on a few inches of strong twine, forming loops at the angles. Sew on, also, eyelets or small loops along the edge which is intended for the luff of the sail, so that it can be laced to the mast.

"You are now ready for your spars, namely, a mast and a

'sprit', the former a couple of feet longer than the luff of the sail, and the latter to be cut off when you find how long you want it. Let these spars be of pine, or spruce, or bamboo—as light as possible, especially the sprit. An inch and a half diameter will do for the mast, and an inch and a quarter for the sprit, tapering to an inch at the top. To 'step' the mast, bore a hole through one of the thwarts (seats) near the bow, and make a socket or step on the bottom of the boat, just under the aforesaid hole—or if anything a trifle farther forward—to receive the foot of the mast. This will hold the mast upright, or with a slight 'rake' aft.

"Lace the luff of the sail to the mast so that its lower edge will swing clear by a foot or so of the boat's sides. Make fast to the loop at D a stout line, ten or twelve feet long. This is called the 'sheet', and gives control of the sail. The upper end of the sprit, C, E, is trimmed so that the loop at C will fit over it but not slip down. The lower end is simply notched to receive a short line called a 'snotter', as shown in the detailed drawing at the right of the cut (Fig. 3). It will be readily understood that, when the sprit is pushed upward in the direction of C, the sail will stand spread out. The line is placed in the notch at E and pulled up until the sail sets properly, when it is made fast to a cleat or to a cross piece at F. This device is in common use and has its advantages, but a simple loop for the foot of the sprit to rest in is more easily made and will do nearly as well. H is an oar for steering. Having thus described the simplest rig possible, we may turn our attention to more elegant and elaborate but not always preferable outfits.

Leg-of-Mutton Rig

"One of the prettiest and most convenient rigs for a small boat is known as the 'leg-of-mutton sharpie rig' (Fig. 4). The sail is triangular, and the sprit, instead of reaching to its upper corner, stands nearly at right angles to the mast. It is held in position at the mast by the devices already described. This rig has the advantage of keeping the

Leg of-mutton Rig

Fig. 4 Leg-of-mutton Rig

whole sail flatter than any other, for the end of the sprit cannot 'kick up', as the phrase goes, and so the sail holds all the wind it receives.

"Fig. 5 shows a device, published for the first time in the *St Nicholas Magazine* for September, 1880, which enables the sailor to step and unstep his mast, and hoist or lower his sail without leaving his seat—a matter of great importance when the boat is light and tottlish, as in the case of that most beautiful of small craft, the modern canoe, where the navigator sits habitually amidships. The lower mast (A, B, Fig. 5) stands about two and a half feet above the deck. It is fitted at the head with a metal ferrule and pin, and just above the deck with two half-cleats or other similar devices (A). The topmast (C, D) is fitted at F with a stout ring, and has double halyards (E) rove through or around its foot. The lower mast being in position (see lower part of Fig. 5), the canoeist desiring to make sail brings the boat's head to the wind, takes the top-mast with the sail loosely furled in one hand, and the halyards in the other. It is easy for him by raising this mast, without leaving his seat, to pass the halyards one on each side of the lower mast and let them fall into place close to the deck under the half-cleats at A. Then, holding the halyards taut enough to keep them in position, he will hook the topmast ring over the pin in the lower mast-head and haul away (see top part of Fig. 5). The mast will rise into place, where it is made fast. A collar of leather,

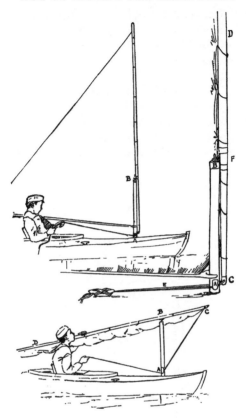

Fig. 5 A New Device

or a knob of some kind, placed on the topmast just below the ring, will act as a fulcrum when the halyards are hauled taut, and keep the mast from working to and fro.

"The advantages of the rig are obvious. The mast can be raised without standing up, and in case of necessity the halyards can be let go and the mast and sail unshipped and stowed below with the greatest ease and expedition, leaving only the short lower mast standing. A leg-of-mutton sail with a common boom along the foot is shown in the cut as

261

the most easily illustrated application of the device, but there is no reason why it may not be applied to a sail of different shape, with a sprit instead of a boom, and a square instead of a pointed head.

The Latteen Rig

is recommended only for boats which are 'stiff'—not tottlish, that is. The fact that a considerable portion of the sail projects forward of the mast renders it awkward in case of a sudden shift of wind. Its most convenient form is shown in Fig. 6.

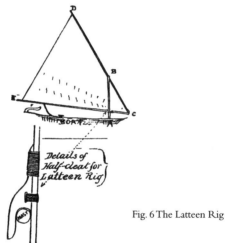

Fig. 6 The Latteen Rig

The arrangement for shipping and unshipping the yard is precisely like that shown in Fig. 5—a short lower mast with a pin at the top and a ring fitted to the yard. It has a boom at the foot which is joined to the yard at C by means of a hook or a simple lashing, having sufficient play to allow the two spars to shut up together like a pair of dividers. The boom (C, E) has, where it meets the short lower mast, a half cleat or jaw, shown in detail at the bottom of the cut (Fig. 95), the circle representing a cross section of the mast. This should be lashed to the boom, as screws or bolts would weaken it. To take in sail, the boatman brings the boat to the wind, seizes the boom and draws it toward him. This disengages it from the mast. He then shoves it forward, when the yard (C, D) falls of its own weight into his hands, and can be at once lifted clear of the lower mast. To keep the sail flat, it is possible to arrange a collar on the lower mast so that the boom, when once in position, cannot slip upward and suffer the sail to bag.

The Cat-Rig,

so popular on the North Atlantic coast, is indicated in Fig. 2. The spar at the head of the sail is called a 'gaff', and, like the boom, it fits the mast with semicircular jaws. The sail is hoisted and lowered by means of halyards rove through a block near the mast-head. The mast is set in the bows—'chock up in the eyes of her', as a sailor would say. A single leg-of-mutton sail will not work in this position, because the greater part of its area is too far forward of amidships. No rig is handier or safer than this in working to windward; but off the wind—running before, or nearly before it, that is—the weight of mast and sail, and the pressure of the wind at one side and far forward, make the boat very difficult and dangerous to steer. Prudent boatmen often avoid doing so by keeping the wind on the quarter and, as it were, taking to leeward.

"This suggests the question of 'jibing', an operation always to be avoided if possible. Suppose the wind to be astern, and the boat running nearly before it. It becomes necessary to change your course toward the side on which the sail is drawing. The safest way is to turn at first in the opposite direction, put the helm 'down' (toward the sail), bring the boat up into the wind, turn her entirely around, and stand off on the new tack. This, however, is not always possible. Hauling in the sheet until the sail fills on the other side is 'jibing'; but when this happens it goes over with a rush that sometimes carries mast and sheet or upsets the boat; hence the operation should be first undertaken in a light wind. It is necessary to know how to do it, for sometimes a sail insists upon jibing very unexpectedly, and it is best to be prepared for such emergencies.

How to Make a Sail

"For the sails of such boats as are considered in this paper, there is no better material than unbleached twilled cotton sheeting. It is to be had two and a half or even three yards wide. In cutting out your sail, let the selvedge be at the 'leech', or aftermost edge. This, of course, makes it necessary to cut the luff and foot 'bias', and they are very likely to stretch in the making, so that the sail will assume a different shape from what was intended. To avoid this, baste the hem carefully before sewing, and 'hold in' a little to prevent fulling. It is a good plan to tack the material on the floor before cutting, and mark the outline of the sail with pencil. Stout tape stitched along the bias edges will make a sure thing of it, and the material can be cut, making due allowance for the hem. Better take feminine advice on this process. The hems should be half an inch deep all around, selvedge and all, and it will do no harm to reinforce them with cord if you wish to make a thoroughly good piece of work.

"For running-rigging, nothing is better than laid or braided cotton cord, such as is used for awnings and sash-cords. If this is not easily procured, any stout twine will answer. It can be doubled and twisted as often as necessary. The smallest manila rope is rather stiff and unmanageable for such light sails as ours.

"In fitting out a boat of any kind, iron, unless galvanized, is to be avoided as much as possible, on account of its liability to rust. Use brass or copper instead.

Hints to Beginners

"Nothing has been said about reefing thus far, because small boats under the management of beginners should not be afloat in a 'reefing breeze'. Reefing is the operation of reducing the spread of sail when the wind becomes too fresh. If you will look at Fig. 6 you will see rows of short marks on the sail above the boom. These are 'reef-points'—bits of line about a foot long passing through holes in the sail, and knotted so that they will not slip. In reefing, the sail is lowered and that portion of it between the boom and the reef-points is gathered together, and the points are tied around both it and the boom. When the lower row of points is used it is a single reef. Both rows together are a double reef.

"Make your first practical experiment *with a small sail and with the wind blowing toward the shore.* Row out a little way, and then sail in any direction in which you can make the boat go, straight back to shore if you can, with the sail out nearly at right angles with the boat. Then try running along shore with the sheet hauled in a little, and the sail on the side nearest the shore. You will soon learn what your craft can do, and will probably find that she will make very little, if any, headway to windward. This is partly because she slides sidewise over the water. To prevent it you may use a 'lee-board'—namely, a broad board hung over the side of the boat (G, Fig. 3). This must be held by stout lines, as the strain upon it is very heavy. It should be placed a little forward of the middle of the boat. It must be on the side away from the wind—the lee side—and must be shifted when you go about. Keels and centre-boards are permanent contrivances for the same purpose, but a lee-board answers very well as a makeshift, and is even used habitually by some canoeists and other boatmen.

"In small boats it is sometimes desirable to sit amidships, because sitting in the stern raises the bow too high out of water; steering may be done with an oar over the lee side, or with 'yoke-lines' attached to a cross piece on the rudder-head, or even to the tiller. In this last case, the lines must be rove through rings or pulleys at the sides of the boat opposite the end of the tiller. When the handle of the oar (H, Fig. 3)—or the tiller (F, Fig. 6) if a rudder is used—is pushed to the right, the boat will turn to the left, and *vice versa.* The science of steering consists in knowing when to push and how much to push—very simple, you see, in the statement, but not always so easy in practice.

"The sail should be so adjusted in relation to the rest of the boat that, when the sheet is hauled close in and made fast, the boat, if left to herself, will point her head to the wind like a weather-cock, and drift slowly astern. If it is found that the sail is so far forward that she will not do this, the fault may be remedied by stepping the mast further aft, or by rigging a small sail near the stern. This is called a 'dandy', or 'steering-sail', and is especially convenient in a boat whose size or arrangement necessitates sitting amidships. It may be rigged like the mainsail, and when its sheet is once made fast will ordinarily take care of itself in tacking.

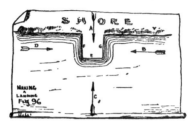

Fig. 7

"Remember that, if the wind freshens or a squall strikes you, the position of safety is with the boat's head to the wind. When in doubt what to do, push the helm down (toward the sail) and haul in the slack of the sheet as the boat comes up into the wind. If she is moving astern, or will not mind her helm—and of course she will not if she is not moving—pull her head around to the wind with an oar, and experiment cautiously until you find which way you can make her go.

"In making a landing, always calculate to have the boat's head as near the wind as possible when she ceases to move. This whether you lower your sail or not.

"Thus, if the wind is off shore, as shown at A, Fig. 7, land at F or G, with the bow toward the shore. If the wind is from the direction of B, land at E with the bow toward B, or at F; if at the latter, the boom will swing away from the wharf and permit you to lie alongside. If the wind is from D, reverse these positions. If the wind comes from the direction of C, land either at F or G, with the bow pointing off shore.

"If you have no one to tell you what to do, you will have to feel your way slowly and learn by experience; but if you have nautical instincts you will soon make your boat do what you wish her to do as far as she is able. *But first learn to swim before you try to sail a boat.*"

Volumes have been written on the subject treated in these few pages, and it is not yet exhausted. The hints here given are safe ones to follow, and will, it is hoped, be of service to many a young sailor in many a corner of the world.

ON GARDENS & GARDENING

The English Garden

JUST before I started home after my recent series of broadcast talks in America, the American people asked me to give a special talk about England, a request to which I acceded the more willingly because I feel that many visitors fail to see the true England.

And in my endeavour to interpret England aright I said this: "If you want to reach the Englishman's heart most quickly, just lean over the gate and praise his garden."

It is indeed much truer to say that we are a race of gardeners than that we are a nation of shopkeepers. Many of us are bad shopkeepers, but practically every Englishman is a good gardener.

This national love of gardens springs from our national love of beauty. Much more than other men is the Englishman susceptible to sweet scents and harmonious blends of colour in his landscapes. He is not impressed by size. What he likes is a rose-plot of his own, where he can watch the results of his own exertion and enterprise.

Whenever I visit a strange house I find that my host and hostess are always more anxious for my opinion on their garden than on their library or their furniture. That is because the furniture and books were not of their own making, whereas the garden usually is.

They have a definite say in the choice of what shall bloom here, and the shapes of this flower-bed and that. More often than not they have dug up the soil themselves, freed the ground of weeds themselves, and planted the seeds and bulbs themselves. A back-breaking job digging, but a marvellous cure for most of the ills that flesh is heir to. It induces the right sort of physical tiredness, and dispels all worry.

271

It is its own reward, quite apart from the reward of seeing two blades grow where one grew before, or being able to conjure colour, scent and beauty out of an overgrown cabbage-patch of ugliness.

Gardening is both the purest and the most disinterested of human pleasure, for in giving pleasure to yourself you give pleasure to all passers-by.

How often do I find myself recalling pleasant haunts of my youth by the flowers that I associate with these places, cottage-gardens in Devon riotously flamboyant with hollyhocks and giant sunflowers, peonies and asters, sweet peas, and roses clustering over the porch.

Gardening is the most democratic of pleasures, for by singular good fortune the loveliest flowers are the most prolific and the cheapest. No flowers give a happier augury that warmer days are coming than the dancing daffodils.

No flowers give a sweeter sense of old-world homeliness than mignonette, wallflowers and sweet-williams. No flower is more graceful than London Pride, more glowing than a marigold, or more calculated to fill the home with happiness than an English rose, and all these are cheap, prolific, and easy to grow.

There is too the symbolic significance of our flowers: "Pansies, that's for remembrance." How often the sight of a simple flower, like a geranium or night-scented stock, has the power to revive most poignant memories that we had thought to be long since buried. How the scent of an early bunch of violets in a city street can take us back on the instant to the garden in the country that we loved long since and lost awhile.

Each month sees the garden put on a fresh panoply. There is the panoply of blue in June when the Canterbury Bells, lupins and delphiniums turn the garden into the Mediterranean Sea. There is the golden panoply of the autumn, and the chill purity of the fresh snowdrops and crocuses of earliest Spring.

There is a peculiar delight in eating peas that you yourself picked and potatoes that you have yourself dug. A garden is only half a garden that is limited to the cultivation of flowers, just as a life is only half a life that is limited to the cultivation of the aesthetic. It is the happy combination of the utilitarian with the beautiful that makes gardening so dear to the average Englishman.

Every evening in the summer, every Saturday afternoon throughout the year, you see city men released from bondage with pitchfork and hoe, barrow and spade setting out to conquer and beautify the land that is entirely their own.

Often they scowl and pretend that they regard it as a further slavery, but in their hearts they are singing, because they are really back to childhood days again, planning a brave new world, here a rock garden, there a stream, here a pool and there a trim lawn.

The explorer and prospector in man at last finds full scope in his garden. That is why life in a flat is to so many men like life to a bird with clipped wings; why life in a flat for children is almost a negation of life altogether; for children, no less than dogs, need room to roam, and the street is no fit place either for dog or child.

Indeed, childhood recollections are more bound up in gardens than anything else, and certainly children owe more to days spent climbing trees in the orchard, making caves under the laurel bushes, watching their own beds of mustard and cress and radishes grow, and helping to pick strawberries, gooseberries, raspberries and beans than to any other single influence at that time.

One may forgive a man who is unable to appreciate music, and blind to the appeal of the great masters of painting, but the man who fails to find a genuine happiness in the sight of a garden and fails to desire to cultivate it, is at least as suspect as the man who does not like dogs.

The great gardens of England so generously thrown open to the public through the summer to help the Queen's nurses, never fail to fill the foreigner with an admiration that surpasses even the admiration he feels for our landscape.

And certainly one of the first things that the average Englishman would do on winning the Irish sweep would be to buy a house containing one of those superb examples of the loveliness that is our national heritage.

But the little gardens of England are no less miraculous. Glance out of any railway carriage window and see what miracles men of limited means and limited accommodation have achieved with a plot of earth about as big as a billiard table.

Unemployed men have turned the arid wilderness of a deserted factory site into a blossoming rose, and men whose lot is cast in an area of chimney pots and squalid streets have contrived to bring an atmosphere of sweetness and light where both were sadly lacking.

But most of us are neither rich enough to own a garden as remarkable as that at Lowther Castle, nor poor enough to have to rely on a window-box for all our colour and scent.

A garden of some sort is within the reach of pretty well everybody. It is usually just laziness or ignorance that prevents us from getting that meed of enjoyment that is our right.

There cannot be too much colour, too many sweet scents, or too many lovely curves in the world. Beauty always serves to increase beauty.

Our gardens serve as perpetual reminders of that happy fact.

S. P. B. Mais.

Of Gardens

GOD Almighty first planted a garden: and, indeed, it is the purest of human pleasures. It is the greatest refreshment to the spirits of man; without which, buildings and palaces are but gross handy-works: and a man shall ever see that when ages grow to civility and elegancy, men come to build stately, sooner than to garden finely; as if gardening were the greater perfection. I do hold it, in the royal ordering of gardens, there ought to be gardens for all the months in the year: in which, severally, things of beauty may be then in season. For December, and January, and the latter part of November, you must take such things as are green all winter; holly; ivy; bays; juniper; cypress trees; yew; pine-apple-trees; fir trees; rosemary; lavender; periwinkle, the white, the purple, and the blue; germander; flags; orange trees; lemon trees; and myrtles, if they be stoved; and sweet marjoram warm set. There followeth, for the latter part of January and February, the mezereon tree, which then blossoms; crocus vernus, both the yellow and the grey; primroses; anemones; the early tulip; hyacinthus orientalis; chamaïris; fritellaria. For March, there come violets, especially the single blue, which are the earliest; the yellow daffodil; the daisy; the almond-tree in blossom, the peach-tree in blossom; the cornelian-tree in blossom; sweet-briar. In April follow the double white violet; the wallflower, the stockgilliflower, the cowslip; flower-de-luces, and lilies of all natures; rosemary-flowers; the tulip; the double piony, the pale daffodil, the French honeysuckle, the cherry-tree in blossom, the damascene and plumb trees in blossom, the whitethorn in leaf, the lilac-tree. In May and June come pinks of all sorts;

especially the blush pink; roses of all kinds, except the musk, which comes later; honeysuckles, strawberries, bugloss, columbine, the French marigold, flos Africanus, cherry-tree in fruit, ribes, figs in fruit, rasps, vine flowers, lavender in flowers, the sweet satyrian, with the white flower; herba muscaria, lilium convallium, the apple-tree in blossom. In July come gilliflowers of all varieties, musk roses, the lime-tree in blossom, early pears and plums in fruit, gennitings codlins. In August come plums of all sorts in fruit; pears, apricots, berberries, filberts, musk melons, monkshoods of all colours. In September come grapes, apples, poppey of all colours, peaches, melo-cotones, nectarines, cornelians, wardens, quinces. In October and the beginning of November come services, medlars, bullaces, roses cut or removed to come late, holly-oaks, and such like. These particulars are for the climate of London; but my meaning is perceived that you may have *ver perpetuum*, as the place affords.

And because the breath of flowers is far sweeter in the air (where it comes and goes like the warbling of musick) than in the hand, therefore nothing is more fit for that delight than to know what be the flowers and plants that do best perfume the air. Roses damask and red, are fast flowers of their smells; so that you may walk by a whole row of them and find nothing of their sweetness; yea, though it be in a morning's dew. Bays likewise yield no smell as they grow; rosemary little; nor sweet marjoram. That which above all others yields the sweetest smell in the air is the violet, especially the white double violet which comes twice a year; about the middle of April, and about Bartholomew-tide. Next to that is the musk-rose; then the strawberry leaves dying, which yield a most excellent cordial smell. Then the flower of the vines; it is a little dust, like the dust of a bent, which grows upon the cluster, in the first coming forth: then sweet briar, then wallflowers, which are very delightful to be set under a parlour or lower chamber window. Then pinks and gilliflowers, especially the matted pink and clove gilliflower: then the flowers of the lime-tree: then the honeysuckles, so they be somewhat afar off. Of bean flowers I speak not, because they are field flowers. But those which perfume the air most delightfully, not passed by as the rest, but being trodden upon and crushed, are three, that is, burnet, wild thyme, and water mints. Therefore, you are to set whole alleys of them to have the pleasure when you walk or tread.

For gardens (speaking of those which are prince-like, as we have done of buildings), the contents ought not well to be under thirty acres of ground, and to be divided into three parts; a green in the entrance; a heath or desert in the going forth; and the main garden in the midst; besides alleys on both sides. And I like well, that four acres of ground be assigned to the green, six to the heath, four and four to either side, and twelve to the main garden. The green hath two pleasures; the one, because nothing is more pleasant to the eye than green grass kept finely shorn; the other, because it will give you a fair alley in the mids; by which you may go in front upon a stately hedge, which is to inclose the garden. But, because the alley will be long, and in great heat of the year, or day, you ought not to buy the shade in the garden by going in the sun through the green; therefore you are of either side the green to plant a covert alley, upon carpenter's work, about twelve foot in height, by which you may go in shade into the garden. As for the making of knots, or figures, with divers coloured earths, that they may lie under the windows of the house, on that side which the garden stands, they be but toys; you may see as good sights many times in tarts. The garden is best to be square, encompassed on all the four sides with a stately arched hedge: the arches to be upon pillars of carpenter's work, of some ten foot high and six foot broad: and the spaces between of the same dimension with the breadth of the arch. Over the arches let there be an entire hedge of some four foot high, framed also upon carpenter's work: and upon the upper hedge, over every arch, a little turret with a belly, enough to receive a cage of birds: and over every space, between the arches, some other little figure, with broad plates of round colour'd glass, gilt, for the sun to play upon. But this hedge I intend to be raised upon a bank, not steep, but gently slope, of some six foot, set all with flowers. Also, I understand, that this square of the garden should not be the whole breadth of the ground, but to leave on either side ground enough for diversity of side alleys; unto which the two covert alleys of the green may deliver you; but there must be no alleys with hedges at either end of this great inclosure; not at the hither end for letting your prospect upon this fair hedge from the green; nor, at the further end, for letting your prospect from the hedge, through the arches, upon the heath.

For the ordering of the ground within the great hedge, I leave it to variety of device; advising, nevertheless, that whatsoever form you cast it into, first it be not too busy or full of work: wherein I, for my part, do not like images cut out in juniper or other garden stuff; they be for children. Little low hedges, round, like welts, with some pretty pyramids, I like well; and in some places fair columns upon frames of carpenter's work. I would also have the alleys spacious and fair. You may have closer alleys upon the side grounds, but none in the main garden. I wish also in the very middle a fair mount, with three ascents and alleys, enough for four to walk abreast; which I would have to be perfect circles, without any bulwarks or embossments; and the whole mount to be thirty foot high; and some fine banqueting house, with some chimneys neatly cast, and without too much glass.

For fountains, they are a great beauty and refreshment; but pools mar all, and make the garden unwholesome and full of flies and frogs. Fountains I intend to be of two natures: the one that sprinkleth or spouteth water; the other a fair receipt of water, of some thirty or forty foot square, but without fish, or slime, or mud. For the first, the ornaments of images gilt, or of marble, which are in use, do well: but the main matter is, so to convey the water as it never stay, either in the bowls or in the cistern; that the water be never by rest discoloured, green, or red, or the like, or gather any mossiness or putrefaction. Besides that, it is to be cleansed every day by the hand. Also some steps up to it, and some fine pavement about it, doth well. As for the other kind of fountain, which we may call a bathing pool, it may admit much curiosity and beauty, wherewith we will not trouble ourselves; as, that the bottom be finely paved, and with images; the sides likewise, and withal embellished with coloured glass, and such things of lustre, encompassed also with fine rails of low statues. But the main point is the same which we mentioned in the former kind of fountain; which is, that the water be in perpetual motion, fed by a water higher than the pool, and delivered into it by fair spouts, and then discharged away under ground by some equality of bores, that it stay little. And for fine devices, of arching water without spilling, and making it rise in several forms (of feathers, drinking glasses, canopies, and the like), they be pretty things to look on, but nothing to health and sweetness.

For the heath, which was the third part of our plot, I wish it to be framed, as much as may be, to a natural wildness. Trees I would have none in it; but some thickets, made only of sweetbriar and honeysuckle, and some wild vine amongst; and the ground set with violets, strawberries, and primroses. For these are sweet, and prosper in the shade. And these to be in the heath, here and there, not in any order. I like also little heaps, in the nature of molehills (such as are in wild heaths) to be set, some with wild thyme, some with pinks, some with germander that gives a good flower to the eye, some with periwinkle, some with violets, some with strawberries, some with cowslips, some with daisies, some with red roses, some with lilium convallium, some with sweetwilliams red, some with bear's-foot, and the like low flowers, being withal sweet and sightly. Part of which heaps to be with standards of little bushes pricked upon their top, and part without. The standards to be roses, juniper, holly, berberries (but here and there, because of the smell of their blossom), red currans, goosberries, rosemary, bays, sweetbriar, and such like. But these standards to be kept with cutting, that they grow not out of course.

For the side grounds you are to fill them with variety of alleys, private, to give a full shade, some of them wheresoever the sun be. You are to frame some of them likewise for shelter, that when the wind blows sharp, you may walk as in a gallery. And those alleys must be likewise hedged at both ends to keep out the wind; and these closer alleys must be ever finely gravelled, and no grass, because of going wet. In many of these alleys, likewise, you are to set fruit-trees of all sorts; as well upon the walls as in ranges. And this would be generally observed that the borders wherein you plant your fruit-trees be fair and large, and low, and not steep; and set with fine flowers, but thin and sparingly, lest they deceive the trees. At the end of both the side grounds I would have a mount of some pretty height, leaving the wall of the enclosure breast high, to look abroad into the fields.

For the main garden I do not deny but there should be some fair alleys, ranged on both sides with fruit-trees and some pretty tufts of fruit-trees, and arbours with seats set in some decent order; but these to be by no means set too thick, but to leave the main garden so as it be not close, but the air open and free. For, as for shade, I would have you rest upon the alleys of the side grounds, there to walk, if you be disposed, in the heat of the year or day; but to make account that the main garden is for the more temperate parts of the year; and in the heat of summer, for the morning and the evening, or overcast days.

For aviaries, I like them not, except they be of that largeness as they may be turffed, and have living plants and bushes set in them, that the birds may have more scope, and natural nestling, and that no foulness appear in the floor of the aviary. So I have made a platform of a princely garden, partly by precept, partly by drawing; not a model, but some general lines of it; and in this I have spared for no cost. But it is nothing for great princes that, for the most part taking advice with workmen, with no less cost, set their things together; and sometimes add statues and such things for state and magnificence, but nothing to the true pleasure of a garden.

Francis Bacon

The Fruit Garden

✳

THERE is no garden which cannot be made to grow fruit, and there is hardly any garden where fruit will not grow really well if care is taken in the preparation of the soil. Even in the little "back-yard" garden of the older town districts, where soot and grime seem such a nuisance, fruit trees will grow and flourish quite well, though the fruit is perhaps not so appetising as when grown in the purer air of country districts. At the same time, fruit trees are so ornamental, and because of their dwarf stature they are so suitable for small gardens, that amateur gardeners ought to pay more attention to possibilities in this direction.

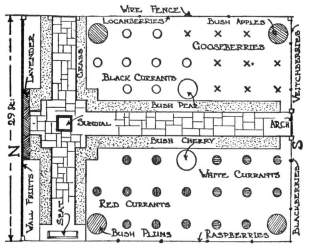

A small fruit garden can be made a decorative garden feature, as shown in this layout.

A standard fruit tree makes an ideal background for a mixed border. It breaks the skyline, and converts a patch of ground from a "glorified allotment on which flowers are grown" to a real garden.

If a flowering tree of any kind is to be included in the garden scheme, it seems a pity that a tree should not be chosen which will not only flower in spring, and carry ornamental foliage in summer, but will bear decorative and profitable fruits in the autumn. Every Nature lover will agree, too, that a tree in winter, outlined in all its naked loveliness against a drifting, cloudy sky, gives character to the landscape as no other feature can. A tree does not altogether change, as seasons pass. Its outline becomes familiar; it ceases to be inanimate and becomes a friend.

WHEN FRUITS FAIL

Quite a number of amateurs have probably been discouraged from growing fruit by hearing of gardens where fruit trees seem to flourish well but do not bear any harvest of fruit. Unless the garden is completely shaded at all times, such as in the case of a garden under, or very close to, tall trees in town districts, a fruit tree could certainly be brought into a healthy-cropping condition and, if possible, the trouble should be traced to its source. It is more than probable that it is due to soil conditions, which can be very simply rectified.

Even in gardens where such trees as apples, cherries, plums and pears cannot find a home some of the other fruits might be grown. For instance, Morello cherries will grow in that most difficult of all positions, on the north side of a tall brick wall. Fan-trained trees grown here would occupy very little garden space and would quickly come into bearing.

CURRANTS ON ROOFS

Loganberries can be grown in the form of a boundary hedge if trained to horizontal wires. I have even heard of successful gooseberries and currants grown as pot plants, cordon trained, on the roofs of town houses, and also of strawberries grown in an ordinary wooden tub; plants were set in holes made in the sides of the tub, while the tub itself was filled with soil into which the roots penetrated. It will therefore be seen that it is only lack of keenness on the part of most amateur gardeners which makes fruit gardens so rare, and those who feel at all inclined to add to the family larder, as well as to their own interest in the garden, and to the general prosperity of the community, by encouraging Nature's generosity need not fear that their plot of ground will not grow fruit.

WHAT TO GROW

The choice of fruits to grow is really the first step in making a fruit garden. With regard to the larger fruit trees, bush trees are the most satisfactory, though standard trees are more ornamental and should be preferred for certain situations. It is advisable, however, for the small orchard to be planted with bush trees, partly because they are easier to prune and spray regularly, and partly because it is easier to gather the fruit from them when it is ripe.

Cordon trees, that is, trees trained so that the flowers, fruit and foliage are all carried on one or two main stems, are frequently used along the sides of paths or against walls where space is very restricted. They are admirable for the purpose, and crop very heavily if they are well trained and cultivated, but the pruning of these trees is a matter for experts (whether amateur or professional), and the novice is advised to ignore this class of tree unless he is prepared to study the subject seriously or to call in the services of an expert about twice a year, in the summer and winter.

The small fruits such as black currants, gooseberries and red currants are grown about five feet apart each way, and can be planted between the bush apples and pears. A small fruit garden is probably best planted with mixed fruits so that a succession and a variety of fruit is available for home use. In the commercial orchard, of course, large acres are devoted to a single variety in order to make the work of pruning, gathering, etc., easier to manage.

SOIL PREPARATION

Any soil that will grow good vegetable crops will grow good fruit. Actually any soil can be brought to this fertile condition by deep digging and manuring. Cold, heavy soils need to be dug to a depth of about two and a half feet in order to break up the soil below and to allow surplus water to drain away. The usual additions to soil to bring it into a normal healthy condition should be made. That is to say light, strawy manure and gritty material of all kinds should be added to clay, and fibrous vegetation should be added to light, sandy soils, together with cow or pig manure, if obtainable. All fruit gardens also need annual dressings of lime.

GREEN MANURING. For the home gardener the small fruit orchard is the only place where green manuring is a practical proposition. This entails the thick sowing of seeds, such as brown mustard or lupin, at the rate of 1 pint to a 10-rod plot, and digging it in as soon as full grown, but before it flowers, thus enriching the ground and rendering it more friable. Friable soil means hard wood, and hard wood results in firmer buds and better crops.

To know whether the soil needs more than an ordinary amount of drainage, a hole three feet in depth should be dug. If water collects in this hole instead of draining away, special precautions should be taken over drainage before any planting is done, to prevent trouble later.

Poor soil will benefit from a good dressing of old stable manure, but fresh manure should not be used at planting time.

PLANTING HINTS

The best time to plant is in late autumn when the leaves are absent from the trees and before the worst of the winter frosts arrive. Actually, fruit trees can be planted at any time during the winter, but if planting is left until rather late in the season it may be that dry weather will occur which would be fatal to the newly-planted trees. No planting should be done when the soil is frosty, and it is far better to

285

heel in the plants, or to store them in a shed, keeping the roots moist, until the weather is suitable for planting. It is best to open out holes for the reception of the roots before the plants arrive from the nursery. The holes should be large enough to allow the roots to be spread out as far as possible almost horizontally. As the tree is put in position, a stake should also be driven in, before the soil is put back into the hole. The roots, as they are spread out, should be examined, and any that are damaged should be cut clearly away. Fine soil will be thrown over the remainder and trodden down firmly before the hole is actually filled in. More treading around the plant will make it firm in the soil, so that it does not sway in the winds. It should be tied immediately to the stake. One important thing to remember is that the stems of fruit trees swell as they grow, and a tie made the first year after planting will probably be too tight the next season.

The planting of all fruits, bush apples, gooseberries and currants, loganberries and even strawberries is on much the same lines; that is to say, the ground must be well dug and well drained. If there is any doubt about drainage, rough material should be put in at the bottom of the deep hole before the soil is filled in again. Also firm planting is essential in all cases, otherwise the roots may be dried out in air pockets in the soil, instead of being in direct contact with moist particles of soil.

FIRST PRUNING

The rule is to prune, not at planting time, but fairly soon afterwards. The reason it is not done at the same time as planting is chiefly that the plant has had one shock, from being moved from nursery to garden, and the pruning would be a double shock, which might prove too much for it. The first pruning should not be too severe, it may be better sometimes to wait until the following winter. But the second season's winter pruning should be drastic, as the more pruning is done while the tree is young, the more likely is it to establish itself and become a strong, healthy specimen. All

standards and bush trees should have their leaders shortened
6 inches or more in the winter after planting, and if the
growth during the first summer seems rather weak, pruning
should be even more severe the following winter; that is to
say, the stems will be cut back to below the point of the first
season's pruning.

SUBSEQUENT PRUNING

It is far better for the amateur gardener to make himself
acquainted with the general principles of pruning than to
worry too much about the particular method of pruning a
particular tree.

The first point to note is that fruit is borne on wood of a
different age, according to the type and variety of tree. For
instance, apples bear fruit on wood that is two years old, after
which the same wood bears fruits from year to year for many
years afterwards. Black currants fruit on stems that have grown
the previous summer, and these stems after fruiting once do not
fruit again. Grapes bear fruit on the current season's growths.

To note these differences with each kind of fruit that is
grown, and to act accordingly, is the real secret of pruning.
For instance, if you are pruning plums, apples, pears, sweet
cherries, or red and white currants, all of which fruit on old
wood, you try to build up a skeleton of main branches, but
whereas with apples you cut to the second *outside* bud of the
laterals to promote outward branching, with plums which
spread too freely you cut to the second inside bud to induce
more upright growth. After the summer growth you cut
back all the young shoots that are not wanted (to extend the
size of the tree) to within about an inch of the old wood.

In the case of the fruits like black currants, raspberries and
loganberries and also the Morello cherry and peaches or
nectarines, where the fruit is carried on the wood that grew
in the previous season, you prune by removing all the wood
that has fruited, leaving only the young shoots to provide the
following year's harvest. This kind of pruning is done
immediately after fruit has been gathered.

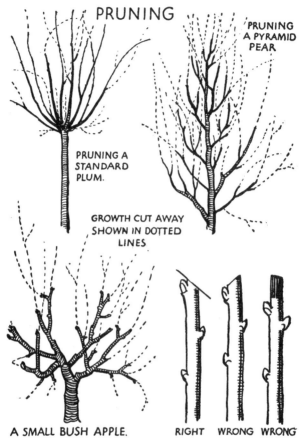

PRUNING

PRUNING
A PYRAMID
PEAR

PRUNING A
STANDARD
PLUM.

GROWTH CUT AWAY
SHOWN IN DOTTED
LINES

A SMALL BUSH APPLE.   RIGHT   WRONG WRONG

Fruit trees need annual pruning to keep them shapely.
Always make the cut towards a bud pointing outwards.

SUMMER PRUNING

Summer pruning, which is the most troublesome to
amateurs, need not be done at all in many cases, and if it is,
is should only be done by those who have made themselves
thoroughly conversant with the reasons for pruning. The

theory of summer pruning is that pinching back the side growths of new wood on the tree will induce the formation of fruit spurs near the base of each stem, that is close the old wood. Instead of these side growths being allowed to grow on until the winter, and to be cut back then, they are pinched off in July about six or nine inches from the old wood. The sap concentrates then in the basal buds, so that the formation of flower buds is encouraged. When winter comes, the pruning is carried out in the normal way; that is to say, the stems are again shortened to just beyond the fruit buds. This type of pruning can only be done with those fruits which regularly make fruit spurs in this way, and not, of course, with such fruits as black currants and raspberries.

One last point about pruning: be very careful to use clean, sharp tools. The damage done by the use of blunt tools or dirty tools cannot afterwards be repaired. It is through carelessness in this matter that diseases and pests find their way into the trees. Also remember that a symmetrical tree is more likely to be healthy than one which is unbalanced. Sun and air reach all the branches if they are well placed, instead of being crowded to one side of the tree, and there is also less likelihood of damage by winds to a tree which is well balanced than in the case of a tree which is lopsided.

PLANTING OF A SMALL FRUIT GARDEN

As a definite scheme for planting a small fruit garden I should recommend a few bush apples, pears and plums, standard cherries, and either loganberries, Morello cherries (fan trained), or other wall-fruits, to cover the walls and fences according to aspect. Bush trees are planted from ten to twelve feet apart. Standard sweet cherries will grow to an enormous size, and as much as twenty-four feet must be left between each.

The first step in planting a fruit garden would be to arrange these larger trees as desired, and as seems most convenient. Bush trees of quickly-maturing type can be chosen to plant between the taller standard trees, so that in years to come, when the tall standard cherries are really at

289

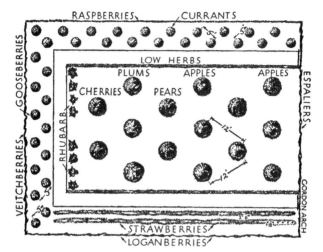

When planting a fruit garden, arrange as far as possible for all the
soft bush fruits to be planted together so that they can
easily be netted against birds.

their best, it may be possible to take out some of the bush
trees altogether, without feeling that it has been a waste of
time to grow them.

HOW STOCK AFFECTS TREES

The age at which a tree comes into bearing depends very
largely on the stock on which it is grafted. By consultation
with the fruit grower from whom the trees are ordered, it is
possible to obtain small bush trees, that will mature quickly,
and provide a good crop of fruit in the first ten years after
planting. These would be used to interplant among varieties
which do not reach their best until the end of the decade,
but which will then need more space.

When the larger trees have been arranged in the fruit
garden, the small bush fruits should be allotted a place. These
must be allowed 5 ft. between the rows. (It is possible to
grow a few vegetable or salad crops between these bushes in
the first two years of their existence, though later the fruits

will occupy the whole of the garden space.) Loganberries and similar berries will be planted about ten feet apart against the fences. Though it is not essential , it is certainly desirable that most of the fruit in a garden should be planted in one section. This makes it possible for a light framework of wood to be erected, over which nets can be stretched during the fruit season, to keep the fruits safe from the attacks of birds. A movable protection is advised, for at other seasons birds do an enormous amount of good in the fruit garden, by devouring insect pests.

REMEMBER THE WHEELBARROW

It is important to allow, in the fruit garden, solid paths or soil tracks over which manure can be wheeled. It is not advisable to plant fruits in grass. The soil should be cultivated round the bole of the tree, for at least five years after planting. It does not seem to harm very old fruit trees if grass grows beneath them, but it has a definitely harmful effect on the health of young trees.

GENERAL HINTS ON MANURING

Cultivation in the fruit garden consists chiefly of keeping down weeds and attending to pruning. Manuring is also important. The condition of a tree can often be judged by the appearance of its leaves. If the leaves have brown edges this indicates lack of potash. Brown, dark centres to the leaves show a need for more phosphatic foods, and undersized leaves of pale colour, show a lack of nitrates in the soil. All fruits need lime annually, and a dressing of potash is also advised.

The most popular fruits in cultivation in the small garden are described in more or less detail in the succeeding pages, together with particular hints as to their cultivation.

APPLES (*Pyrus Malus*). All the apples in cultivation are actually varieties of the common Crab apple. They are probably the most popular of all fruits in the home garden, partly because most varieties can be stored for use as required. They can be grown as ordinary bush trees, or as trained cordons, or espaliers. Standards and half-standards are also obtainable, but these are not so commonly planted, and are not recommended except where an ornamental tree is wanted, for instance, a specimen tree on a lawn.

The best aspect for planting apples (and other fruits) is probably on a slightly northern slope. The reason for this is that frost on the trees in the very early morning is far more harmful if sun shines directly on it, so that it thaws quickly. If it thaws out slowly, frost appears to do little damage. A very low-lying valley is unsuitable for fruit culture of most kinds, but a cold windy hill top is equally unsuitable. If possible, therefore, the site for apples should be on the side of a hill, where there is any preference.

Suitable Soil. Almost any kind of soil is suitable for apple growing. That is to say any kind of soil can be made suitable. Good drainage is absolutely essential as the roots of apples penetrate very deeply. Very chalky sub-soils are possibly less desirable than gravel sub-soils, but actually any kind of soil, if it is deeply dug and suitably manured to make the upper layer of soil porous and friable, will produce good fruit.

In preparing the soil, old decayed stable manure should be used if obtainable, and a good dressing of lime should be given *to every kind of soil* before planting. Chalk is a form of lime that is best suited to gardens where the soil is light and sandy.

The distance apart for apples is according to the type of tree used. Cordons on walls or along side paths are planted 2 feet apart; espaliers are planted 14 feet apart against walls; bush trees are planted 10 to 12 feet apart. (Standards and half-standards would need more room.) Planting should be done in the manner already described, and the trees staked immediately, whatever their kind.

General Cultivation. A newly-planted apple tree is most likely to suffer from the effects of long drought, and to avoid this, a mulch of well-rotted stable manure should be spread over the soil surface round each tree. This also ensures that the tree has a good supply of plant food, so that it makes rapid growth the first season. Stable manure after the first year, is given as required, an annual dressing being usually desirable, until the tree is fully grown.

Regulate Food Supplies. The feeding of apples can be taken as typical of the use of fertilizers all over the fruit garden. The tree must be examined each year to see what amount of new growth it makes, and how it fruits. If a tree makes a large quantity of new stems of healthy appearance, but does not fruit well, it is a sign that it is well supplied with nitrogenous food, but not sufficiently supplied with phosphatic food. If, however, the trees fruit well but make very little new growth, stable manure may be given liberally as this supplies a considerable quantity of nitrogen, and thus promotes the formation of leaf and stem. *All apples should be given a dressing of potash annually*. It is an essential fertilizer for this fruit, and *sulphate of potash* at the rate of one ounce per square yard, or four ounces for each well-established tree, should be applied to the soil annually. It can be given in the form of kainit in November, or pure sulphate of potash (i.e. purified kainit) in spring.

Pruning. When a young tree is supplied from a nursery during the winter months, it is probable that no pruning is required that season, since any that needs to be done will have been done in the nursery. The second winter it should, however, be pruned fairly drastically. As regards subsequent pruning the point to remember is that hard pruning induces vigorous growth. Light pruning only is practised when the tree is growing well, and more fruit then results.

All that the novice needs to do in order to understand the instructions for pruning, is to distinguish between leaders and side shoots, and between fruit and leaf buds. Leaders are the main branches of a tree, that is to say, they are the top, newly-grown parts of these main branches. The side shoots or laterals are the other growths that come from these branches, and these are for the most part pruned back so as to leave the tree with, as it were, a number of cordon stems, radiating from the main trunk.

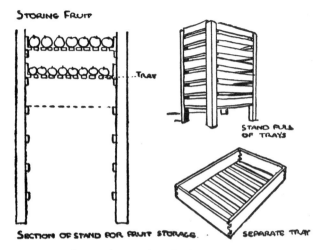

STORING FRUIT

····TRAY

STAND FULL
OF TRAYS

SECTION OF STAND FOR FRUIT STORAGE.   SEPARATE TRAY

Fruit stored in wooden trays through which air can circulate freely
will keep much longer than badly stored crops.

Winter pruning consists in cutting the laterals back to about an inch or two from the old wood. This leaves about four or five buds on the lateral growth. Some of these will develop during the growing season into fresh lateral growths, but some should swell into fruit buds. A fruit bud is, of course, fatter and rounder than a leaf bud.

Pruning in later years consists in repeating this operation, always *leaving the fruit buds and one or two other buds on the laterals*, but cutting away the unwanted ends of the laterals. The leader is treated according to whether an extension of the tree is wanted or not. If the tree is growing healthily, some of the main branches are allowed to remain nearly full length, only the tips being cut off during the winter pruning. When the tree has attained full size the leaders are cut back more severely. The difficulty with apples is that some apples tend to produce fruit buds on the tips of the laterals instead of at the base, near the old wood. As a rule, shortening the laterals in the way described induces the formation of fruit buds near to the old wood, but where these do not readily appear, the laterals are best pruned more lightly, leaving about six buds on them. Fruit buds that are observed at the tops of stems at pruning time are, of course, allowed to remain.

Varieties. The choice of varieties in planting a small fruit garden is rather important, because unless the blossom of each tree can be pollinated, no fruit will set. In some cases the flowers cannot be pollinated unless there is a different variety of the same fruit in flower at the same time. For instance, a Cox's Orange Pippin apple, grown as a single specimen in a garden with no other apple trees near, will crop very poorly, if at all, as this variety is *not self-fertile* (i.e. fruit will not set if the pistil is only pollinated with pollen from its own flowers).

Almost any good catalogue gives full particulars of the varieties which are self-fertile, or non-self-fertile, and the amateur grower is advised to plant, for the most part, the self-fertile kinds, or to be quite certain that he is planting two that will pollinate each other. Self-fertile varieties of apples suitable for planting as single specimens, include "Irish Peach", "Rev W. Wilks", "Lord Derby", "Laxton's Superb" and "Laxton's Epicure".

If a fair-sized fruit orchard is being planned, and a dozen or more varieties are grown, some effort should be made to arrange for a succession of fruit. For instance, "Irish Peach" is ready for gathering in August, but it is not a good apple for keeping. "Laxton's Epicure" is an early apple which would follow "Irish Peach"; "Golden Russet" would come still later and "Laxton's Superb" later still. Another important point is to consider the use to which the fruit is to be put. If apples are wanted for home consumption, those of especially good flavour should be chosen, such as "Cox's Orange", and "James Grieve", or "Laxton's Epicure".

The following brief description of some of the most popular apples will help the amateur to select good varieties:

ALLINGTON PIPPIN. Dessert; Oct.–Dec. Medium, conical, lemon-yellow flushed and striped with bright red; flesh very juicy and crisp with brisk flavour; very vigorous, and a reliable cropper. Light pruning is desirable. Pollinates with Worcester.

BEAUTY OF BATH. Dessert; early Aug. Small, flat, striped and spotted; flesh soft, brisk flavour; neat growth, prolific; much grown for market but good enough for early dessert; gather rather before ripe and store in cool place. Self-sterile. Apt to drop its fruit before quite ripe.

BLENHEIM ORANGE. Culinary or dessert; Nov.-Feb. Large, even shape, golden yellow with red cheek and russet; flesh firm, characteristic flavour. Takes some years to become profitable. Pollinates with Bramley.

BRAMLEY'S SEEDLINGS. Culinary; Nov.-Jan. Very large, flat, green, dull red cheek, acid, cooking frothy; spreading vigorous habit; extremely prolific and the most reliable cooking variety; succeeds on damp and heavy soils and also on dry ones. Partly self-fertile. Pollinates with Blenheim.

CHARLES ROSS. Exhibition and dessert; Oct.-Nov. Very large, fertile, rather upright in growth. Does well on chalk sub-soils.

COX'S ORANGE PIPPIN. Dessert; Nov.-March. Medium, round, orange shaded and striped dull red; flesh soft, very juicy, and of rich flavour; growth and fertility moderate. Self-sterile. It is advisable, therefore, to interplant with Bramley's Seedling, Worcester Pearmain, or Grieve.

DUKE OF DEVONSHIRE. Dessert; March-April. Small, round, yellow with russet; flesh crisp and finely flavoured; hardy and fertile.

ELLISON'S ORANGE. Dessert; Oct. Medium, similar in shape and colour to Cox's Orange; flesh tender, yellow, sweet and of good flavour. A cross between Cox's Orange and Calville Blanc. Does very well in the Midland and Northern Counties.

GRENADIER. Culinary; Aug.-Sept. Large, conical, pale green to yellow, moderate grower, regular cropper; an excellent early codlin. Cooks to a froth.

IRISH PEACH. Dessert; Aug. Small, flat and slightly angular, pale yellow with pretty stripes; flesh soft, juicy, very highly flavoured, fertile. Prune lightly.

JAMES GRIEVE. Dessert; Sept.-Oct. Medium, even in shape, lemon-yellow, striped red; flesh tender, very juicy, of remarkably high flavour; growth vigorous, compact, reliable bearer.

LAXTON'S EPICURE. Sept. Medium, round, pale yellow with crimson flush and stripes. Flesh yellowish, very tender.

LAXTON'S EXQUISITE. Sept.-Oct. Fairly large, round oval, yellow, with strong red flush and stripes, flesh tender, very good flavour. Growth good, rather upright.

LAXTON'S FORTUNE. Dessert; end Sept. Size medium, yellow, flushed and streaked with red, flesh sweet and juicy, highly flavoured. One of the best of the newer apples.

LAXTON'S SUPERB. Dessert; late. Medium, round, flattened, golden yellow with red flush; flesh crisp, sweet and aromatic; very prolific.

NEWTON WONDER. Culinary; Dec.-May. Medium, round and even, beautifully striped and flushed; flesh crisp and acidy, vigorous and hardy; one of the best cooking varieties for orchards or gardens. Interplant with Lane's Prince Albert. Liable to silver leaf in some districts.

REV. W. WILKS. Culinary; Oct.-Nov. Very large, flat, even; pale yellow; extremely fertile, dwarf habit; good cooker.

WORCESTER PEARMAIN. Dessert; Sept. Medium, conical, entirely covered with scarlet; flesh very juicy, crisp and remarkably sweet; habit compact, very regular annual bearer. Partly self-fertile. Pollinates with Allington.

APRICOTS (*Prunus armenaica*). Apricots are cultivated like plums, with the exception of the fact that they are natural dwellers of dry soils. If, therefore, an apricot is growing in a garden where rain soaks frequently down to the roots, it does not succeed well, as excessive rains cause excessive growth which is detrimental to fruit production. The common practice in such a case is to lay sheets of asbestos, or galvanized iron, over the soil surface near the stem of the tree. This, accompanied by very careful attention to drainage before the tree is planted, will encourage fruitfulness.

One of the best varieties for growing in the small garden

is *Breda*, the fruit of which ripens in the middle of August.
(*See also* PLUMS.)

BLACKBERRIES (*Rubus fruticosus*). It may not be
desirable in the very small suburban garden to grow
blackberries, except where they are in special demand. The
newer blackberries such as the "Himalayan Giant" and
"Edward Langley" are exceedingly prolific, and very
decorative, and are admirable for growing trained to wires as
fences. They make enormous growth, however, and must
not be planted nearer than 10 feet apart. The "Himalayan
Giant" blackberry will actually cover 20 feet of fence when
once established, and fruit enormously season after season.

Blackberries should be planted in a situation where the soil
is not likely to dry out, and given a good mulch of manure
each spring so that they do not suffer from drought. Other
culture consists merely in keeping them tied to their supports,
which need constant attention, and in cutting out most of the
old wood after the canes have flowered and fruited.

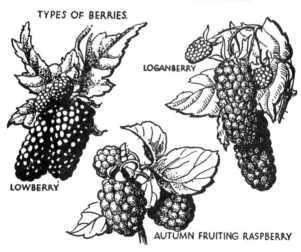

TYPES OF BERRIES.

LOGANBERRY

LOWBERRY

AUTUMN FRUITING RASPBERRY

Climbing fruits are very useful for screening ugly fences and
can be grown in very limited space.

The "Himalayan Giant" blackberry will fruit again on old wood, but as it grows so prolifically, it is really best to cut out the old wood entirely each season, and only train in the new growths.

Increase of stock can be obtained by simple layering.

BULLACE (*Prunus insititia*). Bullaces are not often grown in small fruit gardens, though several varieties are obtainable. They are treated in exactly the same way as ordinary plums.

CHERRIES (*Prunus cerasus*, Wild Cherry. *Prunus avium*, The Gean). Cherries grow to perfection on the chalky hills of Kent, indicating that their roots like to get down into very well-drained, chalky soil. Preparation for cherry planting should, therefore, be thorough. An important point in planting this fruit is to examine the roots carefully, and also the stems, cutting clean away any that are damaged in transit from the nursery. This is necessary because, like all the stone fruits, cherries are susceptible to disease if damaged wood is left.

Standard trees are planted 24 feet apart, bushes 15 feet apart, cordons 2 feet apart. Fan-trained Morello cherries (which are suitable for walls facing north) occupy about 15 feet of wall space.

Pruning is almost unnecessary with most cherry trees, though in the early stages it may be advisable to cut out a little of the feathered growth, weak stems and so on, so as to encourage the formation of long shapely main branches.

In choosing varieties of cherries, succession should be kept in mind as in the case of apples. No self-fertile sweet cherries are known, and it is therefore essential to plant more than one cherry tree unless other cherry trees are grown in neighbouring gardens. A few useful cherries that can be planted in pairs, to pollinate each other, are as follows:

"Bedford Prolific", a dark red early July-fruiting cherry, with "Napoleon Bigarreau", the fruit of which ripens in August. The Napoleon is brilliant scarlet and yellow, and bears enormous sized fruits.

"Frogmore Bigarreau", July, yellow and red fruit, with "Early Rivers", which is ready for gathering at the end of June. Black fruits.

"Napoleon Bigarreau" with "Elton Bigarreau", which fruits in early July, with fruits much the same colour as the Napoleon.

If only one cherry tree can be grown, the best is probably "May Duke", which is partly self-fertile, and will produce some fruit even when grown unaccompanied.

CURRANTS, BLACK (*Ribes nigrum*). Black currants are planted 5 feet apart each way in soil which has been deeply dug and well manured. They like plenty of moisture in the soil, and fruit well in riverside gardens where floods occur during winter. In districts where Big Bud is prevalent, only immune varieties should be grown, as though it is possible to treat Big Bud by applications of lime sulphur, it is far better not to have the worry of this pest in the garden.

General culture of black currants consists in keeping down weeds and in regular systematic pruning. This is done immediately after the plants have fruited, all the old fruiting wood being cut out and only the strongest of the new developing stems allowed to remain. Crowded weak growths should be removed at this season, and also again in winter, if they have appeared in the interim.

Black currants can be increased easily by inserting cuttings 6 inches long, close together, in rows in sandy soil in November. No cold frame or propagating frame is required.

Some of the best varieties for the amateur's garden are "Seabrook's Black" (immune), heavy cropper, long season, "Boskoop Giant", early fruiting, and "September Black".

Black currants grown on stiff soils can be treated with a mixture of 4 ounces of basic slag, and 1 ounce of kainit, to each bush, applied in early winter. In spring this will be followed by an ounce of sulphate of ammonia to each bush. On light soil it is better to use the following mixture, applied in late winter: 2 ounces superphosphate of lime, 1 ounce of sulphate of ammonia, 1 ounce kainit.

CURRANTS, RED (*Ribes vulgare*) **AND WHITE** (*Ribes vulgare album*). These are also planted 5 feet apart each way, unless cordon varieties are being grown. Cordons are not, however, advised for the ordinary garden, because of the extra trouble in keeping them to the trained shape.

On stiff soil, red currants can be dressed with basic slag from 4 to 8 ounces per bush in late autumn, and in winter they will appreciate a dressing of 2 or 3 ounces of kainit to each bush. On chalky soil it is better to use superphosphate of lime at the same rate of kainit, in early spring, in the place of the basic slag.

Pruning consists in cutting back the main stems, cutting out all weak and broken stems so that each is like a cordon. Three or four buds on each lateral growth are sufficient to leave. The red and white currants fruit on the old wood in the same way as apples, and not on the new wood as do black currants.

Good varieties for the amateur's garden are "White Dutch", "Red Dutch", heavy cropper and "Raby Castle", large fruit.

DAMSONS (*Prunis communis*). Damsons are sometimes grown as shelter belts of trees along the most exposed side of a fruit orchard. They are extremely hardy and fruit regularly. The damson will, however, usually give place to the plum in the small garden.

The Merryweather damson is one of the best for all purposes. (Cultivation as for PLUMS.)

FIG (*Ficus carica*). This is best grown in poor soil, such as gravel. Mortar rubble or chalk should be freely added to garden soil before planting.

The fig grows three crops of fruit a year. In this country only one matures, that is, the last of the three. Fruits are

301

formed in autumn and mature the following summer. Any large fruits seen on the trees in September should be removed. No other pruning is needed.

Under Glass figs are grown in large pots. The variety "St John" placed in bottom heat in late October, will produce fruit in March.

The best variety for outdoors is "Brown Turkey", which is also grown under glass.

GOOSEBERRIES. These are planted 5 feet apart each way, like the currants. Gosseberries are not very particular about sunshine, and are very suitable for growing in gardens that are inclined to be shady. They succeed very well under tall standard trees, and in similar positions.

Give an annual mulch of manure in May and light dressing of sulphate of potash in spring. Increase by cuttings in the same way as black currants.

Some of the best varieties are "Lancashire Lad" (red), "Whitesmith" (white), not liable to mildew, "Keepsake" (green), and "Golden Drop".

"Lancashire Lad" is the best variety for garden culture.

If cordon gooseberries are grown, "Lancashire Lad" is a good variety.

The "Worcester" berry is a big bud gooseberry, with a slight black currant flavour, due to its parentage. It is worth growing as a novelty.

GRAPE VINES. Grape vines are grown in this country both outdoors and under glass. Those grown outdoors are usually regarded more as ornamental features of the garden than as fruit bearers, although in some favourable districts, and where plenty of sunshine reaches the vine, heavy crops of small fruits can be obtained from outdoor vines. The pruning of the vine to encourage fruit production does not in any way detract from its beauty as an ornamental feature on a wall, and those who have vines already established would do well to study the methods of pruning applicable to this fruit.

The grapes themselves, when ripening, are very ornamental.

It is very important in growing grape vines under glass to prepare the soil of the border. The soil must be dug to a depth of 3 ½ feet, and a layer of broken clinker and brick bats, fine ash and mortar rubble laid at the bottom. The thickness of this layer should be about 6 inches. It is quite possible to grow good grapes from a vine planted *out*side the greenhouse with its stems entering the greenhouse.

The soil used should be a good rich friable loam, cleansed of all pests. To each barrow-load, a pound of bone-meal and a large potful of mortar rubble are added. Coarse sand should also be added to heavy soil, but no ordinary stable manure should be used.

Grape vines are planted in October, and if more than one is grown, a distance of at least 5 feet should separate each plant.

In heated greenhouses where dessert grapes are grown, the temperature should be kept at about 40–45° in winter, and increased gradually in spring until the flowers appear, when it will be about 60°. Ventilation should be as free as possible, but care must be taken that draughts do not enter on the windy side.

Grapes are syringed freely while the buds are breaking. Moisture is so important at this juncture that if buds do not develop properly, growers frequently tie damp moss over them to encourage them. When the fruits begin to colour, syringing ceases, and more ventilation is given. A thorough soaking with water once a week is better than frequent small doses from a water-can.

The amateur grower is recommended to purchase his fertilizers for vines ready-mixed, as these are prepared with great care, are well-balanced, easy to handle, and clean and efficient in use.

Pruning. It is in the pruning of a grape vine that most amateurs find difficulty, but the pruning principles are quite simple, and can be readily understood by a novice. The vines are restricted to one or more main branches. Large lateral branches are allowed to grow at regular intervals, other buds being rubbed away in the early stages.

Each of these lateral branches is kept free of side stems, apart from short growths which should carry the flowers and fruit. Pruning usually consists in cutting back the side shoots from the lateral branches.

As soon as the foliage has dropped, the shoots are cut back to within two buds of the old wood. As the plants come into growth in the spring both buds develop, but only one is allowed to continue to grow, the other bud being rubbed off. Each shoot as it grows is pinched out when three or four leaves have developed beyond the flower bunch. If a shoot does not show a flower bunch (which will appear not far from the main stem), it is pinched out when it has made about eight pairs of leaves.

As the fruits develop they are thinned, using a pair of sharp-pointed scissors, and cutting out enough fruits from each bunch to allow ample room for the development of the remainder.

The chief troubles of grapes under glass are scorching, scalding and shanking. *Scorching* is due to excessive sunshine and can be prevented by shading the fruits during the hottest sunny days. *Scalding* is due to a sudden rise in temperature and stricter attention to heating and ventilation will remedy this. *Shanking* is the term given when the stalks of the fruits shrivel up before the fruit matures. This may be the result of watering with excessive cold water, or it may be, in the case of vines which are grown outdoors, due to irregular weather conditions. The best variety for planting in the amateur's greenhouse is "Black Hamburg".

The pruning of outdoor vines grown as ornamental coverings for walls, is done on much the same lines as those suggested for indoors, but a large number of lateral growths and longer growths are allowed to remain on the vine during the summer so that the wall is completely covered. Winter pruning (i.e. in January) consists in cutting these back like those of the fruiting vines.

LAXTONBERRIES.   Laxtonberries are a hybrid of somewhat similar character to Loganberries. They appear to be rather less prolific than the Loganberry, and are therefore not to be recommended where only one kind can be grown.

LOGANBERRIES. Loganberries are believed to be a cross between the blackberry and raspberry, but their origin is somewhat obscure. All that is known is that they were first discovered in the garden of Judge Logan.

Like the Himalayan Giant blackberry, they like ordinary good rich soil, well supplied with moisture, and benefit from an annual dressing of stable manure. They are treated in exactly the same way as the Himalayan Giant blackberry, that is, the old canes are cut away after fruiting and new ones tied in their place.

MULBERRY (*Morus nigra*). This is a deciduous tree which grows up to 30 feet in height. A light, rich, moist loam suits it best. No pruning is necessary other than that usually given to ornamental trees in the garden, that is, enough to keep the tree shapely by pruning during the early stages.

If it is desired to increase the stock, a branch can be cut off in autumn and put into some light soil, where it will probably root. Or layering may be done in spring.

NECTARINES (*Prunus persica*). Nectarines are near relatives of peaches, and cultural instructions given for the peach may be taken to apply to the nectarine. They are generally regarded as slightly more hardy than the peach, and more suitable for the open garden. (*See* PEACH.)

NUTS. Cob-nuts (*Corylus avellana*). Are excellent fruits for inclusion in the garden where the soil is rather poor; they should be more commonly grown than they are.

No special cultivation is needed beyond the ordinary soil preparation before planting.

Walnuts (*Juglans*) should also be more common. There are two kinds in commerce: the common European walnut that has been grown here for centuries (*J. regia*) and a newer dwarf walnut (*J. praeparturiens*), which comes into bearing much younger. Walnuts succeed on any soil, and are excellent for town gardens.

PEACH (*Prunus persica*). Peaches require a sheltered corner of the garden, and if they can be grown as wall fruits they are more likely to succeed in midland and northern gardens than if they are in a very exposed position. Fan-trained trees can be planted 15 feet apart. They should be planted in well-prepared soil.

Pruning. As the fruits appear on the young wood of one year old only, it is necessary to keep the tree well furnished with young shoots. During the growing season, the majority of new young shoots are pinched out, leaving only the two strongest at the base of each fruiting stem. One new shoot is also left at the extremity as this practice encourages the sap up beyond the fruit. After the fruit has been gathered, the shoot is cut carefully back to the point just above the two new shoots that were left at the base. These are the fruiting stems for next season.

The best varieties of peaches and nectarines for outdoor culture are: Peaches. "Bellegarde", "Dymond", "Hale's Early".

Nectarines. "Early Rivers", "Lord Napier".

PEARS (*Pyrus communis*). Pear blossom opens early, and is somewhat tender, so that if possible a position sheltered from east winds should be chosen.

Pears succeed only on good rich loam. In ordering pears from a nursery, it is always best to tell the nurseryman what the garden soil is like, as pears on pear stock are more suitable for light soil, while those on quince stock are better for heavy soil.

Standard pears are planted 24 feet apart, half standards 15 feet apart, bushes 10 feet apart, espaliers 15 feet apart, and cordons 2 feet apart.

Pruning of pear trees is done in much the same way as already described for apples. As a rule, however, pruning is less necessary with the pear than with the apple, as the trees often seem to make cordon-like branches naturally, without any assistance from the gardener. In any case it is a mistake to prune too severely while the trees are young.

Fertilizers can be supplied as for apples, and stable manure also given according to the amount of stem and leaf growth made each season.

Lime is a very important fertilizer here as in all parts of the fruit garden. A dressing of nitrate of soda just before the flowers open, often helps to produce quantities of good fruit.

Some of the best varieties of pears for the amateur are described as follows:

BEURRE D'AMANLIS. September; large yellowish green, bronze cheek with small russet patches; excellent cropper as pyramid or standard.

BEURRE D'ANJOU. Nov.-Dec.; large yellow green, slight brown flush; flesh white, melting, with delicate perfume; growth weak, requires a wall or warm corner.

BEURRE DIEL. Oct.-Nov.; very large, yellow, covered with conspicuous brown dots; flesh tender, vigorous, fertile, of good flavour when well grown on quince; requires a wall in colder climates.

BEURRE SUPERFIN. Oct.-Nov.; golden yellow covered thin cinnamon russet; flesh melting, of delicate perfumed flavour; growth moderate, fertile.

CATILLAC. Dec.-April; large, roundish, dull green with brown red flush; flesh firm, cooking well; makes an irregular pyramid on quince, but fruits early; succeeds as a standard, and on north and east walls. One of the best cooking pears.

CONFERENCE. Oct.-Nov.; medium, very long-necked, dark green, with brown russet, flesh of pinkish tinge; vigorous and most regular cropper. Good where only one pear can be grown.

DOYENNE DU COMICE. November; large, pyramidal, lemon yellow, with slight russet; flesh yellowish white; growth vigorous and moderately fertile.

LAXTON'S SUPERB. August; large, flesh very tender and deliciously flavoured.

LOUISE BONNE OF JERSEY.   October; medium, smooth, yellowish-green, with dark red flush and covered prominent dots; flesh white, melting and of distinct flavour.

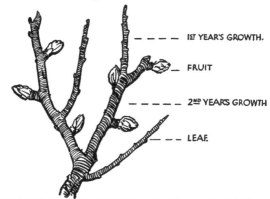

1ST YEAR'S GROWTH.

FRUIT

2ND YEAR'S GROWTH

LEAF.

BRANCH OF PEAR TREE SHOWING DIFFERENCE BETWEEN FRUIT AND LEAF BUDS.
The object of pruning is to promote the formation of fruit spurs, to make a shapely tree that will admit light and air to all branches.

PITMASTON DUCHESS. Oct.–Nov.; enormous, golden yellow, with slight cinnamon russet; flesh yellow, tender, juicy and highly flavoured in good seasons; growth vigorous, fertile; not recommended for standards.

WILLIAMS' BON CHRETIEN. September; medium, yellow with russet dots and faint red streaks; flesh white, fine grained, melting, and of strong musky flavour;   growth vigorous, fertile.

Pears need special care when they are gathered. They are best not allowed to turn colour on the trees, but should be gathered just before they ripen. It is also a useful practice to gather them in batches from the same tree, say at intervals of three or four days, as those that are gathered ripen rather quickly, and the fruit is available by this method for a longer period.

The very late-fruiting pears need plentiful sun before they are gathered and should be left on the trees until the end of September.

PLUMS (*Prunus communis*). Plums are a very useful fruit for small gardens, but some varieties are very regular in fruiting while others are rather erratic. The *Victoria Plum* and *Coe's Golden Drop* are two of the best in this respect.

Greengages are apt to be damaged by frost. They are not self-fertile and should therefore only be grown when other varieties of plums are present. Ordinary good, well-drained soil is required for plums, and trees that are bearing well benefit from a good mulch of stable manure each year. Lime is particularly important in the case of plums and all other stone fruits and so also is a dressing of phosphatic manure each year, such as basic slag in the autumn or superphosphate in spring (4 ounces. per square yard in each case). Kainit can be applied at the same time as basic slag (2-4 ounces. per square yard).

Plums, like cherries and apples, are some of them self-fertile and some self-sterile. The following pairs are satisfactory for the small garden where not many varieties can be grown: "Coe's Golden Drop" with "President". The Golden Drop is a self-sterile yellow dessert plum, ripe at the end of September; and President is a cooker, dark purple, ready for gathering in October. "White Magnum Bonum", a cooking plum of pale creamy yellow, is also suitable for planting with "President".

Other useful varieties of plums for the amateur's garden are as follows:

EARLY TRANSPARENT GAGE (*Early Apricot*). Dessert; early August. Medium, roundish apricot yellow, with crimson spots. Self-fertile.

GOLDEN TRANSPARENT GAGE. Dessert; early October. Very large, golden yellow. Self-fertile.

OULLINS GOLDEN GAGE. Early August. Large oblong, pale yellow with light bloom; flesh firm and very sweet; growth robust. Self-fertile.

PERSHORE. Culinary; August. Medium, oval, yellow, with white bloom; adhering to stone. Self-fertile.

POND'S SEEDLING. Culinary; mid-September. Very large,

oval, very dark red with blue bloom; growth vigorous and spreading. Self-fertile.

PURPLE PERSHORE. Culinary; mid-August. Medium, oval, purplish red. Very vigorous. Self-fertile.

QUINCE (*Rosaceæ*). Several varieties of quince are grown for fruit and many of the ornamental varieties which are recommended for shrubberies in large gardens also bear fruits which can be used for preserves. They appreciate damp soils and can be planted on the margins of ponds. They will also succeed in any ordinary, well-dug garden soil.

Almost no pruning is necessary with this fruit.

RASPBERRIES (*Rubus idæus*). Raspberries are one of the most valuable of all fruits in the home garden; in fact, they may be considered *the* most valuable. The reason for this is that raspberries in good condition are practically unobtainable from shops. By the time the raspberry has been gathered, packed, transported from market to market,

TYPES OF BERRIES

KINGS ACRE BERRY

VEITCHBERRY

RASPBERRY.

Many new types of berries have been introduced lately.
They all enjoy rich soil, especially bone-meal and good drainage.

and then redistributed to consumers, it has lost a good deal of its freshness. Moreover, if the fruit has to be gathered for transport in this way, it cannot be left to ripen on the canes, but must be gathered almost before it is ripe, and this again prevents the finest flavoured fruit from reaching the private household.

Still a third reason why home-grown fruit is best is that certain varieties of raspberries which have the finest flavour, such as "Park Lane", are too soft in texture to be of any use for market culture. These can, however, be grown in the home garden where they are used immediately they are gathered.

Raspberries are planted in rows 5 feet apart, leaving about 18 inches between each cane; or groups of three canes, a few inches apart, can be arranged.

Pruning. With most varieties, pruning consists of cutting out the old canes each season after the fruit has been gathered, cutting them right down to the soil level and leaving only the new canes that are springing up to bear the next season's fruit. A few varieties are called "Autumn fruiting" Raspberries, and these can be cut to the ground each spring instead of each autumn. Fruit will then be produced on canes of the current year's growth. Of these the chief are "Hailsham", "Lloyd George", and "November Abundance". "Lloyd George" is probably still the best variety of Raspberry for general cultivation, and can be treated either as autumn or spring fruiting. As a matter of fact, in many gardens, this variety keeps a supply of fruit all the season.

In winter the soil of the Raspberry plantation may be *lightly* forked, and the canes should be tied to wires stretched along the rows. In early spring a dressing of fertilizer may be applied, mixed as follows: 7 lb. superphosphate of lime, 4 lb. kainit, 2 lb. sulphate of ammonia, applied at the rate of half a pound to each square yard.

STRAWBERRIES. Strawberries are another fruit which it is worth while to grow because of the better condition in which the fruits can be obtained as compared with those of the market.

Unfortunately, Strawberries demand a fair amount of attention and occupy a good deal of garden space without being especially decorative, and they are therefore regarded with disfavour by many owners of small gardens. Where a plot can be given over to them, however, they provide one of the finest of home-grown crops.

A good practice in Strawberry culture is to make a plantation in three sections. A Strawberry plant lasts for about three years, after which it can be discarded as worthless. Every year each plant sends out a plentiful supply of runners, on the ends of which grow tiny new plants which root readily in the surface soil. Each of these rooted runners, if potted up in rich soil, will make a new plant. These plants bear most prolifically in the first and second seasons after planting.

To keep a regular supply of fruit, the grower is advised to scrap one-third of his plants every year and replant the bed with newly-rooted runners *taken from the healthiest plants of his collection.* This last point is important, for it a runner is taken from a plant which has not borne fruit, the runner will in turn bear no fruit.

New plants are generally bought in September or in March. They should be planted 18 inches apart in rows 2 ½ feet apart. (Strawberries can for a season or two be run between two rows of new Gooseberries or Currants which are spaced at 5 feet apart.)

When runners appear in the first season they will be taken off, as they weaken the plants. During the second season one good runner can be allowed to develop from each of the plants, to be rooted and used for September planting. It assists the runner to root if the growing tip, where the tuft of leaves is forming, is pegged down into the surface soil

An annual mulch of stable manure and autumn dressings of fertilizer keep the plants healthy. The fertilizers should consist of an ounce of sulphate of potash per square yard applied in autumn and 3 ounces of superphosphate and 1 ounce of sulphate of ammonia per square yard applied in spring. A little nitrate of soda may be used after the flowers open, to encourage the formation of large fruits. This is of course applied after the soil has been thoroughly soaked with water or rain. During the three years that Strawberries remain in the bed they need frequent hoeing to keep the soil surface free from weeds (except during the time that straw is laid between the rows).

Some growers, especially where the soil is inclined to be dry, put a good dressing of light strawy manure between the rows quite early in the season. This helps to conserve moisture in the soil and also serves the same purpose as the conventional straw mulch which is laid down just before the fruit ripens.

Some of the best varieties of Strawberries for the amateur are as follows: "The Duke", "King George", "Sir Joseph Paxton", "Waterloo", "Givon's Late Prolific". These will provide a succession of fruit for a long period.

VEITCHBERRIES. Veitchberries are hybrid berries of the same type as the Blackberry and Loganberry and treated in the same manner. The fruit is of the colour of a Mulberry and a distinctive flavour midway between the Blackberry and Loganberry. Its greatest use is for preserves.

The chief trouble in connection with this fruit is that it attracts the attention of flies, wasps and birds to such an extent that really ripe fruit is difficult to obtain.

What to Do to Pests Each Month of the Year

January

During calm dry weather fruit-tree spraying should be carried out. Caustic soda or tar-oil winter washes may be used. If pruning is done this month, be sure to gather up and burn all twigs as they may be harbouring pests and diseases.

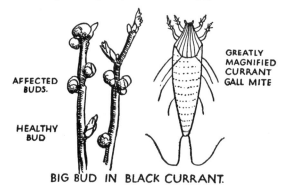

BIG BUD IN BLACK CURRANT.

Blackcurrants need a rich, moist soil and a sunny position to keep them healthy. Spray with lime-sulphur wash to control big bud mite.
It is best applied just as the leaves are opening.

February

Sterilize soil for indoor tomatoes. If you sow peas this month, damp the seed and dip in carbolic powder to keep off mice. Potassium sulphate spray should be used on vines attacked by mildew.

March

Dig naphthalene or other soil fumigants into the ground before seed sowing. Remove by hand "Big Bud" from currants.

April

When sowing your lawn mix carbolic powder with the seed to keep off the birds. All fruit trees liable to be attacked by mildew should be sprayed with Nicotine wash, or in the case of gooseberries use lime sulphur.

May

Greasebanding against Woolly aphis should be renewed early this month. If the Bean aphis or Black Dolphin has appeared on the broad beans, pinch out the affected shoots, and spray with Quassia solution. Cockchafer beetles may be caught by shaking fruit trees over tarred boards or sacks. Arsenate of lead sprays should be used on gooseberries against Sawfly. Raspberries should also be sprayed against moth larvæ.

June

Look out for green-fly on rose trees and spray with soft soap solution. Cuckoo spit insect or Froghopper should be destroyed by hand if possible. Spraying with nicotine soap is fairly effective.

July

Potatoes should be sprayed with Bordeaux Mixture early this month against the potato disease. Plants such as celery and chrysanthemums liable to attack from the leaf-mining maggot should be watched and all affected leaves removed and burned. Spray with soft soap solution. Rose trees sometimes show signs of mildew during this month. Liver of sulphur spray should be used for this.

August

Towards the end of this month potatoes suffering from Potato Disease should have their haulms carefully removed and burned, leaving the tubers in the ground to ripen.

315

Dahlias are usually attacked by earwigs, so inverted flower pot traps should be placed on the tops of their stakes.

September

Raspberries should be sprayed with arsenate of lead against Sawfly. If digging has commenced, a soil fumigant may be applied to the ground, such as naphthalene. This will be especially beneficial where Club Root is prevalent.

October

Greasebanding should be completed by the middle of this month. A good dressing of lime may be given after digging to clean the ground of wireworms, asparagus beetle, club root, moth grubs, cockchafer grubs, etc.

November

This is the month of bonfires. All fruit tree prunings, diseased tops of potatoes, leaves from diseased trees, and tiresome weeds, should be burned and the ashes stored for future use. Go over stores of fruit and vegetables and destroy

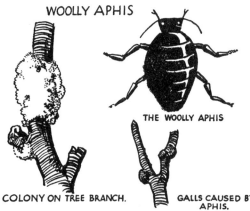

WOOLLY APHIS

THE WOOLLY APHIS

COLONY ON TREE BRANCH.

GALLS CAUSED BY APHIS.

Woolly aphis or American blight frequently attacks old apple trees.
Spraying with tar-oil wash in winter or nicotine soap
in summer are the best remedies.

any showing sign of disease. Woolly aphis may be dealt with by injecting carbon bisulphide into the soil round the roots of affected trees.

December

On calm, dry days fruit tree spraying may be carried out. Greenhouses and frames may be thoroughly cleaned, white-washed and fumigated if they have been visited by any pests or diseases during the past season. Flower pots, and seed boxes and pans should also be cleaned ready for spring sowings.

BENEFICIAL INSECTS

A number of the insects found in the garden, although of rather an alarming appearance, are great friends to the gardener. They are often entirely carnivorous, living on aphides and other small pests. Below are a few particulars of some of the most common, all of which should be allowed to carry out their good work and not destroyed on sight, like insect pests.

Bees. The honey bee is a wonderful worker, and, of course, is a most welcome visitor to the garden. Without his visits practically no seed would develop on some plants, as it is on his body that the pollen is taken from flower to flower to effect fertilisation. The only member of this family that is inclined to be destructive is the leaf-cutting bee but as he only disfigures the leaves, and is easily caught, he does not represent a very great menace. Bees should therefore be treated with courtesy, especially when the fruit blossoms are open. The gardener must avoid the use of poison sprays such as lead arsenate at this critical time.

Beetles. Most ground beetles are carnivorous, living on slugs, grubs and maggots of all kinds. The most familiar are: the *Tiger Beetle*, a rich emerald green, with orange stripes, about ½ inch in length. It covers the ground at a great pace, but, of course, flies as well, and is very difficult to catch. As it does no harm this does not matter. *Carrion Beetles* which are yellow, with a black patch on the thorax, and two on each

317

side of the wing covers, about ½ inch long. Both the larvæ and the beetles feed on carrion, also on snails and slugs. *Burying Beetles*, black with broad orange bands, often an inch long. They also are scavengers, living on dead birds, moles, fish, frogs, etc.

Centipedes. These are entirely insectivorous and should not be mistaken for millipedes, which are very harmful. The centipede is flat and yellow, and has a large number of legs. It runs very fast with a slightly crab-like movement. Millipedes are almost black in colour, rounded in shape and when touched roll into a ball. The millipedes move slowly— a fact which applies to most of the insects that are vegetarian, and therefore harmful. Having no need to catch their food, they approach it in leisurely fashion.

Devil's Coach Horse, or Cock-tail Beetle. This is a narrow black beetle which has a habit of raising its head and tail in a rather threatening manner when touched, hence its name. It feeds on slugs, and other soil pests.

Dragon Flies. These wonderfully beautiful flies, too well known to need description, are insectivorous, and live entirely on minute insects. They have no sting, although they are often called "Horse Stingers".

Hover Flies. The larvæ live almost entirely on aphides, and therefore destroy large quantities. There are several varieties. The common ones seen hovering over rose trees and fruit trees are easily recognisable.

Ichneumon Flies. There are thousands of varieties of this particular insect which varies in size from that of a midge to about 2 inches across the wings. They have long thin bodies and very long legs. They hunt for caterpillars of all kinds, and lay their eggs in the bodies of their victims. The grubs hatch out and feed on the caterpillars, thus killing off large numbers of them. Cabbage caterpillars are a favourite victim.

Lacewing Fly. This is another very beautiful insect, with 4 large gauzy wings, and a thin bright green body. On account of its brilliant golden eyes it is sometimes called the

Golden-eyed Fly. It is mostly found near water, and lays its eggs under leaves, each one being attached by a thin silken thread. The larvæ suck the juices from aphides (green- and black-fly).

Ladybirds, sometimes called Cow Ladies. These live almost entirely on green-fly, and are found on rose trees and other plants subject to this pest. There is no need to describe them, as even the youngest and most amateur gardener knows this charming little spotted beetle.

Spiders feed on insects of all kinds, and are so well known there is no need to describe them.

Wasps (small varieties and Hornets), in spite of the fact that they eat into fruit, are really beneficial. They remove the wings from ordinary house flies, and take the bodies home to their young. They eat grubs in large quantities. Thus hornets and small wasps not only clear the garden of pests, but also fight disease-carrying flies that invade the house.

ON FORMS & FORMING

The Marketing of Small Produce

To the Editor of THE ENGLISH REVIEW, January 1909

DEAR SIR,—Although the back-to-the-land movement is of exceedingly slow growth, and many judges consider that the rural activities of this country will never be notably revived, there has certainly of late been a marked and increasing tendency on the part of people who, for one reason or another, are dissatisfied with the conditions of a city life to take the bold step of endeavouring to earn a living in the country.

It is usually market-gardening, fruit-growing, or poultry-farming that is essayed; and, given the average amount of optimism, what delightfully simple and profitable occupations these are as viewed from the fireside through the medium of nearly all the books that have been written about them! Perhaps a country holiday has introduced rustic proprietors, who are apparently prosperous and content, to the aspirant's notice, and as they plainly lack the advantages of a sound education, and their methods are not the severely scientific ones insisted on by the authors, he falls into the very pardonable error of thinking that he can scarcely fail to secure a comfortable livelihood from the land.

But, unfortunately, in the great majority of instances there is an infinite disparity between the real and the ideal, and I am personally acquainted with several cases in which optimistic and energetic townsfolk have lost all the capital they possessed without acquiring a sufficient understanding of market-gardening or poultry-farming to make these businesses pay. I have heard the term "gardener" used by bookmakers as synonymous with fool, and, in the opinion of perhaps most people who have never handled a spade, gardening is a very simple occupation, but nevertheless, in truth, these same people may be as incapable of making gardening pay as of earning fame on the football field or becoming expert deep-sea fishermen.

I was lately called in to advise two ex-city clerks who had taken up market-gardening in Hertfordshire, and their financial condition and prospects were so deplorable that it seemed best to counsel a speedy return to town.

They had succeeded in raising crops of a kind; but then came the discovery that while a cabbage may cost 1½d. in a shop, its value upon the land is exceedingly small; indeed, in the case of most of their produce, the paying of carriage to London, salesman's commission, &c., would have resulted in a loss. And this is the real problem before the smallholder; it is not very difficult to produce, but unless he is a really skilful cultivator or exceptionally favoured as regards a market, the prices commonly obtained are so small that he will find it a difficult matter to make any profit at all.

Who is to blame for this condition of affairs? It is common to denounce the market salesman or commission agent, and having been a great deal in contact with growers I have heard many stories of his flagrant dishonesty. But on examination these can rarely, if ever, be substantiated; there is either a doubt about the matter or the real victim proves to be an intangible somebody else. Indeed, all my inquiries have proved to be singularly unilluminating. Asked to furnish instances of the dishonesty of market salesmen, the editor of a trade journal writes: "We have no record of cases. It is a matter which is, I think, distinctly difficult to bring home to salesmen, and this probably accounts for our having no record"; while a leading seedsman, who is particularly interested in the matter, writes of the great difficulties of detection, and can only suggest that more precise information might be obtainable in the Channel Islands. But is it a fact that dishonesty of this kind is so difficult to detect? Surely the honesty of salesmen is quite easily tested, and I cannot convict them of systematic malpractices without more direct evidence than I have been able to obtain; indeed, in my own experience their charges are not excessive, and they do their best to satisfy their more dependable customers. As a matter of fact the reason for the deplorable differences between the wholesale and retail prices of garden produce is quite simple—the transformation takes place in the florist's or greengrocer's shop. I recently witnessed a transaction in which, at the cost of a telephone message, a West End florist secured over 100 per cent profit on the sale of some palms (and the grower had been to the expense of tending the plants for several years); but this is, of course, an extreme instance. Indeed I do not condemn these tradesmen; it must be remembered that their goods are exceedingly perishable, and inquiry into the number of failures in the trade will effectually dispel the idea that it is a certain road to affluence. Where a market does not exist the growers deal direct with the shops, but this plan has its disadvantages and it is doubtful if it is more profitable to them. Instances might be given of business being conducted direct with the consumers, with fortunate results, but this is not always practicable, and here, again, the large amount of extra trouble involved is a decided drawback.

As regards the disposal of produce there is a remedy ready to the grower's hands. This is co-operation; it is quite open to the many growers around Worthing or at Hampton-on-Thames, for example, to combine to the extent of effecting a saving in carriage by consigning their produce in bulk, and appointing their own salesman in the principal markets, and if these steps did not prove effective they could go to the further length of opening their own shops. Foreign produce is a great factor in keeping prices down, and were it not for co-operation it is certain that its sale in our market at the prevailing prices would result in a loss. But I am aware of the extreme difficulty of inducing the home growers to combine even to the extent of giving a large order, say, for manure at a much lower rate; the often disastrous principle of "each man for himself" is apparently a national characteristic.

Meanwhile the inexperienced continue to take to market-gardening and fruit-growing to the detriment of the older hands. It has lately been freely stated in the more irresponsible section of the press that fortunes are to be made by adopting the Parisian system of market-gardening in England. Most of the articles that have appeared are so inaccurate and hazy as to be simply mirth-provoking to the established market-gardener, but it is to be feared that they will be the cause of disaster to the inexperienced and the too easily impressed. There is a living to be made from the land in this country, but even more than is the case in other businesses it is only the thoroughly competent and most industrious men who succeed.

ROYAL GARDENS, KEW.   G

Balance-sheet of a
Twenty-five-acre Holding

To the Editor of THE ENGLISH REVIEW, February 1909

DEAR SIR,—For the farmer's financial year ending Michaelmas 1908 the balance-sheet of my twenty-five-acre holding shows a profit of £51. That is to say, my regular man and I have each drawn about the same amount out of the holding. He, however, has put in his whole time, whilst I have only been able to put in about half my time, for on wet days the spade has given place to the pen.

Besides this £100 a year we have had to earn the rent and interest as well, so that looking at the result as a whole it is not unsatisfactory for a small holding which has no special advantages.

It should be borne in mind that the holding is over seven miles from a market town; that the land is of a heavy clay soil, which previous to my occupation had been "farmed out"; and that, being situated on a little hill, the working of it on all sides means an expenditure of extra labour. Labour, indeed, including hay-making and excluding my own, has amounted to quite £65. I found that the cost of mowing, making, carrying and stacking my hay worked out at £1 an acre, were I to charge for my own labour, working sometimes sixteen hours a day, and the voluntary labour of a friend who spent ten days of his summer holiday with me. He came from the city, but his labour, I am thankful to say, was of a more strenuous kind than the ordinary run of voluntary labour.

One or two alterations in my method of working my small holding have resulted in a greater gain. Of the three acres of orchard ground under the spade, I have had an acre or so where half-standards are planted laid down to grass and clover between the fruit trees, so that the mowing-machine can cut this at the same time as it cuts the rest of the hay. I shall thereby increase the size of my haystack and afford extra forage for my bees. This has meant the giving up growing of vegetables for market and resulted in a greater saving of labour, for I am too far from a town to market vegetables successfully. Roots have given place to cabbages on the other two acres of fruit trees, for cabbages require less labour and are more nutritious for cattle.

Spade labour, however, still works out at a loss, for I have carefully observed that labour here is pretty equally divided between stock and the fruit garden and if, therefore, I were to debit the fruit and vegetable account with half-wages it would show a loss.

The details concerning my bottom fruit can be found in *Country Life*, September 26, and I must now unfortunately add to this that my top fruits were a failure this year, the apples bearing practically nothing and the plums very little. The most profitable fruit crops have been strawberries and gooseberries, yet I cannot venture much in growing strawberries, for the strawberry and hay crop come together and it is difficult then to obtain pickers. I have carried out my plan of practically abolishing poultry, which I rank as a sweated industry. There are two or three hens left, but their uninteresting proceedings I have not troubled to record.

The most satisfactory accounts shown are those of horned stock and bees. My cow account shows a decline in gross returns: this can be accounted for by my having one cow less for half the year.

I have discovered one thing, however, about cow-keeping, and that is that winter butter-making really does not pay (the facts concerning which I have already set forth in *Chambers' Journal*). It is true that the price of butter has risen during the year, but in the heart of the country, market fluctuations scarcely affect traditional custom.

The milk, as it comes up from the cow-sheds, is immediately separated, and this separated milk mixed with a cream equivalent is used for weaning calves, the surplus, if any, with the buttermilk, going to the pigs.

Of the twenty-five acres which surround my four-room cottage, twenty-two acres are of grass-land, and three acres under fruit. A little stream trickles through the pasture-land, where two small ponds are held in reserve for any great drought. Everything upon the land, excepting the hedges, has had to be constructed by myself, and by those who have helped me—my cottage, dairy, well, bee-house, cow-shed, pig-sty, cart-shed and calf-shed. The holding is closely surrounded by game preserves, and unless I net my strawberries and currants I do not get any ripe berries to pick. The birds take heavy toll every year, making it extremely difficult to grow fruit with profit, although my apple, plum and damson trees number 750 and my currant and gooseberry bushes over 2,000.

I have given up keeping a pony and cart, finding it more advantageous to hire, not only for the hay-making, but also for marketing my fruit.

Although it has been a bad year for pigs, with feeding-stuff dear and pork cheap, I have managed not to lose money over them. What has brought me the most profit has been rearing and buying in young pedigree jerseys, and selling them as they calve down.

My apiary now consists of twenty-six hives, and the twenty hives which yielded any surplus from honey gave an average of 20 ½ lb. per hive, sold at rates varying from 7½d. to 1s. per lb.

I have credited no sum in the balance-sheet for thirty-six loads of farmyard manure, which during September was carted from my stock-yard and distributed round the fruit trees. At the same time it should be noticed that nothing has been debited to labour in the dairy.

BALANCE-SHEET: MICHAELMAS 1907 TO MICHAELMAS 1908

Dr.

Particulars	£	s.	d.	£	s.	d.
To Cows:						
Cake, straw, bran, &c.	11	4	9			
Service of bulls	1	3	6			
Ploughing and harrowing for seeds	2	1	0			
Mowing, carrying and stacking hay	6	10	9			
Beer for haymakers	0	16	3			
Thatching	0	12	6			
				22	8	9
To Stock Account:						
Value of stock at Michaelmas, 1907	93	0	0			
Cattle bought	14	16	0			
				107	16	0
To Bees:						
Sugar and requisites	1	19	3			
Surrey Bee-Keepers' Association (subscription)	0	5	0			
				2	4	3
To Fruit and Vegetables:						
Straw for strawberries	0	14	2			
Netting	1	0	0			
Manure carting	1	4	0			
Seeds, &c.	0	12	0			
				3	10	2
To Pigs:						
Bran and middlings				8	19	5
To Labour:						
Wages of one man	52	0	0			
Extra labour	5	14	4			
				57	14	4
To Interest on Capital (£964) at 4 per cent.				38	8	0
Rent on ten acres				16	8	0
Tithes				2	8	0
Rates						
Taxes						
Insurance				0	15	0
Repairs				0	13	6
Profit				51	1	2
				£315	**17**	**1**

Cr.

Particulars	£	s.	d.	£	s.	d.
By Cows:						
Butter, 698 lb. at 1s. 3d.	43	12	6			
Milk sold and consumed	17	4	5			
Value of haystack	35	0	0			
				95	16	11
By Stock Account:						
Cows and calves sold	71	9	8			
Value of stock, Michaelmas 1908	88	0	0			
				159	9	8
By Bees:						
Sale of bees, hives, &c.	5	7	7			
Honey (410 lb.) and wax	14	12	9			
				20	0	4
By Fruit and Vegetables:						
Strawberries	8	7	8			
Gooseberries	7	13	0			
Plums	0	15	3			
Damsons	0	7	0			
Currants	0	12	6			
Vegetables consumed	5	4	0			
Vegetables sold	0	13	11			
Rhubarb	1	10	0			
Apples	0	10	0			
				25	13	4
By Pigs:						
11 Pigs sold	7	16	10			
Value of pigs unsold	7	0	0			
				14	16	10
				£315	**17**	**1**

Finally, I wish to make it clear that though I, as a peasant-proprietor, had to expend a good deal of capital on the purchase of the land and on the erection of my cottage and outbuildings, my working capital for stocking the little farm with cattle, fruit trees and implements barely amounted to £10 an acre.

If I were starting again I would not burden myself with the doubtful charm of ownership, which has often bound my hands too tightly to my stake in the country. I would rent land from the County Council and with more money to jingle in my pockets give myself greater scope for development.

F. E. Green

P.S.—With reference to your notes on the marketing of small produce in your January number, the following personal experience may interest you:

One day last May, as an experiment, I sent a bushel of my earliest picking of green gooseberries (Winham's Industry) to Mr. —, reputed to be the largest and best salesman at Covent Garden. The next day I got back a credit note for 9s., less commission, &c., 2s. 3d., extra carriage 1s., thus leaving me a net sum of 5s. 9d. for *one* bushel. On the morning that these were sold, a London greengrocer who attended the market, bought green gooseberries at 7s. 6d. the *half* bushel, and his samples, he informed me, were not as good as mine. I thereupon wrote and complained to the salesman, asking if my smaller price was due to my being shelved as a small grower. The answer came back that I could hardly expect to be treated in the same manner as that in which they handled consignments from large growers!

The following week I took my gooseberries into Dorking, and though the market price had dropped considerably I made 10s. a bushel by selling direct to the greengrocers.

LADIES & GENTLEMEN

Men:
A Hate Song

I hate Men;
They irritate me.

I

There are the Serious Thinkers—
There ought to be a law against them.
They see life, as through shell-rimmed glasses, darkly.
They are always drawing their weary hands
Across their wan brows.
They talk about Humanity
As if they had just invented it;
They have to keep helping it along.
They revel in strikes
And they are eternally getting up petitions.
They are doing a wonderful thing for the Great
Unwashed—
They are living right down among them.
They can hardly wait
For "The Masses" to appear on the newsstands,
And they read all those Russian novels—
The sex best sellers.

II

There are the Cave Men—
The Specimens of Red-Blooded Manhood.
They eat everything very rare,
They are scarcely ever out of their cold baths,

And they want everybody to feel their muscles.
They talk in loud voices,
Using short Anglo-Saxon words.
They go around raising windows,
And they slap people on the back,
And tell them what they need is exercise.
They are always just on the point of walking to San
Francisco,
Or crossing the ocean in a sailboat,
Or going through Russia on a sled—
I wish to God they would!

III

And then there are the Sensitive Souls
Who do interior decorating, for Art's sake.
They always smell faintly of vanilla
And put drops of sandalwood on their cigarettes.
They are continually getting up costume balls
So that they can go
As something out of the "Arabian Nights".
They give studio teas
Where people sit around on cushions
And wish they hadn't come.
They look at a woman languorously, through half-closed
   eyes,
And tell her, in low, passionate tones,
What she ought to wear.
Colour is everything to them—everything;
The wrong shade of purple
Gives them a nervous breakdown.

IV

Then there are the ones
Who are Simply Steeped in Crime.
They tell you how they haven't been to bed
For four nights.
They frequent those dramas

Where the only good lines
Are those of the chorus.
They stagger from one cabaret to another,
And they give you the exact figures of their gambling debts.
They hint darkly at the terrible part
That alcohol plays in their lives.
And then they shake their heads
And say Heaven must decide what is going to become of
    them—
I wish I were Heaven!

I hate Men;
They irritate me.

Persian Gazals

Sufiism; or the Doctrines of the Mystics of Islam

The following remarks on the leading doctrines of the Sufi sect of philosophers—the Mystics of Islam—from a review of Mr. J.W. Redhouse's metrical translation of the First Book of the Mesnevi Jelalu-'d-Din, Er-Rumi, *published in the* Glasgow Herald *of April 25th, 1881, will perhaps render the more obscure passages of the poetry presented in this work somewhat more intelligible to the mere general reader.*

It is a common notion in Europe that all the poetry of Muhammadan countries is simply erotic and bacchanalian, and characterised by extravagant conceits and absurd metaphors. Hafiz is styled by Europeans the Anacreon of Persia, because the subjects of his gazals are love and wine and flowers. But there is more in Oriental poetry than meets the ear; for beneath the literal meaning lies a deep, esoteric, spiritual signification—the love that is celebrated by Hafiz is not human passion, but divine love. And as in the Song of Solomon, which orthodox theologians admit is in a literal sense an epithalamium on the marriage of the sage King of Israel and the Princess of Egypt, the reciprocal love between the soul of man and the Deity is mystically shadowed, so is it in the beautiful poem of the loves of *Layla* and *Majnun*, by the great Persian Nizami. To properly understand and appreciate the finest Oriental poetry it is necessary to possess a thorough knowledge of dervish–doctrine, or Sufiism, of which the leading idea is a mystical union of man with the Creator, through love for Him. For Sufiism has found its ablest exponents in the poets of Islam, and especially in the great poets of Persia—in the *Mesnevi* of Jelalu-'d-Din; the *Mantuku-'t-Tair* of Feridu-'d-Din Attar; the *Bustan* of Sa'di; the *Gulshan-I Raz* of Sa'du-'d-Din Mahmud Shabistari; the gazals of Hafiz, &c. "Under the veil of earthly love and the woes of temporal separation, they disguise the dark riddle of human life and the celestial banishment which lies behind the threshold of existence, and under the joys of revelry and inebriation they figure transports and ecstatic raptures."

Briefly stated, the fundamental doctrine of the Sufis—the Mystics of Islam—is that God is diffused throughout all creation; the soul of man is *of* God, not *from* God, an exile from Him; the body is its prison-house, and life in this world is its period of banishment from God—its home and its source. Before the soul was exiled, it had seen the face of Truth, but here it merely obtains a shadowy glimpse, which "serves to awaken the slumbering memory of the past, but can only vaguely recall it; and Sufiism undertakes, by a long course of education and moral discipline, to lead the soul onward from stage to stage, until at length it reaches the goal of perfect knowledge, truth, and peace." According to dervish-doctrine and practice, there are four stages through which the soul must pass before it reaches its highest—its perfect condition. The first is *nasut*, or humanity, in which obedience to the orthodox law—due observance of the rites and ceremonies of religion—is necessary. Secondly, *tarikat*, or "the way" in which the disciple attains capacity or potentiality; now quitting forms of religion (having risen above them), and adopting spiritual adoration in place of corporeal worship. This stage, which admits the disciple within the pale of Sufiism, is only attained by great piety, virtue, endurance, and resignation to the divine will. The third stage is *'aruf*, knowledge or inspiration; and the fourth and last, *hakikat*, or Truth itself—union with the Deity is now perfect and complete. The Sufi disciple from the first places himself under the guidance of a spiritual instructor, to whom he must in all things be submissive—passive as clay in the hands of the potter, or, to employ the Sufi phrase, as the corpse under the hands of the imam. The dignity of spiritual director—*Khalifa*, as the teacher is designated—is not to be obtained without long-continued fasting and prayer, and by complete abstraction from all earthly things; for the *man* must *die* before the *saint* can be *born*.

Such, in outline, is the doctrine of the Sufis, which differs but little in essentials from that of Buddhism, or from the teachings of Pythagoras, and those of the mystics of modern Europe. Indeed there are many points of resemblance between the mysticism of the Sufis and that of certain sectaries in England during the seventeenth century, who are so wittily satirised in Butler's *Hudibras*; whose boasted "inward light" is there styled, "a dark lanthorn of the spirit". Thus the Sufis, like these sectaries, talk of "love to God", "union with God", "death to self and life eternal in God", "the indwelling in man of the Spirit", "the nullity of works and ceremonies", "grace and spiritual illumination", and so on. The sensual Paradise, with its jewelled mansions and its beauteous huris, described in the Kur'an, is to the Sufis a mere allegory of course; in like manner Law, in his "Serious Call", got rid of the material heaven so minutely described in the Book of the Revelation of St John. In short, Sufiism may be termed the religion of the heart, as opposed to formalism and ritualism.

Muslim poetry, especially that of Persia, is more or less tinged with dervish-doctrine; the parallels are carefully and skilfully maintained between external and sensuous objects and the internal and spiritual emotions of which they are supposed to be the emblems. Therefore, to understand, even partially, the sweet odes of Hafiz, it is necessary to know that by *wine* is meant devotion; *sleep* signifies meditation on the divine perfections; *perfume* represents hope of divine favour; *zephyrs* mean outbursts of grace; *idolators, infidels*, and *libertines* are men of the purest faith, and the *idol* they worship is the Creator; the *tavern* is the cell where the searcher after truth becomes intoxicated with the wine of divine love; the *wine-seller* is the spiritual director; *beauty* is the perfection of the Deity; *curls* and *tresses*, the infiniteness of His glory; *lips*, the inscrutable mysteries of His essence; *down on the cheek*, the world of spirits who surround the Creator's throne; a *black mole* is the point of indivisible unity; *wantonness, mirth,* and *inebriation*, religious ecstasy and perfect abstraction from all mundane thoughts, and contempt for all worldly things. Read with this key to the esoteric meaning, the gazals of Hafiz are no longer anacreontic and bacchanalian effusions, but ecstatic lucubrations on the love of man to his Creator.

W.A. Clouston

Gazals

I LAID my face in her path, but she passed not near me; mine had a hundred kind glances for her, but she gave not one look at me.

O Lord, watch over that young heart-stealer, who suspecteth not the arrow of the sighing anchorite.

The torrent of my tears hath not borne away malice from her heart; not a drop of rain hath left a mark upon that hard marble!

Would that, like a taper, I might expire under her feet, but she would not blow over me like the morning breeze.

O my soul, what heart of stone is so devoid of sense, that it would not make itself a shield against the wounds of thine arrow!

My groanings last night suffered not bird or fish to sleep; but see! that saucy one never once unclosed her eyes from slumber.

Thy sweet lay, O HAFIZ, is so heart-captivating, that every one who heareth it, longeth that it may never be lost to his bosom.

★

MAY thy beauty be perpetually on the increase; may thy tulip-cheek every year preserve its bloom!

May the vision of thy love, which is fixed in my brain, be every day that I live stronger and stronger!

May the forms of all the charmers in the world bow themselves down for ever, as now, in the service of thine image!

May every cypress, which growth in our meadows, be ungraceful for ever, as now, beside thy tall and slender stature!

May the eye, which is not bewitched in looking at thee, instead of pearly tears shed an ocean of blood!

May its glance, that it may steal every heart, be endowed with every trick to work its enchantments!

Is there a soul anywhere which would sorrow thine, may it be deprived of patience, and constancy, and quietude!

May thy ruby-lip, dear as his life to HAFIZ, be ever far from that of the base and the ignoble!

★

THOU lookest at me, and every moment thou augmentest my pain: I look upon thee, and every moment my affection for thee becometh greater!

Thou inquirest not about my condition; I know not what are thy secret thoughts; thou preparest me no medicine; thou knowest not, perchance, even that I am ill!

This is not the way – that thou shouldest cast me to the ground, and pass me by! Ah, come back, and inquire once more, how it is with me; for I would become to thee the dust of thy path!

I will not keep my hand off thy skirt, even when I turn to clay; for when thou passest my grave, my hand shall seize hold of thy garment.

The sorrows of thy love have deprived me of breath:

restore it me again! How long wilt thou take away my breath, and not say to me: "Take it back!"

One night in the darkness I demanded back my heart from thy ringlets! I beheld thy cheek, and quaffed the cup of thy ruby-lip!

I drew thee quickly to my bosom, and thy ringlets burst into flame; I pressed lip to lip, and gave for thy ransom my heart and soul.

When without me thou wanderest for thy pleasure through the green fields, a red tear starteth and courseth down my pale cheek.

Be kind to HAFIZ! Go, say to my enemy: "Resign thy life!" If I but find warmth in thee, what sorrow can I feel from the cold breath of my enemy?

Songs

The Squire and the Chambermaid

NOT far from the town there lived a squire,
  An open-hearted blade,
Long time he had a great desire
  To kiss his chambermaid;
One summer's morn, being full of glee,
  He took her to the shade,
And, underneath the mulberry tree,
  He kissed the chambermaid.

Now the parson's wife at the window high,
  This amorous couple surveyed,
She wished, and did solemnly protest,
  She had been the chambermaid;
When all was o'er young Kitty cried,
  "Kind sir, I'm sore afraid
That woman there will tell your wife
  You've kissed the chambermaid."

Now the squire perceived of a lucky thought,
  And instantly conveyed
Her ladyship unto the spot
  Where he had kissed the maid;
And, underneath the mulberry tree,
  He took her to the shade,
And three times three well kissed was she,
  Much like the chambermaid.

Next morning goes the parson's wife –
    For scandal was her trade –
"I saw your squire, upon my life,
    Kissing the chambermaid!"
"Oh, where, or when?" the lady cried,
    "I'll soon discharge the jade." –
"'Twas underneath the mulberry tree
    I saw him kiss your maid."

"Oh no," replied her ladyship,
    "My spouse you don't degrade,
'Twas I that chanced to take that trip,
    And not the chambermaid."
Both parties parted in a pet,
    Not knowing what was said,
And Kitty keeps her service yet –
    The pretty chambermaid.

I keep my Dogs and Ferrets, too

The following is a poaching song; it is very old.

I KEEP my dogs and ferrets, too,
    I have them in my keeping,
To catch good hares all in the night,
    While the gamekeeper lies sleeping.

My dogs and I went out one night,
    'Twas to view their habitation,
Up jumped poor puss and away ran she
    Straightway to our plantation.

She had not gone so very far in
    Before something caught her running;
So loudly then she cried out, "Aunt!"
    Says I, "Uncle's just a-coming."

345

I then drew out my little pen-knife,
  All quickly for to paunch her;[1]
She turned out one of the female kind,
  How glad I was I catched her!

Now we'll go down to a public inn
  And drink this hare quite mellow,
And I'll spend a crown, and a merry crown, too,
  And be a hearty, bold fellow.

[1] A female hare is considered better eating than a male.

Once I was Single

ONCE I was single, O then,
  Once I was single, O then,
And when I was single, my pockets did jingle,
  And I long to get single again.

Chorus
  Again, and again, and again,
  Again, and again, and again,
 For when I was single, my pockets did jingle,
    And I long to get single again.

 I married a wife, O then,
 I married a wife, O then,
I married a wife, she was the plague of my life,
  And I long to get single again.

 My wife she took fever, O then,
 My wife she took fever, O then,
My wife she took fever, I hope it won't leave her,
  For I long to get single again.

346

My wife she died, O then,
My wife she died, O then;
My wife she died, and I laughed till I cried,
    For I knew I was single again.

I had a funeral, O then,
I had a funeral, O then;
Sweet music did play, I danced all the way,
    For I knew I was single again.

I married another, O then,
I married another, O then;
I married another, much worse than the other,
    And I long to get single again.

I am a Pretty Wench

I AM a pretty wench,
And I came a long way hence,
But for sweethearts I can get none, none, none;
But for sweethearts I can get none.

If it had not been for one,
I should have married, long and gone,
To a weaver that weaves at his loom, loom, loom;
To a weaver that weaves at his loom.

I couldn't have a weaver,
To be my own deceiver,
While the carter he came smiling in my face, face, face;
While the carter he came smiling in my face.

The carter dresses fine,
He drinks strong beer, ale, and wine,
And smokes tobacco, as you may suppose.

If the carter I can't have
I'll go single to my grave,
For I dream of him when I am asleep, asleep, asleep;
For I dream of him when I am asleep.

The carter is the lad,
He's so beautifully clad,
And his breath smells as sweet as the rose, rose, rose;
And his breath smells as sweet as the rose.

KALENDAR OF WILD FLOWERS

No season is dead. In January look for small weeds already flowering, and remember that a weed can be regarded as a flower out of place. GROUNDSEL (1) introduces gold to the year, SHEPHERD'S PURSE (2) has both flowers and seeds, and you will find the first tiny white stars of CHICKWEED (3). This is the main flowering time for CHRISTMAS ROSES (4), though in shelter they may have bloomed earlier. You will find WINTER HELIOTROPE (5) in an old garden and often outside it. YEW (6) and BOX (7) will stiffen a winter posy.

Though most of the dry stems are battered now and berries eaten, save for black IVY berries (8), long grasses still droop gracefully in the lanes. But the best prize is in a cleared patch of copse, for there you will find a few short-stemmed PRIMROSES (9). Pick HAZEL catkins (10) now, and they will soon treble their length and be spilling gold dust in a warm room.

351

February is often the worst month of winter; but if we use the poet's eye we shall see Spring as the infant that "flutters sudden 'neath the breast of Earth A month before the birth". First of the CROCUSES (1) is the orange; then comes the purple, then the white. There are drifts of SNOWDROPS (2); ACONITES (3) pushing up with the frills of their necks; GORSE (4) on the common, smelling almost warm and summery, and little BARREN STRAWBERRY (5) in the short grass. In the woods DOG'S MERCURY (6) is flowering and HONEYSUCKLE (7) is putting out the first leaves of the year. On chalky soil you will find SPURGE LAUREL (8) on a shady bank, shiny green and poisonous, and very rarely, you will find its sweet smelling cousin, DAPHNE (9). Towards the end of the month FERNS (10) uncoil and DAFFODILS come spearing up—look for one carrying a leaf on its point "stabbing winter at a blow" (11).

DAISIES (1) are out, "smell-less yet most quaint". Let them have first place on the page as on the lawn, where soon they will be beheaded. March is golden: KINGCUPS (2) by the pond; COLTSFOOT (3) along the roadside, and glistening LESSER CELANDINE (4) in the ditch. In the garden daffodils bend stiffly in March winds and, if you know where to look, you will find WILD DAFFODILS (5) in the copse. We may have "blackthorn winter" this month when the BLACKTHORN (6) is snowy, and dry frozen ground—but remember "a peck of March dust is worth a king's ransom". GREEN HELLEBORE (7), wild relation of the Christmas rose, is rare, but you may find it in a chalk wood of the South. Watch the trees: the ALDER (8) hangs down purple catkins, the POPLAR (9) red ones, and the ELMS (10), their twigs rosetted with small flowers, wear the pink-purple bloom of a ripe peach.

353

April is the great month in the weald. Spring is in the hazel copses, a green mist in the branches, soon to settle as clouds of new leaves. Walk delicately between cushions of primroses and constellations of ANEMONES (1). You will find the EARLY PURPLE ORCHIS (2) with spotted leaves; LADY'S SMOCKS (3) silver-white in the shade, but pinker where the sun can reach them; and DOG VIOLETS (4) and GROUND IVY (5), both purple-blue. There may be a patch of WILD GARLIC (6) but walk round it, for if it is bruised its onion smell will drown the better scents of spring. Watch for delicate WOOD SORREL (7) in a bed of moss, with its veined white flowers and the young leaves neatly folded down on their pink stems like a shut parasol. PERIWINKLE (8) likes a half-shady bank, and the brittle STITCHWORT (9) stars a sunny one. At the fringe of the wood look up for WILD CHERRY blossom (10), and shell pink CRAB APPLE (11) buds.

May is pink and blue and gold, with YELLOW
ARCHANGEL (1) for her herald: BLUEBELLS (2) in the woods;
magenta CAMPION (3) in the clearings; BUGLE (4) with its
blue flowers and shiny bronze leaves, and YELLOW
PIMPERNEL (5). You may chance on WOODRUFF (6), one of
the Bedstraws, with white waxen flowers and leaves arranged
in ruffs round the stem. The GREATER CELANDINE (7), no
connection of the Lesser but really a poppy, is the only
common flower with yellow juice and because of that
property it was, redundantly, used in treating jaundice. You
will find it growing on a bank usually near a farm or
village. A field pond may be shining white with WATER
CROWFOOT (8), a buttercup, which gets the best of two
worlds with sturdy leaves above and trailing threadlike leaves
below the water. Notice small GERMANDER SPEEDWELL
(9) under the hedge, with flowers of heavenly blue. Best of
all, the COWSLIPS (10) are out.

In June hay rises to its flood, almost submerging the rose-embroidered hedgerows. It is the high month for daisies and buttercups and cloves, for grasses dusty with pollen as mauve as the FIELD SCABIOUS (1). But climb up past the hay, up the edge of the plough—you may find HEARTEASE (2) in passing—to the open down, and lie on a warm turf. There you will smell THYME (3) and, head near the ground, look down the purple veined throat of EYEBRIGHT (4) and watch butterflies on the pink stars of CENTAURY (5). The ROCK ROSES (6) will be out, their petals like crumpled yellow silk, and MILKWORT (7) crimson and blue. Perhaps you will find a BEE ORCHIS (8) or CLUSTERED BELLFLOWER (9). Certainly there will be BUGLOSS (10), royal blue and scratchy, very hard to pick, and wine red SALAD BURNET (11). As you descend to the valley again through a dim hanging wood search for HERB PARIS (12)—one day you will find it.

356

In July, be proud, and walk nose in air for the scent of lime blossom. Wander by a fen river or chalk stream and you will find PURPLE LOOSESTRIFE (1) spearing up through the meadow-sweet. Look for handsome ARROWHEAD (2); FLOWERING RUSH (3); MIMULUS (4) cool and juicy with its feet in the water; little CREEPING JENNY (5) and water FORGET-ME-NOT (6) between the rushes on the edge of the bank. Or if the water meadows are too hot, lie in the shade at the edge of the wood and eat WILD STRAWBERRIES (7) under a bower of HONEYSUCKLE (8).

But if you cannot go to the country at all, picnic on a bombsite near St Paul's before they are all built over. There among the willowherb and ragwort you will find EVENING PRIMROSES (9), and BINDWEED (10) with fragile snowy trumpets, using rusty wire for trellis. Next month the willowherb fluff will be blowing between the buses.

August is the month for the harvest flowers, though with cleaner seed much beauty has been exchanged for more bread. Cornfields seldom harbour POPPIES (1) now, nor blue cornflowers. The wine red CORNCOCKLE (2), once so common, is becoming rare. Look along the roadsides for WHITE CAMPION (3); golden spires of TOADFLAX (4); for great-mullein, grey Goliath of the hedgerow, and its smaller purple-eyed cousin, DARK MULLEIN (5). On the moors listen to bees in BELL HEATHER (6). Eat BILBERRIES (7) while you look for a small parasite, LESSER DODDER (8), wound on a furze bush like a pink cocoon. Squelch through a brown bog to seek GRASS OF PARNASSUS (9); pink BOG PIMPERNEL (10), and insect catching SUNDEW (11). A fly settling on a sundew leaf is caught in the sticky hairs, and the leaf curls over and digests it. In wiry turf there grow slender ST JOHN'S WORT (12) and blue HAREBELLS (13) that rustle if you shake them.

If you go to the sea in September and walk above the ride-rim you may find growing among dusty pebbles and dry seaweed and litter a golden horned SEA POPPY (1)—it has been flowering all summer and now its horns are long—and SEA HOLLY (2), which is really a thistle, all the colours of sea on a cloudy day. In crevices of cliff rocks SAMPHIRE (3) grows right down to high-water mark. It is a seaside relation of the parsleys with aromatic fleshy leaves. On the cliff edge itself are the last few flowers of THRIFT (4) and white SEA CAMPION (5) which had their gay season in June. In a marsh behind dunes you may come on patches of shrubby BOG MYRTLE (6) which smells sweet as you run your fingers through it. Up on the short grass of flanking headlands look for the little white orchis of September, the twisting LADY'S TRESSES (7). SEA LAVENDER (8) and PRICKLY SALTWORT (9) belong to the mud flats of the East coast.

359

October is the month of chestnut harvest. Who does not stoop for a CONKER (1)? SWEET CHESTNUTS (2) should be gathered too, and roasted if possible in a log fire.

The colour of the year is changing: scarlet, unseen in spring, rare in summer, is becoming the focal point of the hedge's colour scheme. The WOODY NIGHTSHADE berries (3) are shiny red and squashy, and SPINDLEBERRIES (4) have split to show the orange seed inside the bright pink cases. Unnoticeable in spring, Spindle is now the glory of any chalk lane. Look for WILD HOP (5) decorating the hedges; PELLITORY (6) growing between the stones of an old wall, and neat white SNEEZEWORT (7), last to bloom in the year's succession. The STINKING IRIS (8), growing on the edge of woods in a limestone district, had dully greyish-mauve flowers, but now its fat seed-cases have split into three parts, each showing a double row of brilliant orange seeds that will last through the winter in your room.

Squirrels must hurry, and we too, for the last of the hedgerow harvest. As you peer in the bushes to see if just one hazel nut has been left, look under the yellow leaves for spring catkins, packed tight for winter storms. You may find a few BEECH NUTS (1), but only every five or seven years is there a heavy crop of beech mast. Nuts may be scarce, but as birds have no storage arrangements there are plenty of berries still: scarlet HIPS (2) and claret HAWS (3), which will serve for jelly, but only in dolls' quantities, PRIVET berries (4), like old-fashioned packets of black-headed pins, and ELDER-BERRIES (5) hanging in heavy clusters. HONEYSUCKLE berries (6) are rose-red and glassy, the berries of BRYONY (7) red and orange and yellow, and bitter black SLOES (8) are ripe. It is a very red and black and gold month. Trails of BLACKBERRY (9) make a good if scratchy decoration. Frothing over nearly every lane is OLD MAN'S BEARD (10). Another name for this wild clematis is Traveller's Joy.

A bunch picked in December has line, not colour, and is a prickly and fragile load. Seek HOGWEED (1) stripped like a scarecrow's umbrella, and bleached NIPPLEWORT (2), SELF-HEAL (3), still neat, and KNAPWEED's ragged cups (4). PLANTAIN (5) is as erect as ever and WOODSAGE (6) keeps its summer curve. These will make a brown etching on your mantelshelf and their shadows will double your design. You may find TEASEL (7) towering over some rough patch, with spines as fierce as when they protected the tiny mauve flowers from insects' feet in July—the "Fullers' Teasel", once used to raise nap on cloth. Stretch for a bunch of ASH seeds (8) and pick up a blown-down twig from the high SCOTS PINE (9). Though the beech trees are bare, the HEDGE BEECH (10) still has leaves to rustle, and OAK leaves (11) cling curled as if carved by Grinling Gibbons. Do not forget the Christmas-pudding HOLLY (12), and perhaps you can claim a sprig of MISTLETOE (13) from an old cottage apple tree.

A PERSIAN CURIOSITY

The Merchant
& the Parrot

THERE was a merchant who possessed a parrot, a beautiful parrot, which he kept in a cage.

The merchant was preparing to make a journey, which he intended to begin with Hindustan;

And the kind-hearted man called before him every man-servant and every maid-servant, and said: "What present shall I bring for thee? Tell me frankly."

Each one of them answered him according to his desire; and to every one the good man promised what he asked.

Then he said to the parrot: "And what present from the regions of Hindustan wilt thou have?"

And the parrot answered: "When thou seest the parrots there, tell them my condition—

"Say: 'A certain parrot is yearning to see you, but is shut out by a cage from the free space of heaven.

"'He sendeth you his benediction, and asketh you to do him justice, and beggeth you to save his life, and to show him the paths of safety.

"'Is it right that I should consume my soul in vain longings, and that I should die here in loneliness?

"'Is it proper that I should be bound in hard shackles, whilst ye dwell amidst green places upon the trees?

"'Is this the kind of faith to keep with a friend—I in a cage and ye in a garden?

"'Call to mind, ye fortunate ones, that verdant lawn, and our morning draught in the midst of the meadows!

365

" 'The remembrance of a friend should be a happy one to friends, as was that of Laila and Mejnun.

" 'My comrades, my precious idols, I am drinking cups of my own blood; drink ye to my remembrance one cup of wine, if ye desire to do me justice.' "

The merchant received the salutation and the message he was to carry to those of its race.

And when he reached the boundaries of Hindustan he saw in the desert a large company of parrots.

Then he stayed his horse and lifted up his voice, and delivered the salutation and the message entrusted to him.

And immediately one of the parrots fluttered excessively, and fell down, and gave up its breath, and died.

Then the merchant repented him of what he had said and done, and exclaimed: "Did I come to bring death to a living creature?

"Perhaps this parrot was a relative of my parrot: perhaps they were two in body and one in soul!

"Why did I do this?—why deliver this message? My heart is on fire, and for this unlucky event I see no remedy.

"The tongue is like flint, and the lip is like iron, and that which is struck in ignorance from the tongue is as flame.

"Do not, foolish man, whether in easy good nature, or in idle boasting, strike flint and steel together!

"For it is dark, and there is much cotton around, and in the midst of cotton wherefore scatter sparks!

"A single word may desolate a world—can convert dead foxes into lions!"

When the merchant had finished his business, he returned once more to his happy home.

For every man-servant he brought a present, and to every maiden he gave a token.

Then said the parrot: "And what present hast thou brought to the captive?—Say! what hast thou seen, and what hast thou said?—Tell it me again."

He replied: "Oh me! that of which I much repent—that for which I could gnaw my hands and bite off my fingers!

"Wherefore did I foolishly carry that unlucky message, which I carried ignorantly?"

It answered: "O merchant, repentance is of small value! What is it that requireth this passion and sorrow?"

He replied: "I delivered thy complaint to a company of parrots, thy fellows.

"One of those parrots took such a share in thine affliction, that its heart broke, and it fluttered, and died."

When the parrot heard what that parrot had done, it too fluttered, and fell, and became cold [*i.e.* died].

When he saw it fall in such wise, the merchant started up, and dashed his cap upon the ground;

And when he saw its colour and condition he leaped up, and tore the breast of his garment, and exclaimed:

"O my parrot, my beautiful, my dear one, what is this that hath befallen thee?—Wherefore art thou thus?

"Alas! and alas! my bird of the melodious voice, who didst breathe the same breath, and knewest my every secret;

"Alas! and alas! bird of the sweet notes, and tones of the harp—pleasant to me as my garden, and sweet as my sweet-basil!"

Then the merchant cast out the dead bird from its cage, and immediately it flew up to a high branch of a tree.

He was amazed at the action of the bird, and was seized with desire to understand this strange mystery;

And turning his face upwards, he said: "O my sweet one, to me sweet as a nightingale, give me, I pray thee, some explanation of what thou hast done."

It replied: "The message thou broughtest me gave me counsel; it said: "Free thyself from speech and voice;

" 'Since it was thy voice which brought thee into bondage;'—and it died itself to confirm the message."

The parrot then gave him one or two counsels, and bestowed upon him a parting benediction.

The merchant said to it: "Depart in peace! thou hast shown me now a new path."

"Farewell! merchant," it replied; "thou hast done me a

mercy; they benevolence hath freed me from the chain and from the net.

"Farewell! merchant; I WAS AWAY FROM MY HOME: may thou, by God's grace, become FREE LIKE ME."

Acknowledgements

Duckworth Overlook would like to thank:

Frances Meynell and Vera Meynell for the original idea of *The Week-End Book*.

Gertrud Watson for the mammoth task of typing the parts of both of *The Week-End Books*.

Associated Country Women of the World for permission to use "Kitchen Folklore", "Many Ways To Take a Holiday", and "Housekeeping On a Great Liner of Today", from *The Countrywoman*. Associated Country Women of the World is an international non-governmental organization for rural women, that is active in over 70 countries. It has consultative status with several United Nations agencies and works closely with its members worldwide to provide education, practical help and support for development programmes. Further information can be obtained from at www.acww.org.uk or by telephone on +44 (0)207 799 3875.

Country Life for their kind permission to reproduce "Liquid Refreshment" from *Country Life Illustrated*, 1901.

Solo Syndication/Associated Newspapers for permission to use chapters from *The Complete Guide to Home Gardens*, M James.